The Complete Study Guide for Scoring High

ENGLISH GRAMMAR
AND USAGE
FOR TEST-TAKERS

by David R. Turner, M.S.

arco 219 Park Avenue South
New York, N.Y. 10003

First Edition (B-3360)
Second Printing, 1977

Published by ARCO PUBLISHING COMPANY, INC.
219 Park Avenue South, New York, N.Y. 10003

Library of Congress Cataloging in Publication Data

Turner, David Reuben, 1915-
  English grammar and usage for test-takers.

  (Arco civil service test tutors)
  1. English language—Examinations, questions, etc.
I. Arco Publishing Company, New York. II. Title.

PE1114.T78   428'.0076   76-3036
ISBN 0-668-04014-9

Printed in the United States of America

CONTENTS

HOW TO USE THIS INDEX
Slightly bend the right-hand edge of the book. This will expose the corresponding Parts which match the index, below.

PART
1
2

PART ONE
ENGLISH GRAMMAR RULES.
NINETEEN QUIZZES ILLUSTRATING EACH OF THE CHAPTERS.

...continued on next page

CONTENTS continued

PART TWO

CORRECT ENGLISH USAGE.

A GLOSSARY CORRECTING COMMON ERRORS.

TWO EXPLANATORY QUIZZES.

WHAT THIS BOOK WILL DO FOR YOU

Knowledge of grammar and English usage is fundamental to almost every exam. Firstly it's required in order to understand and answer the questions correctly. Secondly, many exams ask direct questions involving correct English usage and grammar. This book was written to help you on any exam you might have to take. The grammar is as simple as we could make it, while still solving the problems generally posed by a wide variety of tests. Every significant rule of grammar is concisely explained in eighty indexed pages, reasonably arranged in seven chapters. Each chapter is followed by examination-type questions that explain, clarify, and illustrate the rules in that chapter. Each multiple-choice question is answered both by key letter and by a fuller explanation. These explanations contain frequent references back to the numbered rules of grammar involved. Learning correct English usage should be a pleasure because you will have so many concrete illustrations of the rules which, in the past, were abstract and dry.

If you want to take an exam but are reluctant for fear that your language ability and grammar are a bit rusty, don't sell yourself short. You'll get the greatest help from this book by understanding how it has been organized. You must plan to use it accordingly. Study carefully this concise, readable treatment of grammar and good English and your way will be clear. You will progress directly to your goal. You will not be led off into blind alleys and useless grammatical digressions.

The seven chapters of grammar give you everything you need for successful test-taking. They are divided into numbered sections. Each numbered section is, in turn, subdivided alphabetically so that the grammatical rules and principles are logically presented. This arrangement provides you with ready reference to the Index and to the explanations given for all the questions included. Not only will it help you in preparing for an exam. It will be a valuable, permanent addition to your library.

We believe that you can improve your exam scores measureably with the help of this "self-tutor." It's a carefully thought-out homestudy course which you can readily review in less than twenty hours. It's a digest which you might have been able to assemble after many hundred hours of laborious digging. Since you'll have quite enough to do without that, consider yourself fortunate that we have done it for you.

To prepare for a test you must motivate yourself . . . get into the right frame of mind for learning from your "self-tutor." You'll have to urge yourself to learn. That's the only way people ever learn. Your efforts to score high will be greatly aided because you'll have to do this job on your own . . . perhaps without a teacher. Psychologists have demonstrated that studies undertaken for a clear goal (which you initiate yourself and actively pursue) are the most successful. You, yourself, want to pass this test. That's why you bought this book and embarked on this program. Nobody forced you to do it, and there may be nobody to lead you through the course. Your self-activity is going to be the key to your success in the forthcoming weeks.

Used correctly, your "self-tutor" will show you what to expect and will give you a speedy brush-up on the major problems crucial to your exam. Even if your study time is very limited, you will:

- gain familiarity with your examination;
- improve your general test-taking skill;
- improve your skill in analyzing and answering questions involving reasoning, judgment, comparison, and evaluation;
- improve your speed and skill in reading and understanding what you read—an important ability in learning, and an important component of most tests.

This book will pinpoint your study by presenting the types of questions you will get on the actual exam. You'll score higher even if you only familiarize yourself with these types.

This book will help you find your weaknesses and find them fast. Once you know where you're weak, you can get right to work (before the exam), and concentrate on those soft spots. This is the kind of selective study which yields maximum results for every hour spent.

This book will give you the *feel* of the exam. Many of our practice questions are taken from previous exams. Since previous exams are not always available for inspection by the public, our sample test questions are quite important for you. The day you take your exam you'll see how closely the book conforms.

This book will give you confidence *now*, while you are preparing for the exam. It will build your self-confidence as you proceed. It will beat those dreaded before-test jitters that have hurt so many other test-takers.

This book stresses the modern, multiple-choice type of question because that's the kind you'll undoubtedly get on your exam. In answering these questions you will add to your knowledge by learning the correct answers, naturally. However, you will not be satisfied with merely the correct choice for each question. You will want to find out why the other choices are incorrect. This will jog your memory . . . help you remember much you thought you had forgotten. You'll be preparing and enriching yourself for the exam to come.

Of course, the great advantage in all this lies in narrowing your study to just those fields in which you're most likely to be quizzed. Answer enough questions in those fields and the chances are very good that you'll meet a few of them again on the actual test. After all, the number of questions an examiner can draw upon in these fields is rather limited. Examiners frequently employ the same questions on different tests for this very reason.

By creating the "climate" of your test, this book should give you a fairly accurate picture of what's involved, and should put you in the right frame of mind for passing high.

Arco Publishing Company has been involved with trends and methods in testing ever since the firm was founded in 1937. We have *specialized* in books that prepare people for exams. Based on this experience it is our modest boast that you probably have in your hands the best book that could be prepared to help *you* score high. Now, if you'll take a little advice on using it properly, we can assure you that you will do well.

STUDYING FOR TOP SCORES ON GRAMMAR TESTS

Although a thorough knowledge of the subject matter is the most important factor in succeeding on your exam, the following suggestions could raise your score substantially. These few pointers will give you the strategy employed on tests by those who are most successful in this not-so-mysterious art. It's really quite simple. Do things right . . . right from the beginning. Make successful methods a habit. Then you'll get the greatest dividends from the time you invest in this book.

PREPARING FOR THE EXAM

1. *Budget your time.* Set aside definite hours each day for concentrated study. Adhere closely to this budget. Don't fritter away your time with excessive "breaks." A cup of coffee, a piece of fruit, a look out of the window—they're fine, but not too often.

2. *Study with a friend or a group.* The exchange of ideas that this arrangement affords may be very beneficial. It is also more pleasant getting together in study sessions. Be sure, though, that you ban "socializing." Talk about friends, dates, trips, etc. at some other time.

3. *Eliminate distractions.* Psychologists tell us that study efforts will reap much more fruit when there is little or no division of attention. Disturbances caused by family and neighbor activities (telephone calls, chit-chat, TV programs, etc.) will work to your disadvantage. Study in a quiet, private room. Better still, use the library.

4. *Use the library.* Most colleges and universities have excellent library facilities. Some institutions have special libraries for the various subject areas: Physics library, Education library, Psychology library, etc. Take full advantage of such valuable facilities. The library is free from those distractions that may inhibit your home study. Moreover, research in your subject area is so much more convenient in a library since it can provide much more study material than you have at home.

5. *Answer all the questions in this book.* Don't be satisfied merely with the correct answer to each question. Do additional research on the other choices which are given. You will broaden your background to be adequately prepared for the "real" exam. It's quite possible that a question on the exam which you are going to take may require you to be familiar with the other choices.

6. *Get the "feel" of the exam.* The sample questions which this book contains will give you that "feel." Gestalt (meaning *configuration* or *pattern*) psychology stresses that true learning results in a grasp of the *entire situation*. Gestaltists also tell us that we learn by "insight." One of the salient facets of this type of learning is that we succeed in "seeing through" a problem as a consequence of experiencing *previous similar situations*. This book contains hundreds of "similar situations"—as you will discover when you take the actual exam.

7. *Take the Sample Tests as "real" tests.* With this attitude, you will derive greater benefit. Put yourself under strict examination conditions. Tolerate no interruptions while you are taking the sample tests. Work steadily. Do not spend too much time on any one question. If a question seems too difficult go to the next one. If time permits, go back to the omitted question.

8. *Tailor your study to the subject matter. Skim or scan.* Don't study everything in the same manner. Francis Bacon (1561-1626) expressed it this way: "Some books are to be tasted, others to be swallowed, and some few to be chewed and digested."

9. *Organize yourself.* Make sure that your notes are in good order—also, that your desk top is neat. Valuable time is consumed unnecessarily when you can't find quickly what you are looking for.

10. *Keep physically fit.* You cannot retain information well when you are uncomfortable, headachy, or tense. Physical health promotes mental efficiency. Guarding your health takes into account such factors as these:

a. Sufficient sleep

b. Daily exercise and recreation

c. Annual physical examination

d. A balanced diet

e. Avoidance of eyestrain

f. Mental health

HOW TO TAKE AN EXAM

1. *Get to the Examination Room about Ten Minutes Ahead of Time.* You'll start better when you are accustomed to the room. If the room is too cold, or too warm, or not well ventilated, call these conditions to the attention of the person in charge.

2. *Make Sure that you Read the Instructions Carefully.* In many cases, test-takers lose credits because they misread some important point in the given directions—example: the *incorrect* choice instead of the *correct* choice.

3. *Be Confident.* Statistics conclusively show that success is likely when you have prepared faithfully. It is important to know that you are not expected to answer every question correctly. The questions usually have a range of difficulty and differentiate between several levels of skill. It's quite possible that an "A" student might answer no more than 60% of the questions correctly.

4. *Skip Hard Questions and Go Back Later*. It is a good idea to make a mark on the question sheet next to all questions you cannot answer easily, and to go back to those questions later. First answer the questions you are sure about. Do not panic if you cannot answer a question. Go on and answer the questions you know. Usually the easier questions are presented at the beginning of the exam and the questions become gradually more difficult.

If you do skip ahead on the exam, be sure to skip ahead also on your answer sheet. A good technique is periodically to check the number of the question on the answer sheet with the number of the question on the test. You should do this every time you decide to skip a question. If you fail to skip the corresponding answer blank for that question, all of your following answers will be wrong.

Each student is stronger in some areas than in others. No one is expected to know all the answers. Do not waste time agonizing over a difficult question because it may keep you from getting to other questions that you can answer correctly.

5. *Guess If You Are Nearly Sure*. Guessing is probably worthwhile if you have an intuition as to the correct answer or if you can eliminate one or more of the wrong options, and can thus make an "educated" guess. However, if you are entirely at a loss as to the correct answer, it may be best not to guess. A correction is made for guessing when the exam is scored. A percentage of wrong answers is subtracted from the number of right answers. Therefore, it is sometimes better to omit an answer than to guess.

6. *Mark the Answer Sheet Clearly*. When you take the examination, you will mark your answers to the multiple-choice questions on a separate answer sheet that will be given to you at the test center. If you have not worked with an answer sheet before, it is in your best interest to become familiar with the procedures involved. Remember, knowing the correct answer is not enough! If you do not mark the sheet correctly, so that it can be machine scored, you will not get credit for your answers!

In addition to marking answers on the separate answer sheet, you might also be asked to give your name and other information, including your social security number. As a precaution bring along your social security number for identification purposes.

Read the directions carefully and follow them exactly. If they ask you to print your name in the boxes provided, write only one letter in each box. If your name is longer than the number of boxes provided, omit the letters that do not fit. Remember, you are writing for a machine; it does not have judgment. It can only record the pencil marks you make on the answer sheet.

Use the answer sheet to record all your answers to questions. Each question, or item, has four or five answer choices labeled (A), (B), (C), (D), (E). You will be asked to choose the letter for the alternative that best answers each question. Then you will be asked to mark your answer by blackening the appropriate space on your answer sheet. Be sure that each space you choose and blacken with your pencil is *completely* blackened. If you change your mind about an answer, or mark the wrong space in error, you must erase the wrong answer. Erase as thoroughly and neatly as possible. The machine will "read" your answers in terms of spaces blackened. Make sure that only one answer is clearly blackened. If you erase an answer, erase it completely and mark your new answer clearly. The machine will give credit only for clearly marked answers. It does not pause to decide whether you really meant (B) or (C).

Make sure that the number of the question you are being asked on the question sheet corresponds to the number of the question you are answering on the answer sheet. It is a good idea to check the numbers of questions and answers frequently. If you decide to skip a question, but fail to skip the corresponding answer blank for that question, all your answers after that will be wrong.

7. *Read Each Question Carefully.* The exam questions are not designed to trick you through misleading or ambiguous alternative choices. On the other hand, they are not all direct questions of factual information. Some are designed to elicit responses that reveal your ability to reason, or to interpret a fact or idea. It's up to you to read each question carefully so you know what is being asked. The exam authors have tried to make the questions clear. Do not go too far astray in looking for hidden meanings.

8. *Don't Answer Too Fast.* The multiple-choice questions which you will meet are not superficial exercises. They are designed to test not only rote recall, but also understanding and insight. Watch for deceptive choices. Do not place too much emphasis on speed. The time element is a factor, but it is not all-important. Accuracy should not be sacrificed for speed.

9. *Materials and Conduct At The Test Center.* You need to bring with you to the test center your Admission Form, your social security number, and several No. 2 pencils. Arrive on time as you may not be admitted after testing has begun. Instructions for taking the tests will be read to you by the test supervisor and time will be called when the test is over. If you have questions, you may ask them of the supervisor. Do not give or receive assistance while taking the exams. If you do, you will be asked to turn in all test materials and told to leave the room. You will not be permitted to return and your tests will not be scored.

INDEX TO GRAMMAR RULES

SUBJECT QUIZZES...WITH EXPLANATIONS FOR ALL QUESTIONS

Grammar is a classic stumbling block on the road to lofty examination scores. This section attempts to remove that block, or at least to minimize its damaging effects, by concentrating on material relevant to examination questions.

Since language is a living, active thing, your grasp of correct and effective expression is best measured by a type of question which tests a multitude of grammatical skills.

TWO SAMPLE QUESTIONS EXPLAINED

*DIRECTIONS: Sample question 1 begins with a sentence containing a word in **boldface** type. Following directly are four grammatical descriptions of the **boldface** type. They are lettered (A) (B) (C) (D). Choose the correct grammatical description, and mark your answer **accordingly**.*

QUESTION I

When we finally found him, he was **but** half alive.

(A) conjunction connecting subject and predicate
(B) preposition introducing adverbial phrase **but half alive**
(C) adverb modifying **half**
(D) preposition introducing pronoun **he**

ANSWER I

C REASON: **But**, in this case, means **only**, and is used as an adverb modifying the adverb **half**.

DIRECTIONS: In the following four sentences, select the one sentence that is grammatically INCORRECT. Mark your answer with the letter of that incorrect sentence.

QUESTION II

(A) The ship changed its course on account of there was a storm.
(B) The assassin of Senator Robert F. Kennedy was a dangerously emotional Jordanian.
(C) When we boys go camping, each one brings his own cooking utensils.
(D) For him there will be a great reward.

ANSWER II

A The ship changed its course **because** there was a storm. REASON: The subordinate conjunction **because** is correct — **on account of** may not be used as a conjunction.

1

PART ONE

English Grammar Rules.

Nineteen Quizzes Illustrating Each of the Seven Chapters.

400 Test-Type Questions With Explanatory Answers.

Knowledge of grammar and English usage is fundamental to almost every exam. Firstly it's required in order to understand and answer the questions correctly. Secondly, many exams ask direct questions involving correct English usage and grammar. This book was written to help you on any exam you might have to take. The grammar is as simple as we could make it, while still solving the problems generally posed by a wide variety of tests. Every significant rule of grammar is concisely explained in eighty indexed pages, reasonably arranged in seven chapters. Each chapter is followed by examination-type questions that explain, clarify, and illustrate the rules in that chapter. Each multiple-choice question is answered both by key letter and by a fuller explanation. These explanations contain frequent references back to the numbered rules of grammar involved. Learning correct English usage should be a pleasure because you will have so many concrete illustrations of the rules which, in the past, were abstract and dry.

I. SENTENCE SENSE

1 Parts of Speech

1a Noun

A noun is a word used to name a person, place, thing, or quality.

Kennedy, Paris, desk, truth

1b Pronoun

A pronoun is a word used in place of a noun.

I, we, who, these, each, himself

1c Verb

A verb is a word or group of words that expresses being of the subject or action by or to the subject. The verb, together with any words that complete or modify its meaning, forms the predicate of the sentence.

am, has washed, ran, will be seen

1d Adjective

An adjective is a word that describes or limits (modifies) the meaning of a noun or pronoun.

higher morale, *adjusted net* income, *rolling* stone

1e Adverb

An adverb is a word that modifies a verb, an adjective, or another adverb. It answers the questions where, how or how much, when.

write *legibly*, long *enough*, *very* high production, do it *soon*, go *there*

1f Preposition

A preposition is a word used to relate a noun or pronoun to some other word in the sentence.

at, in, by, from, toward

1g Conjunction

A conjunction is a word used to join words, phrases, or clauses.

and, but, nor, since, although, when

1h Interjection

An interjection expresses strong feeling.

Ah! Nonsense! Shh! Bravo!

2 Relative Frequency of Parts of Speech

A recent study revealed that, of the 300,000 words in our language,

NOUNS VERBS ADJECTIVES ADVERBS	constitute 99.9% of our English words (299,700 words)
PRONOUNS PREPOSITIONS CONJUNCTIONS INTERJECTIONS	constitute 1/10 of one percent of our English words (300 words)

3 Parts of Speech Check

Some parts of speech may be tested as follows:

NOUN: Place *the, a, an,* or *some* before the word.

VERB: If the word is a verb, it will come after one of these: *I, You, He, She, It, We, They.*

ADJECTIVE: Note the position—usually before a noun.

ADVERB: Note the position—usually before a verb.

4 Use Determines Part of Speech

The earliest textbook of grammar was written about 100 B.C. by Denys of Thrace. In it, the author noted that the grammatical function (part of speech) of a word is determined by its use in a given sentence.

4a The foregoing principle holds just as well in modern grammar. Consider, for example, the part of speech of *as* in its various uses:

PRONOUN: He gave me such assistance *as* I needed.
(*as*, here, stands for the relative pronoun *which*. See Section 16e.)

ADVERB and CONJUNCTION } Jim is *as* tall *as* Jack.
(The first *as* is an adverb of degree. See Section 39. The second *as* is a subordinate conjunction. See Section 57b.)

PREPOSITION: Helen obtained a job *as* a secretary.
(*secretary* is the object of the preposition *as*. See Section 13c.)

4b Now consider the versatility of *but*.

ADVERB: I have *but* six cents in my pocket.
(*but*, as an adverb of degree meaning *only*, modifies the adjective *six*. See Section 39.)

PREPOSITION: Everyone *but* Lenny went to the game.
(*but*, as a preposition meaning *except*, introduces the noun *Lenny*. See Section 13c.)

CONJUNCTION: You may win the game *but* he will get the girl.
(*but*, as a coordinate conjunction, connects the two independent clauses. See Section 56b.)

PRONOUN: There is no one *but* believes he will succeed.
(*but*, as a relative pronoun, means *who does not*: There is no one who does not think he will succeed. See Section 16e.)

5 Phrases and Clauses

Phrases and clauses are groups of words which stand for a *noun, adjective,* or *adverb.*

5a Clause

A clause is a group of related words containing a subject and a predicate.

An *independent* (or main) clause makes a complete statement and is not introduced by any subordinating word. When it stands alone, it is a simple sentence.

We shall print the report by the end of the month.

A *dependent* (or subordinate) clause cannot stand alone as a complete sentence; it depends upon some word in the independent clause to complete its meaning. Dependent clauses are classified as:

Adjective: This is the man *who wrote to us for information.*
I have the report *he is looking for.* ("that" understood)

Adverb: *As soon as you have finished the letter,* bring it to my office.

Noun: *Whoever conducts the meeting* will be able to answer your questions.
Can you tell me *what the meeting will be about?*

5b Phrase

A phrase is a group of related words *without a subject and predicate.* A phrase is used as a *noun, adjective,* or *adverb.* Phrases are classified as:

Prepositional: Put the finished letter *on my desk*. (also *adverbial phrase*) The blonde *in the red bathing suit* is my sister. (also *adjective phrase*)

Participial: The man *giving the speech* works in my office. (also *adjective phrase*)

Gerund: *Writing this report* has been

a long and difficult task. (also *noun phrase*)

Infinitive: Our purpose is *to make the report as useful as possible*. (also *noun phrase*) The teacher assigned work *to be done quickly*. (also adjective phrase) She ran *to catch the plane*. (also adverbial phrase)

5c Sentence, clause, phrase differentiated

There are three ways to express a thought: sentence *or* clause *or* phrase.

	DOES IT HAVE COMPLETE THOUGHT?	DOES IT HAVE A SUBJECT AND VERB?
	Yes	*Yes*
SENTENCE	*Example*: Carol went to the movies. Complete thought Subject: *Carol* Verb: *went*	
	No	*Yes*
CLAUSE	*Example*: After the wedding-party was held. Incomplete thought Subject: *wedding-party* Verb: *was held*	
	No	*No*
PHRASE	*Example*: Inside the dark and mysterious house. Incomplete thought No subject No verb	

6 Sentence Classification

To construct sentences which will effectively convey our meaning, we must be able to recognize sentence classification and to know what kind of sentence communicates best. There are four types of sentences:

6a Simple sentence

A simple sentence contains only one clause (an independent clause). This does not mean, however, that it must be short. It may include many phrases, a compound subject or predicate, and a number of modifiers.

The prisoner escaped.
You should set forth your proposal in writing and enclose the latest balance sheets of the corporation.

6b Compound sentence

A compound sentence has two or more independent clauses. Each of these clauses could be written as a simple sentence. There are no dependent clauses in a compound sentence.

> You may discuss this problem with our representative in the Baltimore office, or you may mail your return to this office.

6c Complex sentence

A complex sentence contains one independent clause and one or more dependent clauses.

> When we were reviewing the evaluation reports for February and March, we noted a number of inconsistencies.

6d Compound-complex sentence

A compound-complex sentence contains at least two independent clauses and one or more dependent clauses.

> Since that letter appears to answer your needs, we are enclosing a copy; we hope that it will answer all your questions fully.

7 Functional Classification of Sentence Parts

The parts of speech defined in this chapter are basic to a study of grammar. We can now group these parts according to their *use* and classify them by function as we discuss them in later chapters.

The basic parts of the sentence are the subject, verb, and complement. Modifiers and connectives support this basic sentence—modifiers by making the meaning more exact and connectives by showing the relationship between parts.

7a Subject

The subject of a sentence is the word or group of words which names the thing, person, place, or idea about which the sentence makes a statement. The single words most often used as subjects are nouns and pronouns.

> The *Director* called the meeting for 3 o'clock. (noun)
> *He* wants everybody to attend. (personal pronoun)

Two verbals—the gerund and, less often, the infinitive—may also be the subject of a sentence.

> *Walking* is good exercise. (gerund)
> *To run* is more tiring than to walk. (infinitive)

The demonstrative, interrogative, and indefinite pronouns are among the other parts of speech used as subjects.

> *That* is going to be a difficult task. (demonstrative)
> *What* are your plans for doing it? (interrogative)
> *Everyone* is eager to have you succeed. (indefinite)

A phrase serving as a noun may be the subject of a sentence.

> *Writing that letter* was the smartest thing he did.
> *To make this lesson as comprehensive as possible* is our objective.

An entire dependent clause may be used as the subject.

> *Whoever answers the telephone* will be able to give you the information.
> *Whether the report has been released or not* will determine our action.

7b Verb

The verb tells what the subject itself does (active verb), what something else does to the subject (passive verb), or what the subject is (copulative or linking verb). Every sentence must contain a verb. Verbals, although they come from verbs, cannot serve as verbs in the predicate of a sentence.

The properties of a verb are *number, person, tense, mood,* and *voice.* To indicate these properties we either change the form of the verb itself or add, to the main verb, other verb forms called *auxiliary verbs* — *be, have, can, may, might, shall, will, should, would, could, must, do.*

Number tells whether the verb is singular or plural; *person* tells whether the first person (*I*), second person (*you*), or third person (*he, it, they*) is performing the action. A verb and its subject must agree in number and person. This problem of agreement — so essential to the writing of clear sentences — is discussed in Chapter 3.

Tense is the means by which we show the time of an action — whether it happened in the past, is happening in the present, or will happen in the future. *Mood* (indicative, imperative, subjunctive) indicates the manner of assertion — statement, command, wish, or condition.

Voice is the property of a verb that indicates whether the subject is performing or receiving the action of the verb. A verb in the *active voice* tells what the subject is doing; a verb in the *passive voice* tells what is being done to the subject.

> The *technician completed* the report on time.
> (The verb *completed*, in the active voice, tells what the subject, *technician*, did.)

> The *report was completed* on time.
> The verb *was completed*, in the passive voice, tells what was done to the subject, *report*.)

Verbs may be classified into three types, according to performance.

TRANSITIVE	1) has action and 2) takes a direct object. He *killed* the cat.
INTRANSITIVE	1) has action but 2) takes no direct object. She *fell* down.
COPULATIVE (LINKING)	1) has no action and 2) may take a predicate noun or predicate adjective. Jim *is* captain. (*captain* is predicate noun... also called predicate nominative)

7c Complement

The complement is the word or group of words that comes after the verb and completes its meaning. A complement may be (1) a direct object of the verb, (2) an indirect object of the verb, (3) a predicate nominative, or (4) a predicate adjective.

(1) Direct object:

> He gave the *directions* to his secretary.
> (*Directions* is the direct object of the verb.)

> We are trying *to find a solution to this problem.*
> (The infinitive phrase is the direct object of the verb.)

> Give me *whatever information you have.*
> (The noun clause is the direct object of the verb.)

(2) Indirect object:

> He gave (to) *her* the report.
> (*Her* is the indirect object of the verb; *report* is the direct object.)

> Give (to) *whoever answers the door* this letter.
> (The noun clause is the indirect object of the verb.)

> David did (for) Jerry a big favor.
> (*Jerry* is the indirect object; *favor* is the direct object.)

NOTE: An indirect object must meet all of these requirements:

1. must always be with a direct object.
2. must come after a verb of "giving"
3. must be preceded by "to" or "for" ("to" or "for" may be understood)

The following sentence illustrates how these three requirements for an indirect object are met.

> Her boyfriend bought her a gorgeous mink coat.

1. *Her*, the indirect object, is accompanied by *coat*, the direct object.
2. *Bought*, in a sense, is a verb of "giving."
3. We can say either "bought her" or "bought for her."

(3) Predicate nominative:

The predicate nominative is also called the predicate noun, predicate complement, or subjective complement. The predicate nominative follows the linking verbs and renames the subject. It may be a noun, a pronoun, a verbal, a phrase, or a clause.

Noun:	He is *chairman* of the committee.
Pronoun:	They thought the author was *he*.
Gerund:	My favorite exercise is *swimming*.
Infinitive phrase:	The purpose of this memorandum is *to clarify the matter*.
Noun clause:	The conference leader should be *whoever is best qualified*.

(4) Predicate adjective:

A predicate adjective is an adjective (or adjective phrase) appearing in the predicate and modifying the subject. A predicate adjective occurs only after copulative (linking) verbs.

The flower smells *sweet*.
The meeting we are planning for Tuesday will be *on that subject*.
This material is *over my head*.
He appears *enthusiastic* about the project.

7d Modifiers

Modifiers—single words, phrases, or clauses—are used to limit, describe, or define some element of the sentence. They must attach to a sentence element which is both clear and expressed. A modifier is said to dangle when it cannot attach both logically and grammatically to a definite element in the sentence.

Adjectives describe or limit the meaning of nouns or pronouns.

The *new* employee has been assigned the *difficult* task of analyzing the *statistical* reports on *income* tax.

The report *of the Audit committee* is being studied.
(Prepositional phrase used as an adjective.)

The report *submitted by the Audit committee* is being studied.
(Participial phrase used as an adjective.)

Adverbs modify verbs, verbals, adjectives, or other adverbs. They answer the questions where, how or how much, when, why.

We will hold the meeting *here*. (WHERE?)
She types *rapidly*. (HOW?)
Spending *excessively*, he ran out of funds. (HOW MUCH?)
Bring me the letter *as soon as it is finished*. (WHEN?)
Uncle Don went downtown *to buy a tie*. (WHY?)

7e Connectives

Connectives join one part of a sentence with another and show the relationship between the parts they connect. Conjunctions and prepositions are the most important connectives.

(1) Connectives joining elements of equal rank—

coordinate conjunctions, correlative conjunctions, conjunctive adverbs

Coordinate conjunctions are perhaps the most frequently used connectives. They join sentence elements of equal grammatical importance—words with words, phrases with phrases, independent clauses with independent clauses. The commonly used coordinate conjunctions are:

and, but, or, nor, for, yet

Correlative conjunctions work in pairs to connect sentence elements of equal rank. Each member of a pair of correlative conjunctions must be followed by the same part of speech. Examples of these conjunctions are:

either . . . or, neither . . . nor, not only . . . but also, both . . . and

Conjunctive adverbs connect independent clauses and show a relation between them. Although the clause introduced by the conjunctive adverb is grammatically independent, it is logically dependent upon the preceding clause for its *complete* meaning. These are some conjunctive adverbs:

therefore, however, consequently, accordingly, furthermore, moreover, nevertheless

(2) Connectives joining elements of unequal rank —

subordinate conjunctions, relative pronouns, relative adverbs

Subordinate conjunctions introduce dependent adverb clauses and join them to independent clauses. Some of these conjunctions are:

before, since, after, as, because, if, unless, until, although

NOTE: The subordinate conjunction *that* introduces a noun clause:

When he calls, tell him *that I had to leave for a meeting.*

Relative pronouns not only introduce noun and adjective clauses but also act as pronouns within their own clauses. These pronouns include:

that, which, who, whom, whatever, whichever, whoever

The man *who called for an appointment* has just arrived.
　(Adjective clause)
Tell me the news *that you have heard.*
　(Noun clause)

Relative adverbs introduce subordinate clauses. The most common of these connectives are:

how, where, when, while

(3) Prepositions

A preposition shows the relationship between a word that follows it, called its object, and a word before it to which it relates. Some prepositions are:

to, of, by, from, between, in, over, under, for

7f　Verbals

Verbals are words formed from verbs; however, they can never act as verbs. There are three verbals: infinitive, participle, gerund.

Infinitive (to go, to run, to see, etc.) may act as a noun *or* an adjective *or* an adverb.

I like *to swim.* (noun)
A book *to read* is what the child wants. (adjective)
He went *to play* ball. (adverb)

Participle may be either a present participle (going, seeing, feeling, etc.) or a past participle (having gone, having seen, having felt, etc.). A participle acts *only* as an adjective.

Going to the store, Joe slipped. (adjective)
Having seen the entire movie, Jane left the theatre. (adjective)

Gerund (knowing, running, hearing, etc.) acts *only* as a noun.

Charlie enjoys *running.* (noun)

Now, push forward! Test yourself and practice for your test with the carefully constructed quizzes that follow. Each one presents the kind of question you may expect on your test. And each question is at just the level of difficulty that may be expected. Don't try to take all the tests at one time. Rather, schedule yourself so that you take a few at each session, and spend approximately the same time on them at each session. Score yourself honestly, and date each test. You should be able to detect improvement in your performance on successive sessions.

TEST I. SENTENCE SENSE

TIME: 12 Minutes

DIRECTIONS: In each of the following groups of sentences, select the one sentence that is grammatically INCORRECT. Mark the answer sheet with the letter of that incorrect sentence.

Explanations of the key points behind these questions appear with the answers at the end of this test. The explanatory answers provide the kind of background that will enable you to answer test questions with facility and confidence.

(1)

(A) My brother counseled me to remain silent.
(B) The young recruits deserted their old haunts as quick as possible.
(C) Only part of the speech was delivered.
(D) John said that he would investigate the matter thoroughly.

(2)

(A) Though he said they were all generous contributors, the tone in his voice implied they were not.
(B) The sleeper could not have lain in bed much longer than he did.
(C) It is generally held that English is one of the poorest taught subjects in high school today.
(D) Take my book; if you use Bill's, you will find it's different from mine.

(3)

(A) The Wall Street operator worked strenuously until 3 o'clock and then took things easily for the rest of the day.
(B) Many a challenge in the realm of politics is fraught with pitfalls for the unwary.
(C) It was his intention to give due acknowledgment to whoever sent condolences.
(D) America really did itself proud in the Tokyo Olympics.

(4)

(A) These data have been gathered by compiling the responses to a questionnaire.
(B) That a man should try hard and still fail in spite of his best efforts is better than that he should not try at all.
(C) Whenever one comes upon a fact that one has never known before, the thrill and the satisfaction that come with knowledge.
(D) For you and me, the extra days of vacation will be very welcome.

(5)

(A) Come home with me for dinner, and I shall make you steak and potatoes.
(B) Our youngest son was graduated from a military school last year.
(C) How does weather affect retail sales?
(D) We sell goods received from both government and non-government sources.

(6)

(A) The canoeist found that his fatigue was noticeable after a few hours.
(B) As an executive, you'll probably lose less time from work this year because of illness than any of your employees.
(C) Our union considers it imperative that "no strike" laws be repealed.
(D) The sales manager wanted to know what was the customer complaining about.

(7)

(A) We shall report the accident to the policeman upon his arrival.
(B) Only one of the rooms which is vacant is on the fourth floor.
(C) Many up-to-date plans, some of which were immediately adopted, were submitted by the staff of architects.
(D) We find it to be a sheer waste of time to discuss matters in committee.

(8)

(A) Most Americans read the newspapers, and it is therefore an excellent means of spreading propaganda.
(B) Rather than go with Pat, he decided to stay at home.
(C) His telling the truth in the face of such dire consequences required great moral courage.
(D) He has been rescued by no common deliverer from the grasp of no common foe.

9

(A) To me this is truly a book that, after you have read it, you will find that it has changed your way of viewing your surroundings.
(B) He had to learn the truth; therefore, he decided to visit the hospital.
(C) Turning the bend in the river, you face the rapids just ahead.
(D) We were terrified by sounds: the screaming of the wind, the restless rushing rustle of leaves.

10

(A) I saw two of them, and one waved his hand.
(B) Do not use the word posted when you mean informed.
(C) He was extremely kind to me.
(D) No one was there only Charles.

11

(A) Henry was very grateful for the bonus which Mr. Block sent to him.
(B) If the class had listened carefully, they would of heard when the papers were due.
(C) On arriving at the bus terminal, the mysterious stranger discarded his luggage.
(D) He smiles as my uncle used to smile.

12

(A) The lines on the map are finely drawn.
(B) He spoke very slowly.
(C) The lady looked attractively in her new suit.
(D) The cream tasted sour.

13

(A) School activities are not limited only to books.
(B) To say this often is worth while.
(C) He thought Richard to be me.
(D) Rising, she opened the window.

14

(A) He does not seem able to present a logical and convincing argument.
(B) Each of the goaltenders was trying to protect his respective cage.
(C) He said, "I shall go there directly."
(D) The reason he was late was on account of the delay in transportation.

15

(A) I bought this set of dishes at the local dealer's.
(B) He was extremely kind to me during my last illness.
(C) I have no hope of seeing him again after the case is closed.
(D) The memorandum must be here some place in these files.

16

(A) Henry's failure to do his homework is a daily occurrence now.
(B) Next Friday is Memorial Day.
(C) This is the worst blizzard we have had in the past twenty years.
(D) Neither the defendant or his relatives thought that Sirhan would get a fair trial.

CONSOLIDATE YOUR KEY ANSWERS HERE

TEST I. SENTENCE SENSE

KEY ANSWERS FOR THE FOREGOING QUESTIONS

Check our key answers with your own. You'll probably find very few errors. In any case, check your understanding of all questions by studying the following explanatory answers. They illuminate the subject matter. Here you will find concise clarifications of basic points behind the key answers.

1. B	4. C	7. B	10. D	13. B	16. D
2. C	5. A	8. A	11. B	14. D	
3. A	6. D	9. A	12. C	15. D	

EXPLANATORY ANSWERS CLARIFYING CARDINAL POINTS

The core of the Question and Answer Method . . . getting help when and where you need it. Even if you were able to write correct key answers for the preceding questions, the following explanations illuminate fundamental facts, ideas, and principles which just might crop up in the form of questions on future tests.

Bold-face references in the following answers direct you to paragraphs in the Arco Grammar Text, where fuller explanations are provided.

ANSWER 1.

B The young recruits deserted their old haunts as **quickly** as possible. REASON: An adverb (**quickly**) — not an adjective (**quick**) — modifies the verb (**deserted**). **(1e)**

ANSWER 2.

C It is generally held that English is one of the most **poorly** taught subjects in high school today. REASON: The adverb **poorly** (not the adjective **poorest**) must be used to modify the participle **taught**. **(1e)**

ANSWER 3.

A The Wall Street operator worked strenuously until 3 o'clock and then took things **easy** for the rest of the day. REASON: In the expression **to take things easy** (which is considered acceptable in spoken English), **easy** is used as an adverb. In the original sentence, the idea of theft would be present if we took things **easily**. **(4, 40b)**

ANSWER 4.

C Whenever one comes upon a fact that one has never known before, **one experiences** the thrill and the satisfaction that come with knowledge. REASON: The original sentence is incomplete. **(5a, 24d)**

ANSWER 5.

A If you come home with me for dinner, I shall make you steak and potatoes. REASON: The original sentence lacks necessary subordination. **(6)**

ANSWER 6.

D The sales manager wanted to know what the customer was complaining about. REASON: To avoid awkward expression, get the auxiliary (**was**) and the main part of the verb (**complaining**) together. Incidentally, it would also be correct to move the preposition **about** farther front: . . .**to know about what the customer was complaining. (6)**

ANSWER 7.

B The only vacant room is on the fourth floor. REASON: The original sentence is unclear. **(6, 47)**

ANSWER 8.

A Most Americans read the newspapers, **which** are therefore an excellent means of spreading propaganda. REASON: First, the thought here calls for a complex, not a compound, sentence. Second, the antecedent of the pronoun, **which**, is newspapers. The latter is plural—therefore, the pronoun must be plural. **(6, 15b)**

ANSWER 9.

A From my point of view, after you have read this book, you will find that it has changed your way of viewing your surroundings. REASON: The original sentence is too cumbersome. **(6, 47)**

ANSWER 10.

D No one but Charles was there. REASON: The original sentence is awkward and run-on. **(6a)**

ANSWER 11.

B If the class had listened carefully, they **would have** heard when the papers were due. REASON: The auxiliary is **have**—not **of** (which is a preposition). **(7e)**

ANSWER 12.

C The lady looked **attractive** in her new suit. REASON: The copulative verb (**looked**) takes a predicate adjective (**attractive**). **(7c)**

ANSWER 13.

B To say this often is **worthwhile**. REASON: The adjective **worthwhile** is a solid word. **(7c)**

ANSWER 14.

D The reason he was late was **the delay** in transportation. REASON: The predicate noun after the copulative verb (**was**) is **delay**. The original sentence is awkward. **(7c)**

ANSWER 15.

D The memorandum must be **some place** in these files. REASON: **here** is unnecessary. **(1e)**

ANSWER 16.

D Neither the defendant **nor** his relatives thought that Sirhan would get a fair trial. REASON: The correlative conjunction is **neither-nor**. **(7e)**

TEST II. PARTS OF SPEECH

TIME: 25 Minutes

The tests of English expression are designed to find out whether the candidate can write correctly and effectively, whether he can organize his ideas properly, and whether he can suit his language to the particular task he is engaged in. They test for correctness, effectiveness, sensitivity, and organization in written English. The objective or semi-objective exercises illustrated in this chapter enable examiners to find out how the candidate solves a number of different writing problems. The variety of questions asked insure that no candidate is discriminated against and that each candidate gives a fair picture of his ability.

*DIRECTIONS: Most questions in this test begin with a sentence containing a word or expression in **boldface** type. Then follow four grammatical descriptions of the **boldface** type. They are lettered (A) (B) (C) (D). Choose the correct grammatical description, and mark your answer sheet with the letter of the correct answer.*

Explanations of the key points behind these questions appear with the answers at the end of this test. The explanatory answers provide the kind of background that will enable you to answer test questions with facility and confidence.

The teacher used **well** as five different parts of speech.

(A) adverb
(B) noun
(C) adjective
(D) verb

Have you seen **him** since last night?

(A) adverb
(B) conjunction
(C) adjective
(D) pronoun

Obstinacy **is** the strength of the weak.

(A) noun
(B) pronoun
(C) conjunction
(D) verb

The teacher made the **very** mistake against which he had warned his pupils.

(A) adverb
(B) reflexive pronoun
(C) adjective
(D) noun in apposition

I have come **this** far but I shall go no farther.

(A) pronoun
(B) adverb
(C) adjective
(D) noun

"Comrades, leave me here a **little**, While as yet 'tis early morn."

(A) direct object
(B) adjective
(C) adverb
(D) pronoun

Since summer, I have merely marked time.

(A) adverb
(B) conjunction
(C) preposition
(D) adjective

The Marine Corps trains all recruits to shoot **straight**.

(A) adverb
(B) adjective
(C) noun
(D) incorrect usage

He went home, **for** his father had sent for him.

(A) preposition
(B) conjunction
(C) expletive
(D) appositive

Do you realize that the young man **now** addressing the audience is our principal?

(A) adjective modifying **man**
(B) adverb modifying a verb
(C) adverb modifying a participle
(D) preposition governing a gerund

The decision, **unfortunately,** came too late.

(A) an adverb modifying the verb **came**
(B) an adverb modifying the adverb **too**
(C) an adverb modifying the adjective **late**
(D) an independent adverb

For the guests to leave early was a serious mistake.

(A) subordinating conjunction
(B) preposition introducing **guests**
(C) expletive
(D) preposition introducing **to leave**

Of the following, the sentence that contains a preposition is

(A) Her makeup retouched, she went on as though nothing had happened.
(B) John looked up expectantly.
(C) The sailors fighting the fire inside shouted horrible oaths.
(D) We sent him a letter concerning your predicament.

Alas! Thou art like a star beyond my reach.

(A) adjective
(B) adverb
(C) interjection
(D) noun

There is always time **for** courtesy.

(A) noun
(B) verb
(C) conjunction
(D) preposition

The four most frequently used parts of speech are

(A) nouns, verbs, adjectives, adverbs
(B) pronouns, prepositions, conjunctions, interjections
(C) adjectives, adverbs, pronouns, prepositions
(D) verbs, adjectives, adverbs, conjunctions

The part of speech that usually appears before a noun is a(n)

(A) preposition
(B) adverb
(C) verb
(D) adjective

All that a man owns will he give for his life.

(A) subject of **owns**
(B) object of **will give**
(C) in apposition with **that**
(D) subject of **will give**

Ring out the old, ring **in** the new.

(A) noun
(B) pronoun
(C) adverb
(D) preposition

He offered to drive **as** many as wished to attend.

(A) adverb
(B) conjunction
(C) preposition
(D) relative pronoun

He is such a man **as** can be expected to pay his debts.

(A) relative pronoun
(B) subordinating conjunction
(C) preposition
(D) adverb

Such of you **as** are tired may leave.

(A) preposition
(B) adverb
(C) relative pronoun
(D) correlative conjunction

He has no thought but **to succeed**.

(A) verb of elliptical clause
(B) object of preposition
(C) in apposition with **thought**
(D) modifies **thought**

The defendant chose an outstanding attorney as his **lawyer**.

(A) subject of elliptical clause
(B) objective complement
(C) object of preposition
(D) direct object

The nervousness of the untrained driver was such **as** might have been expected.

(A) relative pronoun
(B) subordinating conjunction
(C) coordinating conjunction
(D) preposition

Bob is **as** agile as anyone can be.

(A) conjunction
(B) preposition
(C) adverb
(D) pronoun

The color of her gown was such a red **as** makes the eyes ache.

(A) preposition
(B) adverb
(C) relative pronoun
(D) conjunction

There is no school **but** is affected by the ruling.

(A) adjective
(B) preposition
(C) adverb
(D) pronoun

The paths of glory lead **but** to the grave.

(A) relative pronoun
(B) coordinate conjunction
(C) adverb
(D) preposition

Although he worked without stopping, he was **but** three-quarters finished when the bell rang.

(A) preposition
(B) conjunction
(C) adverb
(D) incorrect usage

There was nobody **but** despised him for his cowardice.

(A) conjunction
(B) adverb
(C) relative pronoun
(D) preposition

No one **but** a child would have such energy.

(A) subordinating conjunction
(B) preposition
(C) coordinating conjunction
(D) adverb

"Beyond my window in the night is **but** a drab inglorious street."

(A) pronoun
(B) preposition
(C) conjunction
(D) adverb

TEST II. PARTS OF SPEECH

CONSOLIDATE YOUR KEY ANSWERS HERE

	A	B	C	D	E
1	☐	☐	☐	☐	☐
2	☐	☐	☐	☐	☐
3	☐	☐	☐	☐	☐
4	☐	☐	☐	☐	☐
5	☐	☐	☐	☐	☐
6	☐	☐	☐	☐	☐
7	☐	☐	☐	☐	☐
8	☐	☐	☐	☐	☐
9	☐	☐	☐	☐	☐
10	☐	☐	☐	☐	☐
11	☐	☐	☐	☐	☐
12	☐	☐	☐	☐	☐
13	☐	☐	☐	☐	☐
14	☐	☐	☐	☐	☐
15	☐	☐	☐	☐	☐
16	☐	☐	☐	☐	☐
17	☐	☐	☐	☐	☐
18	☐	☐	☐	☐	☐
19	☐	☐	☐	☐	☐
20	☐	☐	☐	☐	☐
21	☐	☐	☐	☐	☐
22	☐	☐	☐	☐	☐
23	☐	☐	☐	☐	☐
24	☐	☐	☐	☐	☐
25	☐	☐	☐	☐	☐
26	☐	☐	☐	☐	☐
27	☐	☐	☐	☐	☐
28	☐	☐	☐	☐	☐
29	☐	☐	☐	☐	☐
30	☐	☐	☐	☐	☐
31	☐	☐	☐	☐	☐
32	☐	☐	☐	☐	☐
33	☐	☐	☐	☐	☐
34	☐	☐	☐	☐	☐
35	☐	☐	☐	☐	☐
36	☐	☐	☐	☐	☐
37	☐	☐	☐	☐	☐
38	☐	☐	☐	☐	☐
39	☐	☐	☐	☐	☐
40	☐	☐	☐	☐	☐

Correct Answers For The Foregoing Questions

Check our key answers with your own. You'll probably find very few errors. In any case, check your understanding of all questions by studying the following explanatory answers. They illuminate the subject matter. Here you will find concise clarifications of basic points behind the key answers.

1.B	6.C	11.D	16.A	21.A	26.C	31.C
2.D	7.C	12.B	17.D	22.B	27.C	32.B
3.D	8.A	13.D	18.B	23.B	28.D	33.D
4.C	9.B	14.C	19.C	24.C	29.C	
5.B	10.C	15.D	20.A	25.A	30.C	

EXPLANATORY ANSWERS CLARIFYING CARDINAL POINTS

The core of the Question and Answer Method . . . getting help when and where you need it. Even if you were able to write correct key answers for the preceding questions, the following explanations illuminate fundamental facts, ideas, and principles which just might crop up in the form of questions on future tests.

Bold-face references in the following answers direct you to paragraphs in the Arco Grammar Text, where fuller explanations are provided.

ANSWER 1.

B REASON: **Well** is a noun in this case since it is the direct object of the verb **used**. **(1a, 4)**

ANSWER 2.

D REASON: The personal pronoun **him** stands for a noun. **(1b)**

ANSWER 3.

D REASON: **Is** is a copulative verb connecting the subject (**obstinacy**) and the predicate noun (**strength**). **(1c)**

ANSWER 4.

C REASON: **Very** is an adjective modifying the noun **mistake**. **(1d)**

ANSWER 5.

B REASON: **This**, ordinarily a pronoun or an adjective, is used here as an adverb modifying the adverb **far.** **(1e)**

ANSWER 6.

C REASON: **Little** is used as an adverb of degree, modifying the verb **leave.** Actually, we have an ellipsis here — **a little while** — in which **while** is an adverbial objective. **(1e, 13h)**

ANSWER 7.

C REASON: **Since** is a preposition in this case because it introduces the noun **summer.** Together (**Since summer**) we have a prepositional phrase. **(1f)**

ANSWER 8.

A REASON: **Straight** is an adverb (telling "how") modifying the infinitive **to shoot.** **(1e)**

ANSWER 9.

B REASON: **For**, which means the same as **because** in this sentence, is a subordinate conjunction. **(1g)**

ANSWER 10.

C REASON: **Addressing** is a participle (verbal adjective) modifying **man. Now** is an adverb modifying **addressing.** **(1e)**

ANSWER 11.

D REASON: **Unfortunately** is an independent adverb modifying the rest of the sentence rather than a particular element in the sentence. **(1e, 62)**

ANSWER 12.

B REASON: **For** is a preposition, the object of which is **guests. Guests**, in turn, is the subject of the infinitive **to leave.** The entire phrase, **For...early**, is the subject of the verb **was.** **(1f, 7a, 13c)**

ANSWER 13.

D REASON: **Concerning** is a preposition—the object of the preposition is **predicament.** Note that **on** in the first sentence is an adverb; so are **up** and **inside** in the second and third sentences. **(1f, 7e)**

ANSWER 14.

C REASON: **Alas!** is an interjection because it expresses strong feeling. **(1h)**

ANSWER 15.

D REASON: **For** is a preposition introducing the noun **courtesy.** **(1f)**

ANSWER 16.

A REASON: Nouns, verbs, adjectives, and adverbs constitute 99.9% of all our English words. **(2)**

ANSWER 17.

D REASON: The adjective customarily appears before a noun. **(3)**

ANSWER 18.

B REASON: **All** is an adjective used as a noun and acts as the direct object of the verb **will give.** **(4, 7c)**

ANSWER 19.

C REASON: **In** is an adverb of place modifying the second **ring.** **(4, 39)**

ANSWER 20.

A REASON: The first **as** is an adverb of amount modifying the adjective **many.** Incidentally, the second **as** is used as a relative pronoun (**who**) with conjunctive force. **(4a)**

ANSWER 21.

A REASON: **As** is equivalent to the relative pronoun **who.** **(4a, 16e)**

ANSWER 22.

C REASON: **As** refers to the pronoun **you**—it also acts conjunctively in the clause **as are tired may leave.** **(4a)**

ANSWER 23.

B REASON: To succeed is an infinitive used as a noun and acts as the object of the preposition **but**. **(4b, 7f)**

ANSWER 24.

C REASON: The noun **lawyer** is the object of the preposition **as** (which means **for** in this case). **(4a, 13c)**

ANSWER 25.

A REASON: **As**, in this sentence, really means which. **As**, therefore, acts as a relative pronoun whose antecedent is **nervousness**. **(4a)**

ANSWER 26.

C REASON: The first **as** is an adverb of degree modifying the adjective **agile**. The second **as** is a subordinate conjunction. **(4a)**

ANSWER 27.

C REASON: **As** in this sentence refers to the adjectival noun **red**. **As** also acts conjunctively in the clause **as makes the eyes ache**. One could readily replace **as** with the relative pronoun **which**. **(4a)**

ANSWER 28.

D REASON: **But** is a relative pronoun whose antecedent is **school**. When **but** is so used as a relative pronoun, it has negative significance and means **which not**. **(4b)**

ANSWER 29.

C REASON: **But**, in this sentence, means **only**. It is used as an adverb of degree modifying the adverbial phrase **to the grave**. **(4b)**

ANSWER 30.

C REASON: **But**, in this case, means **only**, and is used as an adverb modifying the adverb **three-quarters**. **(4b)**

ANSWER 31.

C REASON: **But** here is a relative pronoun after a negative (**nobody**). In this sentence, **but** means **who not**. **(4b)**

ANSWER 32.

B REASON: **But** here is a preposition (meaning **except**) introducing the noun **child**. **(4b)**

ANSWER 33.

D REASON: **But** means **only** in this case and is used as an adverb of degree. **(4b)**

TEST III. SENTENCES AND THEIR PARTS

TIME: 18 Minutes

*DIRECTIONS: Most questions in this test begin with a sentence containing a word or expression in **boldface** type. Then follow four grammatical descriptions of the **boldface** type. They are lettered (A) (B) (C) (D). Choose the correct grammatical description, and mark your answer sheet with the letter of the correct answer.*

Explanations of the key points behind these questions appear with the answers at the end of this test. The explanatory answers provide the kind of background that will enable you to answer test questions with facility and confidence.

Which is a compound sentence?

(A) We wish you every success in this new business venture.
(B) Although he has plenty of money in the bank, he refuses to buy enough food for his needs.
(C) I want to go but I have no ticket.
(D) The boss is sick and tired of all this nonsense.

Of the following, the one sentence that may correctly be defined as complex is:

(A) The fighter, clutching the ropes, arose at the count of nine; but the referee would not permit him to continue.
(B) This is the house he built with his own hands.
(C) We called him on four occasions; however, he never once answered.
(D) In spite of all the intervening years of quarrel and hatred, George and Tony shook hands and embraced.

A compound-complex sentence must have at least two independent clauses and _____ or more dependent clauses.

(A) one
(B) two
(C) three
(D) four

Which is **not** a simple sentence?

(A) Running in the hall, the child fell.
(B) Smith is a Democrat and Jones is a Republican.
(C) After deciding upon the car with the red interior, he decided to buy a motorcycle.
(D) Call me tonight.

Show **me** a happy person and I'll show you a busy one.

(A) predicate noun
(B) indirect object
(C) object of preposition
(D) direct object

I shall do it even though it is **against my better judgment**.

(A) adverbial modifier
(B) predicate adjective
(C) appositive
(D) objective complement

Manner, not gold, is woman's best **adornment**.

(A) simple subject
(B) predicate noun
(C) indirect object
(D) transitive verb

It will be necessary **to call** again in the morning.

(A) modifies **necessary**
(B) object of verb
(C) modifies **again**
(D) subject of verb

Our single and absorbing purpose now is **to complete** the spring planting.

(A) modifier of **purpose**
(B) objective complement
(C) predicate nominative
(D) subject of **is**

Pass the butter, if **you** please.

(A) subject of verb
(B) object of verb
(C) object of infinitive
(D) none of these

In the sentence, "Looking out of the plane window, we marveled at the beauty of the flashing neon signs which gave me the impression of living jewels against a background of black velvet."

(A) **beauty** is the object of the verb **marveled**
(B) **me** is an indirect object
(C) **impression** is an indirect object
(D) **velvet** is the object of the preposition **against**

His conceit proved his **undoing**.

(A) predicate nominative
(B) direct object of **proved**
(C) subject of **proved**
(D) indirect object of **proved**

Her face and hands were prematurely wrinkled from prolonged **tanning** at the beach.

(A) participle
(B) infinitive
(C) predicate verb
(D) gerund

Tom's **seeing** his old enemy after a lapse of twenty years, during which he had no cause to retain his animosity, was no excuse for his uncontrolled behavior.

(A) modifier of **enemy**
(B) modifier of **he**
(C) subject of main clause
(D) nominative absolute

Completely **irreconcilable** were the viewpoints expressed by the board members.

(A) subject of the sentence
(B) predicate noun
(C) predicate adjective
(D) modifies **completely**

There is a **but** attached to every statement he makes.

(A) preposition
(B) relative pronoun
(C) noun
(D) co-ordinating conjunction

Despite the page's bantering manner, his story **rang** true.

(A) transitive verb
(B) copulative verb
(C) passive verb
(D) unidiomatic verb

He was chosen **president**.

(A) objective complement
(B) object of verb **was chosen**
(C) in apposition with pronoun **he**
(D) predicate nominative

Modifiers are

(A) verbs and nouns
(B) prepositions and conjunctions
(C) adjectives and adverbs
(D) pronouns and interjections

I have never seen such carrots **as** these.

(A) relative pronoun
(B) preposition
(C) subordinating conjunction
(D) conjunctive adverb

The architect recommended **strengthening** the outer wall.

(A) participle modifying **wall**
(B) participle modifying **architect**
(C) gerund object of the verb
(D) predicate verb

A man's reach **should** exceed his grasp.

(A) correlative conjunction
(B) concrete noun
(C) auxiliary verb
(D) copulative verb

The teacher, having given each **pupil** an assignment, turned her attention to the visitor.

(A) nominative absolute
(B) indirect object
(C) objective complement
(D) direct object

Although ignored by reviewers, this book is well worth **reading**.

(A) gerund used as predicate nominative
(B) appositive of **worth**
(C) participle used as predicate adjective
(D) object of an adjective

CONSOLIDATE YOUR KEY ANSWERS HERE

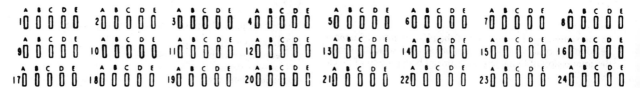

Correct Answers For The Foregoing Questions

(Check your answers with these that we provide. You should find considerable correspondence between them. If not, you'd better go back and find out why. On the next page we have provided concise clarifications of basic points behind the key answers. Please go over them carefully because they may be quite useful in helping you pick up extra points on the exam.)

1. C	5. B	9. C	13. D	17. B	21. C
2. B	6. B	10. B	14. C	18. D	22. C
3. A	7. B	11. B	15. C	19. C	23. B
4. B	8. D	12. A	16. C	20. A	24. D

TEST III. SENTENCES AND THEIR PARTS

EXPLANATORY ANSWERS CLARIFYING CARDINAL POINTS

The core of the Question and Answer Method . . . getting help when and where you need it. Even if you were able to write correct key answers for the preceding questions, the following explanations illuminate fundamental facts, ideas, and principles which just might crop up in the form of questions on future tests.

Bold-face references in the following answers direct you to paragraphs in the Arco Grammar Text, where fuller explanations are provided.

ANSWER 1.
   C   REASON: **I want to go** and **I have no ticket** are independent clauses connected by the coordinate conjunction **but**.   **(6b)**

ANSWER 2.
   B   REASON: A complex sentence has an independent clause (**This is the house**) and a subordinate clause ([**which**] **he built with his own hands**). Note that the relative pronoun **which** is understood in the subordinate clause. The first and third sentences are compound. The fourth sentence is simple.   **(6c)**

ANSWER 3.
   A   REASON: A compound-complex sentence contains at least two independent clauses and one or more dependent clauses.   **(6d)**

ANSWER 4.
   B   REASON: We have here a compound sentence which contains two independent clauses.   **(6a)**

ANSWER 5.
   B   REASON: **Me** is an indirect object — the preposition **to** is understood. **Person** is the direct object.   **(7c, 13b)**

ANSWER 6.
   B   REASON: **Against . . . judgment** is a prepositional phrase after the copulative verb **is**. Since the phrase refers to, and describes, the subject **it**, the phrase acts as a predicate adjective.   **(7c)**

ANSWER 7.
   B   REASON: **Adornment** is a predicate noun after the copulative verb **is**. **Adornment** refers to, and means the same as, the subject **manner**.   **(7c)**

ANSWER 8.
   D   REASON: **To call** is an infinitive used as a noun and acts as the subject of **will be**. It is an expletive.   **(7a, 18a)**

ANSWER 9.
   C   REASON: **To complete** is an infinitive used as a noun after the copulative **is**.   **(7c)**

ANSWER 10.
   B   REASON: **If you please** is elliptical for **if it will please you**. It is obvious, then, that **you** is the direct object of the verb **please**.   **(7c)**

ANSWER 11.

B REASON: **Me** is an indirect object (to **me**) after the verb **gave**. The direct object is **impression**. **(7c)**

ANSWER 12.

A REASON: **Undoing** is a predicate noun after the copulative verb **proved** (which in this sentence has the meaning of the copulative verb **was**). **Undoing** refers to, and means the same as, the subject **conceit**. **(7c)**

ANSWER 13.

D REASON: **Tanning** is a gerund (verbal noun) used as the object of the preposition **from**. **(7f)**

ANSWER 14.

C REASON: **Seeing** is a gerund—as a gerund, it is a noun. **Seeing** acts as the subject of the main clause verb **was**. **(7a)**

ANSWER 15.

C **Viewpoints** is the subject of the copulative verb **were**. The predicate adjective **irreconcilable** refers to the subject. **(7c)**

ANSWER 16.

C REASON: **But** is used as a predicate noun after the copulative verb **is**. **(7c)**

ANSWER 17.

B REASON: The copulative verb is **rang**. A copulative verb may couple up the subject (**story**) with a predicate adjective (**true**). **(7b)**

ANSWER 18.

D REASON: In the active form, the sentence would read: "They chose him president." In this active form, **president** is an objective complement. In the passive form, **president** means the same as the subject **He**. **President** is, therefore, a predicate noun (nominative). **(7c)**

ANSWER 19.

C REASON: Adjectives modify nouns or pronouns and adverbs modify verbs, verbals, adjectives, and other adverbs. **(7d)**

ANSWER 20.

A REASON: **As** in this sentence, may be substituted for the relative pronoun **which**. The dependent clause is, therefore, **as these** (**are**). **carrots** is the antecedent of **as**. **(7e)**

ANSWER 21.

C REASON: **Strengthening** is a gerund used as the direct object of **recommended**. **(7f, 13a)**

ANSWER 22.

C REASON: **Should** is the first part of the verb **should exceed**. **(7b)**

ANSWER 23.

B REASON: **Pupil** is an indirect object and **assignment** is a direct object after the participle **given**. Incidentally, the preposition **to** is understood before **pupil**. **(7c)**

ANSWER 24.

D REASON: **Worth** is the only adjective that takes the objective (accusative) case. **Reading**, then, is a gerund (verbal noun) used as the object of **worth**. **(7f)**

TEST IV. PHRASES AND CLAUSES

TIME: 24 Minutes

*DIRECTIONS: Each question in this test begins with a sentence containing a word or expression in **boldface** type. Then follow four grammatical descriptions of the **boldface** type. They are lettered (A) (B) (C) (D). Choose the correct grammatical description, and mark your answer sheet with the letter of the correct answer.*

Explanations of the key points behind these questions appear with the answers at the end of this test. The explanatory answers provide the kind of background that will enable you to answer test questions with facility and confidence.

1

After the chauffeur had driven for a half hour, we began to realize that he did not know **where he was going**.

(A) noun clause
(B) adverbial clause
(C) adjective phrase
(D) adjective clause

2

"And we are here as on a darkling plain
Swept with confused alarms of struggle and flight
Where ignorant armies clash by night."

(A) adverbial clause modifying verb, **are**
(B) adjective clause modifying **flight**
(C) adjective clause modifying **alarms**
(D) adjective clause modifying **plain**

3

Every move he made was **in defiance** of an order.

(A) adverbial phrase modifying **made**
(B) prepositional phrase used as predicate adjective
(C) prepositional phrase, object of **made**
(D) prepositional phrase modifying **order**

4

He returned, after many years, to the neighborhood **where he had spent his boyhood.**

(A) adjective clause modifying **neighborhood**
(B) adverbial clause modifying **returned**
(C) noun clause in apposition with **neighborhood**
(D) adverbial phrase

5

He suffered such trouble **that he became deranged**.

(A) adverbial clause modifying **such**
(B) adjective clause modifying **trouble**
(C) adjective clause modifying **he**
(D) noun clause in apposition with **trouble**

6

There is no reason **why you cannot do this yourself**.

(A) noun clause in apposition with **reason**
(B) adverbial clause modifying **is**
(C) noun clause, subject of the verb
(D) adjective clause modifying **reason**

7

During the hurricane we found that **inside the barn** was the safest place.

(A) adverb phrase modifying **place**
(B) adverb phrase modifying **safest**
(C) prepositional phrase used as subject
(D) prepositional phrase in apposition with **place**

8

We hoped **we could arrive on time**.

(A) an adverbial clause
(B) an adjective clause
(C) a noun clause
(D) an incorrect usage

S1857

9

I am very happy **that you have reached the decision** you have.

(A) noun clause
(B) adjective clause
(C) adverbial clause
(D) appositive

10

He who buys what he does not need steals **from himself**.

(A) collective noun
(B) compound adjective
(C) prepositional phrase
(D) nominative absolute

11

Young people always talk of a time **when they will be rich**.

(A) adjective clause
(B) noun clause
(C) adverbial clause
(D) adverbial phrase

12

This is the reason **I did not answer the letter** that you sent me last week concerning tomorrow's program.

(A) main clause
(B) noun clause
(C) adverbial clause
(D) adjective clause

13

That he is a cheat and a liar seems to be common knowledge.

(A) adjective clause modifying **knowledge**
(B) noun clause subject of the verb
(C) adverbial clause modifying verb
(D) adverbial phrase modifying verb

14

After much urging, on our part, for instructional materials, he gave us enough books **to distribute to our class**.

(A) an infinitive phrase used as a substantive
(B) a gerund phrase used as a substantive
(C) a prepositional phrase used as an adjective
(D) an infinitive phrase used as an adjective

15

The thought **that he would have to face his father's wrath** made him ill.

(A) adjective clause modifying **thought**
(B) noun clause, subject of **made**
(C) adverbial clause modifying **made**
(D) adjective clause in apposition with subject

16

Whatever he does, he does with style and verve.

(A) adjective clause modifying **he**
(B) noun clause, subject of the main verb
(C) nominative absolute construction
(D) noun clause, object of the main verb

17

To believe such a strange tale was more than we were able to do.

(A) noun clause
(B) noun phrase
(C) prepositional phrase
(D) infinitive clause

18

None knew him but trusted him to the end.

(A) contains a noun clause in apposition
(B) contains a past participle
(C) contains an adjective clause
(D) contains an adverbial clause

19

There was such tension in the air **that we could not relax**.

(A) modifies **was**
(B) modifies **air**
(C) modifies **such**
(D) modifies **tension**

20

Whatever you cannot understand, you cannot possess.

(A) noun clause, subject
(B) noun clause, object
(C) noun clause, predicate nominative
(D) none of these

Bernstein's muscle-flexing and bodily contortions were apparent in the scherzo, **where they more than a little detracted from the beautiful playing of the solo horn passages by James Chambers.**

(A) independent clause
(B) noun clause
(C) adverbial clause
(D) adjective clause

Although it almost cost him his life, the boy was true **to his promise.**

(A) prepositional phrase used as an adjective
(B) prepositional phrase used as an adverb
(C) prepositional phrase used as a noun in apposition
(D) prepositional phrase used as a predicate nominative

So convincing were his tone and manner that I had no idea **that his story was false.**

(A) appositive noun clause
(B) adjective clause modifying **idea**
(C) adverbial clause modifying **had**
(D) noun clause acting as object of **convincing**

A common criticism of programmed instruction is **that the answers required of students are too simple and too stereotyped.**

(A) adjective clause modifying **criticism**
(B) adjective clause used as predicate complement
(C) noun clause used as object of the verb
(D) noun clause used as predicate complement

I looked at my wrist watch or held it to my ear every few minutes, wondering **why it moved so slowly.**

(A) noun clause
(B) adverbial clause of cause
(C) adjective clause modifying **reason** (understood)
(D) coordinate clause

It was a night **when everything seemed enchanting.**

(A) adverbial clause
(B) adjective clause
(C) participial phrase
(D) noun clause in apposition with **night**

It is true **that he is not coming to school.**

(A) adverbial clause modifying **true**
(B) noun clause after **is**
(C) noun clause used as objective complement
(D) noun clause in apposition with **it**

Although we agree upon what is to be done, it has not yet been decided **who will do it.**

(A) subordinate clause, apposition
(B) noun clause, objective case
(C) retained object
(D) relative clause, modifying verb

His first contention, **that his group should be given preferential treatment,** was quickly disputed.

(A) adjective clause modifying a noun
(B) absolute construction
(C) adverbial clause modifying an adjective
(D) noun clause in apposition

The day **when he arrived at the summit** was one of his pleasantest memories.

(A) adverbial phrase
(B) adjective clause
(C) adverbial clause
(D) past participial phrase

At the second blow, the champion staggered **as if he were about to go down.**

(A) a noun clause used as object of **staggered**
(B) an adverbial clause used to modify **staggered**
(C) an adjective clause used to modify **champion**
(D) an incorrect usage

TEST IV. PHRASES AND CLAUSES

CONSOLIDATE YOUR KEY ANSWERS HERE

	A	B	C	D	E
1					
2					
3					
4					
5					
6					
7					
8					
9					
10					
11					
12					
13					
14					
15					
16					
17					
18					
19					
20					
21					
22					
23					
24					
25					
26					
27					
28					
29					
30					
31					
32					

KEY ANSWERS FOR THE FOREGOING QUESTIONS

1.A	5.A	9.C	13.B	17.B	21.D	25.A	29.D
2.D	6.D	10.C	14.D	18.C	22.B	26.B	30.B
3.B	7.C	11.A	15.A	19.C	23.B	27.D	31.B
4.A	8.C	12.D	16.D	20.B	24.D	28.A	

EXPLANATORY ANSWERS CLARIFYING CARDINAL POINTS

The core of the Question and Answer Method . . . getting help when and where you need it. Even if you were able to write correct key answers for the preceding questions, the following explanations illuminate fundamental facts, ideas, and principles which just might crop up in the form of questions on future tests.

Bold-face references in the following answers direct you to paragraphs in the Arco Grammar Text, where fuller explanations are provided.

ANSWER 1.

A   REASON: **Where he was going** is a clause used as a noun acting as the direct object of **did know**.   (5a)

ANSWER 2.

D   REASON: **Where . . . night** is a clause used as an adjective to describe the noun **plain**.   (5a)

ANSWER 3.

B   REASON: **In defiance**, obviously a prepositional phrase, comes after a copulative verb (**was**) and refers to the subject **move**.   (5b, 7c)

ANSWER 4.

A   REASON: **Where he . . . boyhood** is an adjective clause modifying the noun **neighborhood**.   (5a)

ANSWER 5.

A   REASON: **That he became deranged** is an adverbial clause showing the extent of the adjective **such**.   (5a)

ANSWER 6.

D   REASON: The clause **why you . . . yourself** describes the noun **reason**.   (5a)

ANSWER 7.

C   REASON: **Inside the barn** takes the place of a noun which acts as the subject of the verb **was**.   (5b, 7a)

ANSWER 8.

C   REASON: Having a subject (**we**) and a verb (**could arrive**), but not expressing a complete thought, the underlined portion of the sentence is a clause. The clause is used as a noun since it is the direct object of the verb **hoped**.   (5a)

ANSWER 9.

C   REASON: The clause **that you . . . decision** is adverbial—it tells "why" in modifying the adjective **happy**.   (5a)

ANSWER 10.

C   REASON: Since **from himself** begins with a preposition, it is a prepositional phrase. Functionally, it is an adverbial phrase of manner modifying the verb **steals**.   (5b, 54)

ANSWER 11.

A   REASON: **When . . rich** is a clause used as an adjective to modify the noun **time**.   (5a)

ANSWER 12.

D   REASON: A clause contains a subject and a verb but does not express a complete thought. An adjective clause modifies a noun. It is clear that **I did not answer the letter** fulfills the requirements of a clause. Since it modifies the noun **reason**, it is an adjective clause.   (5a)

ANSWER 13.

B   REASON: **That he . . . liar** is a noun clause acting as the subject of the verb **seems**.   (5a)

ANSWER 14.

D   REASON: **To distribute to our class** is an infinitive phrase used as an adjective to modify the noun **books**.   (5b)

ANSWER 15.

A   REASON: **That he would . . . wrath** is a clause used as an adjective to modify the noun **thought**.   (5a)

ANSWER 16.

D   REASON: **Whatever he does** is a clause used as a noun. The clause is the direct object of **does**.   (5a, 7c)

ANSWER 17.

B   REASON: The infinitive (**to believe**) and its attendant words comprise a phrase. This phrase acts as a noun since it is the subject of **was**.   (5b)

ANSWER 18.

C   REASON: There is an ellipsis here: none knew him but **those who** trusted him to the end. The adjective clause **who trusted him to the end** modifies the pronoun **those**.   (5a)

ANSWER 19.

C   REASON: **That . . . relax** is a clause used as an adverb of result. The clause modifies the adjective **such**.   (5a, 39)

ANSWER 20.

B   REASON: **Whatever . . . understand** is a noun clause used as the direct object of **possess**.   (5a)

ANSWER 21.

D   REASON: The clause, **where they . . . Chambers**, is used as an adjective modifying the noun **scherzo**.   (5a)

ANSWER 22.

B REASON: **To his promise** is a phrase (incomplete thought with no subject and no verb). It modifies the predicate adjective **true**.   **(5b)**

ANSWER 23.

B REASON: **That his . . . false** is a clause used as an adjective to modify the direct object **idea**.   **(5a)**

ANSWER 24.

D REASON: The entire clause **that the answers . . . too stereotyped** is used as a noun after the copulative verb **is**. The clause is, therefore, a predicate noun. A predicate noun is the noun form of the predicate complement. A predicate adjective is also a form of a predicate complement.   **(5a, 12d)**

ANSWER 25.

A REASON: **Why it . . . slowly** is a clause because it is incomplete though it has a subject and a verb. Since the clause acts as a noun—it is the direct object of the participle **wondering**—it is a noun clause.   **(5a, 13a)**

ANSWER 26.

B REASON: **When . . . enchanting** is a clause used as an adjective modifying the noun **night**.   **(5a)**

ANSWER 27

D REASON: **That the . . . school** is a noun clause which refers back to, and means the same as, the subject **it**.   **(5a, 12)**

ANSWER 28.

A REASON: **Who will do it** is a noun clause which refers back to, and means the same as, the subject **it** (of the main clause).   **(5a, 12)**

ANSWER 29.

D REASON: **That his group . . . treatment** is a noun clause which refers to, and means the same as, the immediately preceding subject of the sentence (**contention**).   **(5a, 12)**

ANSWER 30.

B REASON: The boldface part contains a subject (**he**) and a verb (**arrived**), yet does not express a complete thought—it is, therefore, a clause. Since it modifies the noun **day**, it is an adjective clause.   **(5a)**

ANSWER 31.

B REASON: The clause in boldface is used to explain how the champion staggered - the clause modifies the verb staggered.   **(5a)**

II. NOUNS AND PRONOUNS AND THEIR CASES

8 Naming Words

Nouns are the principal "naming" words; certain kinds of pronouns also name things and persons. Both nouns and pronouns serve as *subject* and as *complement*.

If the writer is to use them effectively, he should refresh his knowledge of the kinds or classes of nouns and pronouns and of the peculiar characteristics that may cause them to be troublesome.

Let us consider, first, the characteristics (the grammatical properties) that nouns and pronouns have in common.

9 Characteristics of Nouns and Pronouns

Both nouns and pronouns have three properties: gender, case, and number.

9a **Gender** states the sex of the object being named. In English there are four genders: masculine, feminine, common, and neuter. Since the problem of gender is not very troublesome, very little emphasis will be placed on it in this book.

>Masculine: *uncle, David* (male sex)
>Feminine: *nun, Martha* (female sex)
>Common: *teacher, driver* (either sex)
>Neuter: *table, loyalty* (absence of sex)

9b **Case** is the property of a noun or pronoun which shows, either by inflection (change in the form of the noun or pronoun) or by position, the relation of the noun or pronoun to other parts of the sentence. English has three cases: nominative, objective, and possessive.

9c **Number** is the property by which we indicate whether one thing or more than one is being named. In English, we recognize two numbers: singular and plural.

10 Recognizing Nouns

Nouns are the principal naming words. To use them effectively, the writer needs background information about (1) the kinds or classes of nouns and (2) the grammatical properties of nouns.

A noun names a person, thing, idea, place, or quality. There are five classes of nouns: proper, common, collective, concrete, and abstract.

10a A **proper** noun names a particular place, person, or thing. The writer's chief problem with proper nouns is recognizing them so that he can capitalize them.

>*Atlanta, Mr. Jones, the Commissioner of Education, Form 1040*

10b A **common** noun names a class or group of persons, places, or things.

>*hope, banana, education, form*

10c A **collective** noun, singular in form, names a group or collection of individuals. The chief problem with collective nouns is determining the number of the verb to use with the collective noun. For this reason, it is discussed at length in Chapter 3, under agreement of subject and verb.

>*committee, jury, council, task force*

10d A **concrete** noun names a particular or specific member of a class or group.

>*apple*, not *fruit*; *typist*, not *personnel*

10e An **abstract** noun names a quality, state, or idea.

>*justice, truth, objectivity*

11 Recognizing Pronouns

Pronouns are the second line of naming words. They stand in place of nouns. The six classes of pronouns are: personal, relative, interrogative, indefinite, demonstrative, and intensive and reflexive.

11a The **personal** pronoun shows which person (first, second, or third) is the subject. Personal pronouns are troublesome because of their many forms; they change form to indicate number, person, and case.

11c The **interrogative** pronoun is the same in form as the relative pronoun, but different in function. The interrogative pronoun asks a question.

>*who*
>*whom* refer to persons
>
>*what* refers to things
>*which* refers to persons or things

As adjectives, *which* and *what* may be used.

>. . . which book? . . . what time?

11d The **indefinite** pronouns listed here are singular, as are most indefinites. Their chief problem, that of number, is discussed in detail in Chapter 3.

>*another, anyone, each, either, everyone, no one, nothing . . .*

PERSONAL	PRONOUNS	NOMINATIVE CASE	OBJECTIVE CASE	POSSESSIVE CASE*
SINGULAR	1st person	I	me	mine (my)
	2nd person	you	you	yours (your)
	3rd person	he, she, it	him, her, it	his, hers (her, its)
PLURAL	1st person	we	us	ours (our)
	2nd person	you	you	yours (your)
	3rd person	they	them	theirs (their)

*Possessive case personal pronouns in parentheses are used as adjectives only.

11b The **relative** pronoun serves two purposes: (1) it takes the place of a noun in the clause it introduces, and (2) like a conjunction, it connects its clause with the rest of the sentence.

>*who, whom, which, that, what, whoever, whomever, whichever, whatever*

The relative pronoun, like the personal pronoun, changes form to indicate number, person, and case. The number and the person of relative pronouns are discussed in Chapter 3; this chapter discusses their function in indicating case.

11e The **demonstrative** pronouns (*this, that, these, those*) point out or refer to a substantive which has been clearly expressed or just as clearly implied. They may be used as pronouns.

>*These* are the letters he wants.

or as adjectives.

>Bring me *those* letters.

NOTE: Do not use the personal pronoun *them* as an adjective. Use either of the demonstratives *these* or *those*, instead.

>Not: Give *them* letters to the messenger.
>But: Give *those* letters to the messenger.
>or: Give *them* to the messenger.

11f The **reflexive** pronouns are compound personal pronouns:

> *myself, yourself, yourselves, himself, themselves, ourselves, herself, itself*

A reflexive pronoun emphasizes or intensifies a meaning. It is not set off by commas.

> I *myself* will see that it is done.
> The director *himself* gave the order.
> I will take it to him *myself*.

A reflexive pronoun appears as the direct object of a verb; its antecedent, as the subject of the verb.

> I taught *myself* how to type.
> He hurt *himself* when he fell.

It can, however, be the object of a preposition,

> He finished the assignment by *himself*.
> He was beside *himself* with joy.

the indirect object of a verb,

> I bought *myself* a new suit yesterday.

or a predicate nominative.

> I am just not *myself* today.

In formal usage, the reflexive pronoun is not used where the shorter personal pronoun can be substituted for it with no change in meaning.

> Not: Both the Director and *myself* endorse the policy.
> But: Both the Director and *I* endorse the policy.

NOTE: Most errors (usually in oral communication) in the use of these pronouns are such careless errors as:

> The use of *hisself* for *himself*.
> The use of *theirselves* for *themselves*.
> The use of *myself* instead of the personal pronoun *me* or *I* in such constructions as "The secretary and *myself* were assigned to do this work."

CASE

Case is the property of a noun or pronoun which shows, either by inflection (change in form) or by position, the relation of the word to other parts of the sentence.

English has three cases: nominative, objective, and possessive.

All nouns and a few pronouns keep the same form in the nominative and in the objective cases. Consequently, we must depend on the position of these words in the sentence to indicate their function. Since nouns don't change form to indicate nominative and objective case, our only real difficulty with them comes in the formation and use of the possessive.

On the other hand, some pronouns are inflected (change form) in the nominative and objective cases, as well as in the possessive. Because of this, the case of pronouns causes us more trouble than does the case of nouns, and pronouns are more frequently misused.

12 Nominative Case

The nominative (or subjective) case is used primarily to name the subject of a verb or the predicate complement after a linking verb (such as *seem, appear,* or any form of *be*).

If either the subject or predicate complement is compound, both members must be in the nominative case.

> Not: Either *she* or *me* will be responsible.
> But: Either *she* or *I* will be responsible.
> (Either *she* will be... or *I* will be....)

NOTE: An appositive, which is a word or group of words standing next to another word and denoting the same person or thing, is always in the same case as its antecedent (the word it stands in apposition to). Therefore, *if the antecedent is in the nominative case*, the appositive must also be in the nominative case. If the antecedent is in the objective case, the appositive is also in the objective case.

> Not: The representatives, *John and me*, are to meet on Friday.
> But: The representatives, *John and I*, are to meet on Friday.
> (*John and I* are to meet. . . .)

12a Subject of a verb in a main clause.

A noun or pronoun serving as the subject of a verb (except the subject of an infinitive) is in the nominative case.

> *I* was late for work this morning.
> (*I* is in the nominative case.)

> *He* is planning to finish his report this week.

> *He* and *I* have been assigned a new case.
> (Both words joined by the coordinate conjunction are in the nominative case.)

> Neither *he* nor *I* had heard of this before.

> The culprits, *she and I*, were reprimanded.
> (The appositive, *she and I*, is in the nominative case because its antecedent, *culprits*, is the subject of the sentence.)

12b Subject of a relative clause

A relative pronoun (*who, whoever, which, whichever*) used as the subject of a clause is in the nominative case.

> Give the letter to *whoever answer the door.*

The clause itself may be a subject or, as in this example, an object; however, the case of the relative pronoun depends upon its use *within the clause.*

> The award will go to him *who completes the course with the highest score.*
> (The antecedent of the relative pronoun—*him*—is in the objective case, but *who* is in the nominative case because it is the subject of the clause.)

> *Whoever is selected* must report on Monday.
> (The clause is the subject of the sentence; the relative pronoun is in the nominative case because it is the subject of the clause.)

The pronoun *who* used as the subject of a verb is not affected by a parenthetical expression such as *I think, he believes, they say* intervening between the subject and the verb.

> He is the person *who* I think is best qualified.
> (Disregard "I think"; *who* is the subject of the clause.)

> We asked Susan, *who* we knew *had always been* a student of English.
> (Ignore "we knew": *who* is the subject of the clause.)

> Mr. Jones is the attorney *who* we suppose *will prepare* the brief.
> ("We suppose" is a parenthetical expression; *who* is the subject of the clause.)

To know when to use *who* or *whom*, the following two steps should help you.

Take this sentence—

> Tell me (*who, whom*) you think should wash the dishes.

STEP ONE: Change the who/whom part of the sentence to its natural order.

> You think (*who, whom*) should wash the dishes.

STEP TWO: Substitute *he* for *who*, *him* for *whom*.

> You think (*he, him*) should wash the dishes.

You would, of course, say *he* in this case. Therefore, the original sentence should be

> Tell me *who* you think should wash the dishes.

12c Subject of clause introduced by *than or as*

If the word following *than* or *as* introduces a clause, even if part of the clause is understood, that word must be in the nominative case. But if the word following *than* or *as* does not introduce a clause, it must be in the objective case. To test whether the word should be in the nominative or objective case, complete the clause.

He has been here longer than *she*. (than *she has*)

Mary is a better stenographer than *I*. (than *I am*)

They were as late as *we* in filing the report. (as *we were*)

We were told as promptly as *they*. (as *they were*)

In the following examples, the word following *than* or *as* may be in either the nominative or the objective case, depending on the intended meaning. If there is any chance your meaning might be misunderstood, complete the clause.

She likes this work better than I. (than *I lik it*)

She likes this work better than *me*. (than *she likes me*)

I have known John as long as *she*. (as *she has*)
I have known John as long as *her*. (as *I have known her*)

12d Words following forms of *be* (predicate nominative)

A noun or pronoun following a form of the verb *be* (except for the infinitive if it has its own subject) must be in the nominative case. (This word is called the *predicate nominative*—or, if a noun, the *predicate noun*.) The general rule applying to this construction is that the word following the verb *be* must be in the same case as the word before the verb. Imagine that the verb *be* has the same meaning as the equals sign (=) in mathematics.

Not: They thought I was *him*.
But: They thought I was *he*. (*I = he*)

Not: I am expecting my secretary to call. Is that *her?*
But: I am expecting my secretary to call. Is that *she?*

A noun or pronoun following the infinitive *to be* is in the nominative case if the infinitive has no subject. For a discussion of the case of the noun or pronoun following an infinitive when the infinitive has a subject, see section 13e.

He was thought to be *I*.
My brother was taken to be *I*.

NOTE: You may have trouble when one or both of the members of the compound subject or predicate nominative are pronouns. Try this simple test: Decide which case would be appropriate if *one* pronoun were the simple subject or predicate nominative, and then use the same case for both.

Example:
The new *chairmen* are *he* and *I*.
Reverse positions:
He and I are the new *chairmen*.

Example:
If any one of the agents is chosen, *it* should be *he*.
Reverse positions:
If any one of the agents is chosen, *he* should be *it*.

Example:
The *author* was thought to be *I*.
Reverse positions:
I was thought to be the *author*.

12e Direct address

Direct address is a construction used parenthetically to direct a speech to some particular person. Nouns or pronouns in direct address are in the nominative case and are set off by commas. This construction will cause little trouble, since proper names, which are the main examples of direct address, do not change form to indicate case.

James, come here for a minute.
It is true, *sir,* that I made that remark.
Tell me, *Doctor,* is he showing much improvement?

12f Nominative absolute

The nominative absolute is a phrase that consists of a noun or a pronoun and a participle. It modifies the whole sentence but is grammatically independent of the rest of the sentence. The noun or pronoun in a nominative absolute construction is in the nominative case.

We left the office together, HE *having finished his work.*

(The phrase beginning *he having finished* . . . is a nominative absolute phrase modifying the main clause. The pronoun *he* is the subject of the *action implied* by the participle *having finished*; it is in the nominative case.)

HE *having been elected chairman*, I am sure the meeting will have outstanding results.

13   Objective Case

The objective (or accusative) case is used chiefly to name the receiver or object of the action of a verb, or to name the object of a preposition.

When one part of a compound expression (joined by a coordinate conjunction) is in the objective case, all other parts of the same expression must also be in the objective case.

> When you reach the station call either *him* or *me*.
> (*Call him* . . . or *call me*)
> The work was given to *you* and *me*.
> (*To you* . . . *to me*.)

When the antecedent of an appositive is in the objective case because it is serving a function that requires that case, the appositive must also be in the objective case.

> The director has appointed *us, you and me,* to the committee.
> (*has appointed you* . . . *has appointed me*)
> He gave *us auditors* a copy of the report.
> (*he gave us* . . .)
> The principle is basic to *us Americans.*
> (*is basic to us*)

13a   Direct object of a verb or verbal

A noun or pronoun serving as the direct object of a verb or verbal is in the objective case.

> The driver returned *him* to his home.
> (*Him* is the object of the verb *returned*.)
> My supervisor called *him* and *me* to his office.
> (The compound object *him and me* is the object of the verb *called*.)
> They will invite *us secretaries* to the meeting.
> (*Us*, as well as its appositive *secretaries*, is the object of the verb *invite*.)
> *Whomever* you called before the meeting might like a copy of this report.

(The relative pronoun *whomever* is the object of the verb *called* in the relative clause; the entire clause is the subject of *might like*.)

But: Call *whoever* is responsible before the meeting.

(The whole relative clause *whoever is responsible* is the object of the verb *call*; but *whoever* is in the nominative case because it is the subject of its clause.)

I enjoyed meeting *him*.

(*Him* is the object of the gerund *meeting*)

I didn't intend to ask *them* again.

(*Them* is the direct object of the infinitive *to ask*.)

Having called *him* and told *him* of our plan, we left the office.

(The first *him* is the direct object of the participle *having called*; the second *him* is the object of the participle *having told*.)

We have a letter from his company thanking *us* for our courtesy.

(*Us* is the direct object of the participle *thanking*.)

13b   Indirect object of a verb or verbal

A word used as the indirect object of a verb or verbal is in the objective case.

> The supervisor gave *me* the report.
> (*Me* is the indirect object of the verb *gave*.)

> The supervisor assigned *him* and *me* the task of reviewing the study.
> (The compound object *him and me* is the indirect object of the verb *assigned*.)

> The representative showed *us secretaries* the operation of the new typewriter.
> (*Secretaries*, is the indirect object of the verb *showed*.)

> A letter giving *him* authority to represent the company is being prepared.
> (*Him* is the indirect object of the participle *giving*.)

> To tell *us* the latest developments, the Director held a staff meeting.
> (*Us* is the indirect object of the infinitive *to tell*.)

Offering the book to the *child*, the teacher smiled.
> (*Child* is the indirect object of the participle *offering*.)

13c Object of a preposition

A noun or pronoun serving as the object of a preposition is in the objective case.

The rebels fought with *fury*.
> (*Fury* is the object of the preposition *with*.)

An anchor could not be made of *wood*.
> (*Wood* is the object of the preposition *of*.)

We shall arrive in Denver before *noon*.
> (*Noon* is the object of the preposition *before*.)

From whom did you receive the letter?
> (*Whom* is the object of the preposition *from*.)

NOTE: *But* is a preposition when *except* may be substituted for it with no change in meaning.

Everyone is going BUT *me*.
> (Everyone is going EXCEPT *me*.)

A special troublemaker is the compound object *you and me* after the preposition *between*. Do not say *between you and I*; say *between you and me*.

13d Subject of an infinitive

A noun or pronoun used as the subject of an infinitive is in the objective case.

I want *him* to have this copy.
> (*Him* is the subject of the infinitive *to have*.)

We expect *him* to be elected.
> (*Him* is the subject of the infinitive *to be elected*.)

Please let *us* know if you are coming.
> (*Us* is the subject of the infinitive (*to*) *know*.)

They invited *him and me* to attend the reception.
> (*Him and me* is the compound subject of the infinitive *to attend*.)

The Director asked *us secretaries* to attend the meeting.
> (*Us*, and its appositive *secretaries*, is the subject of the infinitive *to attend*.)

Whom do they expect to be the next chairman?
> (*Whom* is the subject of the infinitive *to be*.)

Whom will we invite to speak at the convention?
> (In natural order—*we will invite* WHOM *to speak* . . . *Whom* is the subject of the infinitive *to speak*.)

13e Word following infinitive to be

In section 12d we saw that the verb *to be* takes the same case after it as before it. Since the subject of an infinitive is in the objective case, a word following the infinitive is also in the objective case.

They thought him to be *me*.
> (Reverse, to test choice of case: They thought *me* to be *him*.)

We assumed the author of the letter to be *him*.
> (Reverse: We assumed *him* to be the *author*. . . .)

They did not expect the representatives to be *him and me*.
> (Reverse: They did not expect *him and me* to be the *representatives*.)

We had expected the group selected to be *us secretaries*.
> (Reverse: We had expected *us secretaries* to be the *group selected*.)

13f Subject of a participle and of a gerund

The subject of a participle is in the objective case. The problem comes in determining whether a verbal is a participle or a gerund. Both may have the same form (the *ing* form of the verb), but only the subject of the *participle* is in the objective case. The subject of the *gerund* is in the possessive case. This technique may help you choose the correct case: When the *doer* of the action is stressed, the verbal is a participle performing its adjective function as a modifier of its subject; when the *action itself* is the important thing, the verbal is a gerund—a verbal noun.

> Imagine *him flying* an airplane.
> (The element being stressed here is the pronoun *him*; therefore the verbal *flying* is a participle modifying *him*, and the pronoun *him* is in the objective case.)

> Imagine *his flying* to Paris.
> (Here we are stressing not *him* but his *flying*; therefore the verbal *flying* is a gerund, and the pronoun *his* is in the possessive case.)

> *His rushing* to catch the plane was in vain.
> (We are talking about his *rushing*, not the person himself; therefore *rushing* is a gerund, and its subject must be in the possessive case.)

> We watched *him rushing* to catch the plane.
> (Here we are stressing *him*. The verbal *rushing* is a participle modifying *him*; therefore, the subject, *him*, is in the objective case.)

NOTE: In the gerund expression *its being*, the subject that follows must be in the objective case.

> In our search for the thief, we never thought of its being *him* (not *he*).
> (The possessive *its* has an expletive function here. See 18a.)

13g Objective complement

Verbs of naming, selecting, making, and the like often take an objective complement which is a noun (or adjective) that completes the meaning of the direct object.

> I call this headache a *nuisance*.
> Paul's rashness makes his friends *uneasy*.
> We consider him a perfect *gentlemen*.

13h Adverbial objective

A noun used as an adverb to modify a verb is called an adverbial objective.

> I slept two *hours*.
> Turn your head this *way*.
> Thomas is sixteen *years* old.

13i Retained object

A retained object occurs in a sentence which has a passive verb. The retained object was originally an object after the active verb.

> Mable was given a *lesson* by the teacher.
> (The verb, *was given*, is a passive verb. The retained object is *lesson*.)
> The teacher gave Mable a *lesson*.
> (The verb, *gave*, is an active verb. The direct object is *lesson*.)

> The boy was asked by his mother *whether he had bought the milk*.
> (The verb, *was asked*, is a passive verb. The retained object is the entire clause *whether . . . milk*.)
> His mother asked the boy *whether he had bought the milk*.
> (The verb, *asked*, is an active verb. The direct object is the entire clause *whether . . . milk*. Incidentally, *boy* is an indirect object.)

> The girl was taught *to type*.
> (the verb, *was taught*, is a passive verb. The retained object is the infinitive, *to type*.)
> The maid taught the girl *to type*.
> (The verb, *taught*, is an active verb. The direct object is *to type*.)

13j Cognate object

A cognate object is a noun which comes after an intransitive verb and which, through its similarity to the verb, expresses the action already expressed by the verb.

> The horse ran a good *race*.
> He smiled a sickly *smile*.
> They lived a *life* of ease.

14 Possessive Case

The possessive (or genitive) case is used to indicate possession.

14a Possessive of singular words

To form the possessive of singular words not ending in *s* (including the indefinite pronouns), add the apostrophe and *s*.

> the *agent's* report; the *Director's* office; the *secretary's* desk; *anyone's* guess; somebody's coat.

NOTE: When *else* is used with an indefinite pronoun, form the possessive by adding the apostrophe and *s* to *else*, rather than to the indefinite pronoun.

somebody's coat	but: somebody *else's* coat
anyone's idea	but: anyone *else's* idea

To form the possessive of a singular word ending in *s* or an *s*-sound, add the apostrophe alone if the possessive and the regular forms of the word are pronounced alike. If the possessive form is pronounced with an additional *s*-sound, add both the apostrophe and *s*.

Singular form	Possessive form
boss	boss's (pronounced *boss-es*)
hostess	hostess' (pronounced *hostess*) or hostess's (pronounced *hostess-es*)

NOTE: To form the possessive of a proper name ending in *s* or an *s*-sound, follow this same method. If the possessive form is pronounced with an additional *s*-sound, add both the apostrophe and *s*. If the regular and the possessive forms of the proper name are pronounced alike, add the apostrophe alone to form the possessive.

Either: Charles'	or:	Charles's
Either: James'	or:	James's
Either: Mr. Simmons'	or:	Mr. Simmons's
But: Roberts'	not:	Roberts's

The apostrophe is omitted in some organizational or geographical names that contain a possessive thought. Follow the form used by the organization itself.

Harpers Ferry	*Pikes Peak*
Governors Island	*Citizens National Bank*

Do not use the apostrophe in forming the possessive of the personal and relative pronouns. The possessive forms of these pronouns are:

Relative: whose

Personal: *her, hers* (not *her's*), *his, their, theirs, our, ours, my, mine, your, yours, its*

NOTE: *Its* is the possessive form of the personal pronoun *it*; *it's* is a contraction of *it is*. Similarly, *whose* is the possessive form of the relative pronoun *who*, and *who's* is a contraction of *who is*. The examples below illustrate the correct use of these words.

Its operation is simple.
It's (*it is*) simple to operate.

Don't use that typewriter; *its* ribbon needs changing.
Don't use that typewriter; *it's* in need of a new ribbon.

Whose typewriter is that?
Who's (*who is*) going with me?

Theirs is in the closet.
There's very little time left.

14b Possessive of plural words

To form the possessive of a plural word not ending in *s*, add the apostrophe and s

men's, children's, women's, people's

To form the possessive of a plural word ending in *s*, add the apostrophe only.

All of the *District Directors'* reports have been received.

NOTE: Avoid placing the apostrophe before the final *s* of a word if the *s* is actually a part of the singular or plural form. To test, first form the plural; then add the correct possessive sign.

Not: *Ladie's*   But: *Ladies'*

(*Ladies* is the plural form; since the word ends in *s*, add the apostrophe alone to form the possessive, *ladies'*.)

14c Use of the *of* phrase to form possessive

Use an *of* phrase instead of an apostrophe or an apostrophe and *s* to form the possessive of inanimate things.

Not: A corporation's long-term capital gain is taxed. . . .
But: The long-term capital gain of a corporation is taxed. . . .

Not: The *bill's passage* will no doubt mean higher taxes.

But: The *passage of the bill* will no doubt mean higher taxes.

EXCEPTION: The apostrophe and *s* is used to form the possessive of inanimate objects denoting time, measure, or space. The illustrations below are examples of this idiomatic usage. Notice the placement of the apostrophe to indicate singular or plural.

a day's work	two weeks' notice
five days' pay	six months' course
a dollar's worth	a stone's throw
two dollars' worth	his money's worth
an arm's length	a snail's pace

Use the *of* phrase in forming the possessive to avoid the "piling up" of possessives.

Not: The *taxpayer's wife's income* must be reported.

But: The *income of the taxpayer's wife* must be reported.

Not: The *committee's treasurer's report* was read.

But: The *report of the committee's treasurer* was read.

Use the *of* phrase to form the possessive of names consisting of several words, in order to avoid an awkward construction.

Not: The local chapter of the National Association of Radio and Television Broadcasters' first meeting was held Thursday.

But: The first meeting of the local chapter of the National Association of Radio and and Television Broadcasters was held Thursday.

Not: The Director of the Alcohol and Tobacco Tax Division's report....

But: The report of the Director of the Alcohol and Tobacco Tax Division....

Sometimes both the *of* phrase and the possessive are needed to express meaning accurately.

Not: This is the *Commissioner's picture.*
  (Could mean: This is a portrait of him.
  or: This is his property.)

But: This is *a picture of the Commissioner.* (his portrait)

or: This is *a picture of the Commissioner's.* (his property)

Use the *of* phrase to avoid adding a possessive to a pronoun that is already possessive.

Not: We are going to a *friend of mine's* house.

But: We are going to the *house of a friend of mine.*

14d Possessive of compound words

Form the possessive on the last word of a compound word, whether or not the compound is hyphenated. A point to remember is that, even though the plural of a compound word is formed by adding "s" to the principal noun in the compound, the possessive is always formed by adding the *sign of the possessive* to the *last word in the compound.*

Singular possessive	*Plural*
notary public's	notaries public
comptroller general's	comptrollers general
supervisor in charge's	supervisors in charge

Plural possessive

notaries public's
comptrollers general's
supervisors in charge's

If a possessive is followed by an appositive or an explanatory phrase, form the possessive on the explanatory word.

That was *Mr. Smith the auditor's* idea.
I was acting on my *attorney Mr. Brown's* advice.
Have you read the *Senator from Arizona's* speech?

If the appositive or explanatory words are set off by commas, the possessive may be formed on both the main word and the explanatory word.

Either: This is *Mary, my secretary's,* day off.
Or: This is *Mary's, my secretary's,* day off.

Either: I sent it to *Mr. Roberts, the collector's*, office.

Or: I sent it to *Mr. Roberts', the collector's*, office.

NOTE: The methods just illustrated are grammatically correct ways to show possession; they do, however, sound awkward. To be more effective (and just as correct), try using an *of* phrase to form the possessive of compound words.

Not: This is the supervisor in charge's office.
But: This is the office of the supervisor in charge.

Not: I was acting on my attorney Mr. Brown's advice.
But: I was acting on the advice of my attorney, Mr. Brown.

Not: I sent it to Mr. Roberts', the collector's office.
But: I sent it to the office of Mr. Roberts, the collector.

14e Joint, separate, and alternative possession

When two or more people possess the same thing jointly, form the possessive on the last word only.

She is *Mr. Roberts and Miss Henry's* secretary.
(She is secretary to both people.)
These pictures are from *John and Mary's* vacation trip.
I bought my coat at *Woodward and Lothrop's* (*store* understood).

NOTE: When one of the words involved in the joint possession is a pronoun, each word must be in the possessive.

This is *John's, Bob's*, and *my* office.
Have you seen *Mary's* and *his* new home?

When it is intended that each of the words in a series possess something individually, form the possessive on each word.

Barbara's and *Mary's* typing are certainly different.
The *Secretaries'* and the *Accountants'* associations are meeting here this week.

When alternative possession is intended, each word must be in the possessive.

I wouldn't want either *John's* or *Harry's* job.
Is that the *author's* or the *editor's* opinion?

14f Possessive of abbreviations

Possessives of abbreviations are formed in the same way as are other possessives. Ordinarily the possessive sign is placed after the final period of the abbreviation.

Singular Possessive	Plural	Plural Possessive
M.D.'s	M.D.s	M.D.s'
Dr.'s	Drs.	Drs.'
Co.'s	Cos.	Cos.' or Cos'.
Bro.'s	Bros.	Bros.'

Enclosed is Johnson *Bros.'* bill for their work.
John Blank, *Jr.'s* account has been closed.
(Note that there is no comma after *Jr.* when the possessive is used).

14g Parallel possessives

Be sure that a word standing parallel with a possessive is itself possessive in form.

Not: *His* work, like an *accountant*, is exacting.
But: *His* work, like an *accountant's*, is exacting.

Not: The *agent's* job differs from the *auditor* in that. . . .
But: The *agent's* job differs from the *auditor's* in that. . . .

Not: *His* task is no more difficult than his *neighbor*.
But: *His* task is no more difficult than his *neighbor's*.

14h Possessive with a gerund

A noun or pronoun immediately preceding a gerund is in the possessive case. A gerund is a verbal noun naming an action. A participle, which may have the same form as a gerund, functions as an adjective; its subject is in the objective case.

Our being late delayed the meeting.
Mr. Jones' being late delayed the meeting.
You can always depend on *his* doing a good job.
Jim's writing the letter made all the difference.
Washington's being the capital makes it different from other cities.

NOTE: There are three exceptions to this general rule:

(1) The possessive of an inanimate object is not usually formed by the apostrophe and *s*. When the subject of a gerund is a noun standing for an inanimate object, use the objective case, an *of* phrase, or a subordinate clause, whichever is most appropriate.

Not: The *desk's refinishing* is almost complete.
But: The *refinishing of the desk* is almost complete.
(*of*-phrase)

Not: The possibility of the *meeting's ending* soon is doubtful.
But: The possibility of the *meeting ending* soon is doubtful.
(objective case)

Not: We missed our ride because of the *meeting's lasting so late*.
But: We missed our ride because the *meeting lasted so late*.
(subordinate clause)

(2) Do not use the possessive case for the subject of a gerund unless the subject immediately precedes the gerund. If subject and gerund are separated by other words, the subject must be in the objective case.

Not: I can see no reason for a *man's* with his background *failing* to pass the test.
But: I can see no reason for a *man* with his background *failing* to pass the test.
(Without intervening words: I can see no reason for a *man's failing* to pass the test.)

Not: I concede the difficulty of *his*, because of his interest, *being* completely fair.
But: I concede the difficulty of *him*, because of his interest, *being* completely fair.

(3) There are no possessive forms for the demonstrative pronouns *that, this, these,* and *those*. Therefore, when these words are used as subjects of a gerund they do not change form.

Not: We cannot be sure of *that's* being true.
But: We cannot be sure of *that* being true.

Not: What are the chances of *this'* being sold?
But: What are the chances of *this* being sold?

Now, push forward! Test yourself and practice for your test with the carefully constructed quizzes that follow. Each one presents the kind of question you may expect on your test. And each question is at just the level of difficulty that may be expected. Don't try to take all the tests at one time. Rather, schedule yourself so that you take a few at each session, and spend approximately the same time on them at each session. Score yourself honestly, and date each test. You should be able to detect improvement in your performance on successive sessions.

TEST V. NOUNS, PRONOUNS, AND THEIR CASES

TIME: 25 Minutes

DIRECTIONS: In each of the following groups of sentences, select the one sentence that is grammatically INCORRECT. Mark the answer sheet with the letter of that incorrect sentence.

Explanations of the key points behind these questions appear with the answers at the end of this test. The explanatory answers provide the kind of background that will enable you to answer test questions with facility and confidence.

(A) In the event that a typist is not coming in, she is to call the office at 7:30 a.m. or as close to that time as possible.
(B) The notation on the "While You Were Out" slip said that Mr. Lane of the board of directors had called.
(C) Decisions of these kinds may have to be made by you if no supervisor is available.
(D) What kind of information did the customer request?

2

(A) A reconciliation was effected by the guidance counselor.
(B) We shall all have benefited if fear of man's annihilation becomes a thing of the past.
(C) They had already investigated the truth of his allegations.
(D) He was driving somebody else's car, not our's.

3

(A) The teacher asked, "Is this coat your's or John's?"
(B) Some students apparently learn easily; others have to be tutored individually.
(C) A state cannot remain sovereign if it yields control of its boundaries to other nations.
(D) The meeting had scarcely started when a member raised a point of order.

4

(A) "Your's is not to question why!" she declaimed from the stage.
(B) Had you explained how colossal the task would become, she would not be in this predicament now.
(C) In the melee, he thought the disputant to be me.
(D) A number of Europeans were hanged during the Crusades.

5

(A) Our club sent two representatives, Charles and I, to Miami Beach.
(B) From a neighbor he borrowed a shovel that was broken.
(C) Each of us held his breath.
(D) The sergeant had had many close calls; for example, he had once been left for dead by the enemy.

(A) The villagers suffered from the depredations of the enemy.
(B) These books are ours, but that one on the library table is hers.
(C) Mary will join with you and I in attempting to persuade the superintendent to repair the damage.
(D) The old man was careful not to deplete his strength.

(A) In his effort to reach a wise decision about these truants, the attendance officer conferred many times with the dean and I.
(B) An old miser who picked up yellow pieces of gold had something of the simple ardor, something of the mystical materialism, of a child who picks out yellow flowers.
(C) Corruption of language has reached higher proportions in America than anywhere else.
(D) Dealers were instructed to replace all four wheels.

8

(A) Why not join Gwen and myself at the concert?
(B) TV can be an invaluable aid to the teacher in presenting material clearly, effectively, and dramatically.
(C) I think we should treat them with a mixture of respect and irreverence: respect for their learning and experience, irreverence for any alleged infallibility.
(D) The apocryphal Acts of Paul is the work which contains a description of his appearance.

9

(A) The alternative suggested by him is even less desirable than your plans.
(B) Many of our modern insignia date back to medieval times.
(C) The book is popular with those who have never seen the Orient.
(D) Give the message to whomever arrives first.

10

(A) The lilacs, the early roses, and the lush warmth of the morning smelled fragrant as odors from the gardens of Heaven.
(B) I found it to be fruitful to study the plan in detail.
(C) Let's you and I confront him together.
(D) Maugham has the ability to hold his reader's attention.

11

(A) Her work, like any computer programmer, is difficult.
(B) His alternative was to stand or run.
(C) His wish is that the house be finished by Christmas.
(D) If you wait but ten minutes you will see her.

12

(A) Few of us, at the end of a project, are altogether satisfied that we have done our best.
(B) Only the following are needed: a hammer, nails, some boards, and a simple plan.
(C) In spite of his youth, no faster runner than him will be found in our school.
(D) Address the letter to Mr. William Brown, 25 East Ocean Street, Hamilton, California.

13

(A) If you work hard, you will soon be as efficient as him.
(B) Mr. Oldschmidt, the custodian, washes our windows regularly, but he does not think that he should wax the floors.
(C) The students demand that the honor system be retained for at least one more year.
(D) The committee feels that a man whose speech is poor should not be selected.

14

(A) I didn't approve my friend's talking so much at the meeting.
(B) Let's you and I decide that the prize should go to whoever tried hardest.
(C) I have no knowledge of or interest in such a topic as this.
(D) She is a person whom we know people can trust.

15

(A) The author who's works I admire most is Galsworthy.
(B) Trapped in a high fork of the tree, the cat could be reached only by a man using the firemen's longest ladder.
(C) The art critic challenged my statement that the vase was unique, stating that he had seen a replica in England.
(D) That there is only one solution for any set of problems is difficult to prove.

16

(A) Neither of these two men has won a reputation in his field.
(B) Students in the field of education often find statistical data rather involved.
(C) After living through the cold winters of the North, people welcome the thaws of spring.
(D) Offer the nomination to whomever commands the respect of the people.

17

(A) He feels ill, but his sister looks worse.
(B) The Joneses are going to visit their friends in Chicago.
(C) "Robinson Crusoe," which is a fairy tale to the child, is a work of social philosophy to the mature thinker.
(D) I was appreciative of all his efforts, especially of him doing that one job for me.

18

(A) This production is inferior to that of a few years ago.
(B) They carefully tested the effectiveness of this novel procedure.
(C) Just between you and I, his theories won't work.
(D) The book contains several allusions to Teutonic mythology.

19

(A) Henry maintains that he has already read the article in its entirety.
(B) A large number of people signed the petition.
(C) We appreciate you going to all this trouble for us.
(D) Acoustics is a subdivision of science.

20

(A) We studied some mathematics, very well taught; some science, very badly taught; also some plays of Shakespeare, taught worst of all.
(B) They teased him mercilessly, but there was no doubt of him being able to take it and come back for more.
(C) In this country there are few chances of diversion—a shift in weather, perhaps, or something arriving in the mail.
(D) I find Henry James' prose style difficult.

(A) Remains of an ancient civilization were found near Mexico City.
(B) It is interesting to compare the interior of one of the pyramids in Mexico with the interior of one of the pyramids in Egypt.
(C) In two days' journey you will be reminded of political upheavals comparable to the volcanic eruptions still visible and audible in parts of Mexico.
(D) There is little danger of the law being broken.

(A) Five dollars is too much to pay for a book in that condition.
(B) I have no doubt that America taking a strong, consistent attitude in the world crisis at this time will both strengthen the Western powers and weaken the Soviet.
(C) In all your years as dormitory master have you ever seen two students so devoted to each other?
(D) Not a word, not a single word did I ever hear him utter in protest.

(A) He would not accept of my hospitality.
(B) He is a pleasant person until challenged.
(C) We still don't know to whom to turn.
(D) It is the shutters swinging in the wind.

(A) They choose only such women as measure up to their high scholastic standards.
(B) Because of the strictness of her upbringing, she was not allowed to partake in any of the school dances.
(C) They wanted both Louise and he to join the club.
(D) Do you think that everything is all right in the house and in the yard?

(A) His vociferous pleading made no impression upon the old judge.
(B) Only fear of reprisals restrained him.
(C) Where is the girl who he recommended?
(D) "The United States needs assurance by action—not words—that its citizens will be safe," was the official's reply.

(A) These kinds of excuses are hard to accept.
(B) The teacher asked three of us, Dan, Edward and I, to carry the plants down to the office.
(C) Neither of those men has decided to stay on.
(D) The Federal Reserve banks are now interested in hiring people who have been graduated from college recently.

(A) Why should he mind your having taken the stapler?
(B) It has been functioning as a graduate school ever since.
(C) He led his captors a merry chase.
(D) All sorority members declined except she.

(28)

(A) Give the position to whomever you think is best qualified in all respects.
(B) The consensus, as far as I can determine it, is that his official conduct amounts to malfeasance.
(C) Whatever his personal feelings about his colleagues may be, he should keep his professional relationships on a high plane.
(D) All boys in the school are expected to participate in the athletic program.

(29)

(A) It is hard to conceive of their not doing good work.
(B) Who won—you or I?
(C) He reading the speech caused much comment.
(D) Their finishing the work proves that it can be done.

(30)

(A) The company has moved into its new building.
(B) They will approve of him going to the concert.
(C) That business is good appears to be true.
(D) It was he who won the prize.

(31)

(A) Them that honor me I will honor.
(B) They that believe in me shall be rewarded.
(C) Who did you see at the meeting?
(D) Whom are you writing to?

(32)

(A) Bob has an advantage over Al, for he knows the subject well.
(B) Give the parcel to whomever pays for it.
(C) Her husband is a career officer in the State Department.
(D) Regardless of our wishes in the matter, she intends to leave Saturday morning.

(33)

(A) The company published its new catalogue last week.
(B) The man who he introduced was Mr. Carey.
(C) The Rolls-Royce is the fastest car in England.
(D) He finished the job satisfactorily.

(A) Barbara's and Tommy's mother comes from a family of actors and actresses.
(B) Great teachers must have native gifts, for, like poets, they are born, not made.
(C) Brought to the U.S. late in life, Einstein, one of the world's most renowned scientists, developed into an ardent American.
(D) The only uninterested spectator I noticed in the courtroom was a feeble old man half asleep near the door.

(A) Answer the door to whomever rings the bell.
(B) When the packages for us men arrived, there was a wild rush to open them.
(C) When a member of the group received a cake or a box of candy from home, he was expected to share it.
(D) Bill Simpson is one of the four men in our squad who have been on the honor list every term of their service.

CONSOLIDATE YOUR KEY ANSWERS HERE

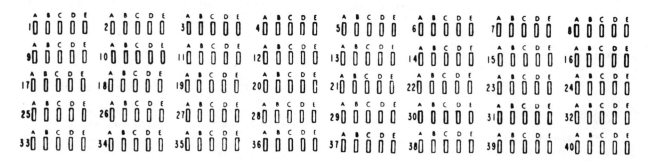

Correct Answers For The Foregoing Questions

(Check your answers with these that we provide. You should find considerable correspondence between them. If not, you'd better go back and find out why. On the next page we have provided concise clarifications of basic points behind the key answers. Please go over them carefully because they may be quite useful in helping you pick up extra points on the exam.)

1.B	6.C	11.A	16.D	21.D	26.B	31.C
2.D	7.A	12.C	17.D	22.B	27.D	32.B
3.A	8.A	13.A	18.C	23.A	28.A	33.B
4.A	9.D	14.B	19.C	24.C	29.C	34.A
5.A	10.C	15.A	20.B	25.C	30.B	35.A

TEST V. NOUNS, PRONOUNS, AND THEIR CASES

EXPLANATORY ANSWERS CLARIFYING CARDINAL POINTS

The core of the Question and Answer Method ... getting help when and where you need it. Even if you were able to write correct key answers for the preceding questions, the following explanations illuminate fundamental facts, ideas, and principles which just might crop up in the form of questions on future tests.

Bold-face references in the following answers direct you to paragraphs in the Arco Grammar Text, where fuller explanations are provided.

ANSWER 1.

B The notation on the "While You Were Out" slip said that Mr. Lane of the **Board** of **Directors** has called. REASON: The important words of a title are capitalized. **(10a)**

ANSWER 2.

D He was driving somebody else's car, not **ours**. REASON: The possessive pronoun (**ours**) has no apostrophe. **(11a)**

ANSWER 3.

A The teacher asked, "Is this coat **yours** or John's?" REASON: The possessive pronoun is **yours**, without an apostrophe. **(11a)**

ANSWER 4.

A "**Yours** is not to question why!" she declaimed from the stage. REASON: The possessive pronoun has no apostrophe. **(11a)**

ANSWER 5.

A Our club sent two representatives, Charles and **me**, to Miami Beach. REASON: The direct object of the pronoun requires the **me** form. **(11a, 13a)**

ANSWER 6.

C Mary will join with you and **me** in attempting to persuade the superintendent to repair the damage. REASON: The object of the preposition is **me**. **(11a, 13c)**

ANSWER 7.

A In his effort to reach a wise decision about these truants, the attendance officer conferred many times with the dean and **me**. REASON: The objects of the preposition **with** are **dean** and **me**. **(13c)**

ANSWER 8.

A Why not join Gwen and me at the concert? REASON: The direct object is **me**. The reflexive pronoun (**myself**) has no place here. **(11f)**

ANSWER 9.

D Give the message to **whoever** arrives first. REASON: This sentence, complete without the ellipsis, says: "Give the message to the one whoever arrives first." We see that **whoever** (whose antecedent is **one**) is the subject of the verb **arrives**. A subject must be in the nominative case (**whoever**). **(12b)**

ANSWER 10.

C Let's you and **me** confront him together. REASON: The direct object of **Let** is is **us** ('s). The words you and me constitute an appositive of the direct object (**us**). The appositive must be in the same case as the noun that precedes it. Therefore, say **Let's you and me**. **(13)**

ANSWER 11.

A   Her work, like any computer **programmer's**, is difficult. REASON: The possessive form (**programmer's**) must be used since it stands parallel with the possessive pronoun–adjective **her**.   **(14g)**

ANSWER 12.

C   In spite of his youth, no faster runner than **he** will be found in our school. REASON: The subject of the **than clause** verb is nominative (**he**).   **(12c)**

ANSWER 13.

A   If you work hard, you will soon be as efficient as **he**. REASON: We mean **as efficient as he is efficient**.   **(12c)**

ANSWER 14.

B   Let's you and me decide that the prize should go to whoever tried hardest. REASON: The direct object of **let** is **us** (**'s**). The words **you** and **me** constitute an appositive of the direct object (**us**). The appositive must be in the same case as the noun that precedes it. Therefore, say **Let's you and me**...   **(13)**

ANSWER 15.

A   The author **whose** works I admire most is Galsworthy. REASON: **who's** means **who is**.   **(14a)**

ANSWER 16.

D   Offer the nomination to **whoever** commands the respect of the people. REASON: The subject of the verb (**commands**) is **whoever**. Note that the sentence has an ellipsis: Offer the nomination **to the one** whoever commands.   **(12b, 13b)**

ANSWER 17.

D   I was appreciative of all his efforts, especially of **his** doing that one job for me. REASON: The modifier of the **gerund** (doing) must be an adjective (**his**).   **(14h)**

ANSWER 18.

C   Just between you and **me**, his theories won't work. REASON: The object of the preposition (**between**) is **me**.   **(13c)**

ANSWER 19.

C   We appreciate **your going** to all this trouble for us. REASON: The gerund (which is a noun) needs a possessive adjective (**your**).   **(14h)**

ANSWER 20.

B   They teased him mercilessly, but there was no doubt of **his being** able to take it and come back for more. REASON: **being** is a gerund and requires the possessive adjective (**his**).   **(14h)**

ANSWER 21.

D   There is little danger of the **law's** being broken. REASON: A noun immediately preceding the gerund is in the possessive case.   **(14h)**

ANSWER 22.

B   I have no doubt that **America's** taking a strong, consistent attitude in the world crisis at this time will both strengthen the Western powers and weaken the Soviet. REASON: The possessive form must be used in transforming the noun **America** to a possessive adjective to modify the gerund **taking**.   **(14h)**

ANSWER 23.

A   He would not **accept my hospitality**. REASON: The direct object (**hospitality**) follows **accept** — not the preposition **of**.   **(13a)**

ANSWER 24.

C   They wanted both Louise and **him** to join the club. REASON: The direct objects of wanted are **Louise** and **him**. (not **he**).   **(13a)**

ANSWER 25.

C Where is the girl **whom** he recommended? REASON: The relative pronoun (**whom**) is the direct object of the verb (**recommended**). **(13a)**

ANSWER 26.

B The teacher asked three of us, Dan, Edward and **me**, to carry the plants down to the office. REASON: **Dan, Edward, me,** are appositive direct objects of the verb **asked. I** can never act as an object. **(13a)**

ANSWER 27.

D All sorority members declined **except her.** REASON: The object of the preposition (**except**) is in the objective case (**her**). **(13c)**

ANSWER 28.

A Give the position to **whoever** you think is best qualified in all respects. REASON: The subject of the clause **whoever is best qualified** must be in the nominative case (**whoever**). **(12b)**

ANSWER 29.

C **His reading** the speech caused much comment. REASON: The gerund (**reading**) is modified by the possessive adjective-pronoun **his.** **(14h)**

ANSWER 30.

B They will approve of **his going** to the concert. REASON: The gerund **going** is properly modified by the possessive adjective-pronoun **his.** **(14h)**

ANSWER 31.

C **Whom** did you see at the meeting? REASON: The direct object of the verb (**did see**) is in the objective case (**whom**). **(12b, 13a)**

ANSWER 32.

B Give the parcel to **whoever** pays for it. REASON: The subject of the verb **pays** is in the nominative case (**whoever**). **(12b)**

ANSWER 33.

B The man **whom** he introduced was Mr. Carey. REASON: The direct object of the verb **introduced** is in the objective case (**whom**). **(12b, 13a)**

ANSWER 34.

A **Barbara** and Tommy's mother comes from a family of actors and actresses. REASON: The first **'s** would be redundant. **(14e)**

ANSWER 35.

A Answer the door to **whoever** rings the bell. REASON: The nominative form is required for the subject (**whoever**) of the clause. Incidentally, the object of the preposition **to** is **the one** (understood). **(12b)**

TEST VI. NOUNS, PRONOUNS, AND THEIR CASES

TIME: 17 Minutes

DIRECTIONS: In each of the following groups of sentences, select the one sentence that is grammatically INCORRECT. Mark the answer sheet with the letter of that incorrect sentence.

Explanations of the key points behind these questions appear with the answers at the end of this test. The explanatory answers provide the kind of background that will enable you to answer test questions with facility and confidence.

(1)

(A) Do you really believe that my attitude is different from what it was?
(B) There are very good grounds for such action.
(C) Both teachers and supervisors are involved in instruction.
(D) None of my three sons is taller than me.

(2)

(A) Who do you believe to be the best student in the senior class?
(B) The finalist is Smith, whom few people would have supposed to be a strong contender.
(C) Even after we had explained the regulations to him, he could not seem to understand that economics was required for graduation.
(D) To raise the standard of living it is not enough to divide the riches of the few.

(3)

(A) A curious friend of my mothers' happened to overhear the conversation.
(B) The more you borrow, the more you spend.
(C) The day turned out to be a sweltering one, the thermometer registering in the nineties.
(D) The appearance of leaden skies led to consternation among the leaders.

(4)

(A) He talks as if he were tired.
(B) He amended his declaration to include additional income.
(C) I know that he would have succeeded if he had tried.
(D) Whom does Mrs. Jones think wrote the play?

(5)

(A) Of all my friends he is the one on whom I can most surely depend.
(B) We value the Constitution because of it's guarantee to freedom.
(C) The audience was deeply stirred by the actor's performance.
(D) Give the book to whoever comes into the room first.

(6)

(A) The dog had lain in the car's shadow so long we had forgotten all about him.
(B) Is the fountain pen yours or theirs?
(C) Although we had less time to complete the test on Friday, we made fewer errors.
(D) "Whose coming in our car?" Mr. Porter asked.

(A) The instructor could not but laugh at the predicament of the student.
(B) "The teachings of the Bible should be employed as guideposts for the maintenance of ethical standards," declared the minister.
(C) Do you think that you have more information than us?
(D) All birds which prey upon destructive pests are helpful to those whose livelihood is derived from agriculture.

(A) His work was admired by a critic who's judgment we respect.
(B) The story is interesting but of doubtful authenticity.
(C) He has set aside a vast sum of money for the development of thermonuclear military weapons.
(D) The guard was willing to act, provided no danger was present.

S1857

(A) Spending the money, he felt like a wealthy man.
(B) He prefers we to believe he is a descendant of a distin guished Colonial official.
(C) Although the table was supposed to be stationary, i was readily moved.
(D) His impromptu decisions were usually quite sound.

(A) When I arrived, he was already there.
(B) My diagnosis is worth more than a surgeon's.
(C) I use all my pens without fear of them leaking.
(D) When I arrived, they were all ready to go.

(A) I'll never agree to John changing his job.
(B) He gained admittance to the ball park.
(C) Please advise me what to do.
(D) The wound was aggravated by rubbing.

12

(A) I move that the report of the committee be accepted.
(B) A library aide must give great attention to detail.
(C) The finger of suspicion was obviously being pointed at the two of us, the lawyer and I.
(D) I move that the agenda be suspended for the duration of the emergency.

13

(A) John, who's mother is a teacher, is not as good a student as many other friends I have with no academic backgrounds in their families.
(B) On the other side of the coin, many of our major industrial concerns have been subjected to a constant stream of abuse.
(C) Vote for whoever, in your opinion, is most worthy of your consideration.
(D) He was graduated at the head of his class.

(A) She was incredulous when I told her the incredible story.
(B) She was told that the symptoms would disappear within a week.
(C) If possible, I should like to sit in front of the very tall couple.
(D) Punish whomever disobeys our commands.

(A) Henry maintains that he has already read the article in its entirety.
(B) A large number of people signed the petition.
(C) We appreciate you going to all this trouble for us.
(D) The biennial election of Congressmen is held in the even-numbered years.

(A) If I were you, I should be careful of who my friends are.
(B) Neither of them is willing to admit that his actions were exceptionable.
(C) Merrihew, who I never thought was even in the running, has won.
(D) I should be unfair to both she and you if I did not warn you that, in my estimation, you are committing an egregious blunder.

(A) The driver did all that it was possible to do.
(B) He agreed to phone you before now.
(C) I thought it to be he.
(D) We expected to stay there.

(A) The spectators thought the winner of the third race to be he.
(B) He it was who told the tale of hidden treasures.
(C) I inferred from his remarks that he had enjoyed himself.
(D) It was not his father's influence that led him to choose that kind of work.

(A) It is not quite clear whether it was his friend or him who had requested the favor.
(B) He was so fast that he finished the work in half an hour.
(C) If the chairman is absent, who's to take his place?
(D) Each member of the club is expected to present his report at the end of this month.

(A) I knew him to be the ringleader.
(B) Who did you ask to go to the dance?
(C) Everyone has studied his lesson.
(D) The material used in this cabinet was oak and white pine.

(A) The advisor announced at the close of the meeting, "Every one of you girls in the group, remember, is to bring her own lunch tomorrow."
(B) Three months pass in no time at all when you spend your vacation traveling in Europe.
(C) The audience is requested to remain seated during intermission.
(D) Specialization in the undergraduate colleges has fostered departmentalization of the teaching function.

(A) Luckily, we happened to find a really tame deer.
(B) In her autobiographical essays, she often alludes to her early life in Wales.
(C) Were your reactions similar to hers?
(D) He was my uncle, my mother's brother, who I hadn't seen for ten years.

(A) The attorney cited a ruling of the Supreme Court as an instance of the application of this principle.
(B) We took Jean, Mary, and she to the dance.
(C) I apologize; I really should have known your new address.
(D) John said that he would transfer to another school at the end of the year.

CONSOLIDATE YOUR KEY ANSWERS HERE

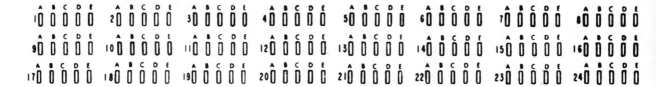

Correct Answers For The Foregoing Questions

(Check your answers with these that we provide. You should find considerable correspondence between them. If not, you'd better go back and find out why. On the next page we have provided concise clarifications of basic points behind the key answers. Please go over them carefully because they may be quite useful in helping you pick up extra points on the exam.)

1.D	5.B	9.B	13.A	17.C	21.B
2.A	6.D	10.C	14.D	18.A	22.D
3.A	7.C	11.A	15.C	19.A	23.B
4.D	8.A	12.C	16.D	20.B	

TEST VI NOUNS, PRONOUNS, AND THEIR CASES

EXPLANATORY ANSWERS CLARIFYING CARDINAL POINTS

The core of the Question and Answer Method . . . getting help when and where you need it. Even if you were able to write correct key answers for the preceding questions, the following explanations illuminate fundamental facts, ideas, and principles which just might crop up in the form of questions on future tests.

Bold-face references in the following answers direct you to paragraphs in the Arco Grammar Text, where fuller explanations are provided.

ANSWER 1.

D None of my three sons is taller **than I.** REASON: We really mean **taller than I am tall.** It is clear, then, that **I,** being the subject of the **I am tall** clause, is in the nominative case. **(12c)**

ANSWER 2.

A **Whom** do you believe to be the best student in the senior class? REASON: The subject of the infinitive should be in the objective case (**Whom**). **(13d)**

ANSWER 3.

A A curious friend of my **mother's** happened to overhear the conversation. REASON: **mothers'** means belonging to several mothers; **mother's** means belonging to one mother. Note that the double possessive **of my mother's** is idiomatically acceptable, though **of my mother** is more logical. **(14a)**

ANSWER 4.

D **Who** does Mrs. Jones think wrote the play? REASON: The subject of the relative clause is in the nominative case (**who**). **(12b)**

ANSWER 5.

B We value the Constitution because of **its** guarantee to freedom. REASON: **it's** means **it is.** **(14a)**

ANSWER 6.

D "**Who's** coming in our car?" Mr. Porter asked. REASON: The possessive form **whose** is misused here. **(14a)**

ANSWER 7.

C Do you think that you have more information than **we**? REASON: The subject of the **than** clause (**than we do**) is **we** (nominative case). **(12c)**

ANSWER 8.

A His work was admired by a critic **whose** judgment we respect. REASON: **who's** means **who is.** **(14a)**

ANSWER 9.

B He prefers **us** to believe he is a descendant of a distinguished Colonial official. REASON: The subject of the infinitive must have an objective case form (**us**). However, we could correctly say, "He prefers that we believe . . ." **(13d)**

ANSWER 10.

C I use all my pens without fear of **their** leaking. REASON: The gerund **leaking** is modified by the possessive adjective-pronoun **their.** **(14h)**

ANSWER 11.

A I'll never agree to **John's changing** his job. REASON: The gerund **changing** is modified by the possessive noun **John's.** **(14h)**

ANSWER 12.

C The finger of suspicion was obviously being pointed at the two of us, the lawyer and **me**. REASON: **me** is used as an object of the preposition (**at**). **(13c)**

ANSWER 13.

A John, **whose** mother is a teacher, is not as good a student as many other friends I have with no academic backgrounds in their families. REASON: The relative pronoun (**whose**) must be used here. The expression **who's** means **who is**. **(14a)**

ANSWER 14.

D Punish **whoever** disobeys our commands. REASON: The subject of the subordinate clause (**whoever disobeys our commands**) is in the nominative case (**whoever**). **(12b)**

ANSWER 15.

C We appreciate **your** going to all this trouble for us. REASON: The gerund (**going**) must be modified by an adjective (**your**) —not a pronoun (**you**). **(14h)**

ANSWER 16.

D I should be unfair to both **her** and you if I did not warn you that, in my estimation, you are committing an egregious blunder. REASON: As object of the preposition **to**, **her** is the correct form. **(13c)**

ANSWER 17.

C I thought it to be **him**. REASON: The subject (**it**) of the infinitive is in the objective case. It follows that the predicate noun (which means the same as the subject) is in the objective case (**him**). **(13e)**

ANSWER 18.

A The spectators thought the winner of the third race to be **him**. REASON: The word **race**, as the subject of the infinitive **to be**, is in the objective case. The predicate noun must, accordingly, be in the objective case—therefore **him**. **(13e)**

ANSWER 19.

A It is not quite clear whether it was his friend or **he** who has requested the favor. REASON: The copulative verb (**was**) requires a predicate nominative (**he**). **(12d)**

ANSWER 20.

B **Whom** did you ask to go to the dance? REASON: The subject of the infinitive (**to go**) is in the objective case (**whom**). **(13d)**

ANSWER 21.

B Three months pass in no time at all when you spend your vacation **by traveling** in Europe. REASON: In the original sentence, **vacation** could be misinterpreted as an adjective modifying the gerund **traveling**. **(13c)**

ANSWER 22.

D He was my uncle, my mother's brother, **whom** I hadn't seen for ten years. REASON: The direct object of **had seen** is **whom** (in the objective case). **(13a)**

ANSWER 23.

B We took Jean, Mary, and **her** to the dance. REASON: The direct object of **took** must have an objective case form (**her**). **(13a)**

TEST VII. CASES

TIME: 26 Minutes

*DIRECTIONS: Each question in this test begins with a sentence containing a word or expression in **boldface** type. Then follow four grammatical descriptions of the **boldface** type. They are lettered (A) (B) (C) (D). Choose the correct grammatical description, and mark your answer sheet with the letter of the correct answer.*

Explanations of the key points behind these questions appear with the answers at the end of this test. The explanatory answers provide the kind of background that will enable you to answer test questions with facility and confidence.

(1)

Our **luxuries** are always masquerading as necessities.

(A) retained object
(B) gerund
(C) neuter noun
(D) predicate adjective

(2)

We are confident that **justice** will eventually triumph.

(A) proper noun
(B) collective noun
(C) concrete noun
(D) abstract noun

(3)

Everybody talks about the weather but nobody does anything about **it**.

(A) direct object
(B) expletive
(C) subordinate conjunction
(D) personal pronoun

(4)

Let us discuss only such matters **as** concern us directly.

(A) conjunctive adverb
(B) relative pronoun
(C) preposition
(D) correlative conjunction

(5)

In case of a fumble, the ball is given to **whoever** recovers it.

(A) incorrect – it should be **whomever** because it is the object of the preposition **to**
(B) incorrect – it should be **whomever** because it is a retained object
(C) correct – it is subject of **recovers**
(D) correct – it is a predicate nominative

(6)

What did the boy who was defeated say he dropped while running?

(A) subject of predicate verb
(B) object of **say**
(C) object of **was defeated**
(D) object of **dropped**

(7)

Talk to a man about **himself** and he will listen for hours.

(A) reflexive pronoun
(B) verb in future tense
(C) abstract noun
(D) simple subject

(8)

It is imperative, if the class is to be orderly, **that the students be occupied throughout the hour.**

(A) in apposition with **it**
(B) modifier of verb
(C) modifier of **imperative**
(D) object of the verb

S1857

The building was old and dilapidated, **a condition** which made it necessary for us to close it.

(A) in apposition with the principal clause
(B) the subject of the subordinate clause
(C) the predicate nominative of the principal clause
(D) none of the preceding

Death, be not proud, though some have called thee mighty and dreadful.

(A) retained object
(B) personal pronoun
(C) nominative of direct address
(D) noun in apposition

Mr. Browne, who had for many years devoted himself to various works of charity, was unanimously elected **chairman** of the Community Chest Fund of the entire county.

(A) object of the verb
(B) objective complement
(C) retained object
(D) predicate adjective

It is the first time anyone has called this ship **unseaworthy** for coastwise service.

(A) predicate adjective
(B) objective complement
(C) adverb modifying **has called**
(D) adjective modifying **service**

"Are there no water-lilies, smooth as cream,
With long stems dripping **crystal**?"

(A) adjective modifying **stems**
(B) object of the preposition, **with**
(C) adjective modifying **dripping**
(D) object of **dripping**

His decision having been made, the President called for an itinerary for his trip.

(A) subject of clause
(B) subject of sentence
(C) objective noun
(D) nominative absolute

What **color** shall I paint the backdrop for the third **scene**?

(A) subject of verb
(B) object of verb
(C) predicate nominative
(D) objective complement

He ran a **race** that was noteworthy not for its **speed**, but for its methodical nature.

(A) objective complement
(B) predicate nominative
(C) subject of **was**
(D) cognate object

Harmony, what Pythagorean discipline will ring from discord?

(A) object of preposition **from**
(B) appositive of **discord**
(C) direct object of **ring**
(D) nominative by direct address

The general made every effort to wrest from sure **defeat** victory and even the **spoils** of war.

(A) object of the preposition
(B) object of the infinitive
(C) in apposition with **victory**
(D) objective complement

He was asked by the reporters **whether he would plead the Fifth Amendment**.

(A) predicate adjective
(B) predicate nominative
(C) adverbial clause
(D) retained object

We know **him** to be undisputed master of the new technique.

(A) object of **know**
(B) in apposition with **master**
(C) subject of the infinitive
(D) object of the infinitive

The ship having left port, we settled down to a **long cruise**.

(A) participial phrase
(B) gerund
(C) adjective phrase
(D) nominative absolute

He would take orders from no one but his **counselor** at camp.

(A) subject of verb in an elliptical clause
(B) object of **but**
(C) object of **from**
(D) object of verb in an elliptical clause

He was awarded **the place** I lost.

(A) object of **was awarded**
(B) retained object
(C) adverbial clause modifying **awarded**
(D) indirect object

When he retired, he was given a gold **watch**.

(A) direct object
(B) indirect object
(C) predicate noun
(D) retained object

You can tell the size of a man by the size of the thing that makes him **angry**.

(A) adverb of agree
(B) definite article
(C) participle
(D) objective complement

The **series** won, they settled down to a real winter vacation in the south.

(A) subject of the verb **won**
(B) noun in direct address
(C) adverbial objective
(D) part of nominative absolute

Let **us** go now that evening has come.

(A) subject of infinitive
(B) subject of verb
(C) object of preposition
(D) object of infinitive

Here you should lie, ye **Kings** of old.

(A) subject of **should lie**
(B) direct object of **should lie**
(C) nominative by direct address
(D) none of these

Offering the arresting **officer** a bribe was a sad mistake.

(A) direct object
(B) indirect object
(C) objective complement
(D) subject of **was**

I call the painting a **masterpiece**.

(A) objective complement
(B) object of **call**
(C) object of **painting**
(D) in apposition with **painting**

We asked **Dr. Jones** to be our sponsor.

(A) object of **asked**
(B) subject of **to be**
(C) in apposition with **sponsor**
(D) indirect object

We believed **her** to be the woman of whom you spoke.

(A) object of the verb **believed**
(B) subject of infinitive **to be**
(C) pronoun in apposition with **whom**
(D) object of infinitive **to be**

There was little we could do but **entertain** our unexpected guests.

(A) verb in subordinate clause
(B) infinitive, predicate nominative
(C) infinitive, in apposition with **little**
(D) infinitive, objective case

Our job well done, we put away our tools.

(A) appositive of the subject
(B) adverbial clause
(C) subject
(D) nominative absolute

The principal preoccupation was **eavesdropping** on the conversation of others.

(A) gerund
(B) participle
(C) progressive form of verb
(D) objective complement

CONSOLIDATE YOUR KEY ANSWERS HERE

KEY ANSWERS FOR THE FOREGOING QUESTIONS

Check our key answers with your own. You'll probably find very few errors. In any case, check your understanding of all questions by studying the following explanatory answers. They illuminate the subject matter. Here you will find concise clarifications of basic points behind the key answers.

1.C	6.D	11.C	16.D	21.D	26.D	31.B
2.D	7.A	12.B	17.D	22.B	27.A	32.B
3.D	8.A	13.D	18.B	23.B	28.C	33.D
4.B	9.A	14.D	19.D	24.D	29.B	34.D
5.C	10.C	15.D	20.C	25.D	30.A	35.A

TEST VII. CASES

EXPLANATORY ANSWERS CLARIFYING CARDINAL POINTS

The core of the Question and Answer Method . . . getting help when and where you need it. Even if you were able to write correct key answers for the preceding questions, the following explanations illuminate fundamental facts, ideas, and principles which just might crop up in the form of questions on future tests.

Bold-face *references in the following answers direct you to paragraphs in the Arco Grammar Text, where fuller explanations are provided.*

ANSWER 1.

C   REASON: **Luxuries** is a neuter noun because it is without sex.   **(9a)**

ANSWER 2.

D   REASON: An abstract noun names a quality, state, or idea.   **(10e)**

ANSWER 3.

D   REASON: **It** is a personal pronoun because it is used instead of the name of a thing. In this sentence, **it** is the object of the preposition **about**.   **(11a)**

ANSWER 4.

B   REASON: A relative pronoun is one which refers to a noun and at the same time serves as a connective. It is clear that **as** in this sentence refers to **matters** — it also acts conjunctively in the clause **as concern us directly**.   **(11b)**

ANSWER 5.

C   REASON: **Whoever** is a relative pronoun whose antecedent is **person** (understood). Since **whoever** is the subject of the clause, it takes the nominative form.   **(11b)**

ANSWER 6.

D   REASON: Turn the sentence around — "The boy who was defeated did say he dropped what while running." **What**, then, is an interrogative pronoun acting as the direct object of **dropped**.   **(11c, 18a)**

ANSWER 7.

A   REASON: **Himself**, reflecting the previous noun **man**, is a reflexive pronoun. In the sentence given, it is the object of the preposition **about**.   **(11f)**

ANSWER 8.

A   REASON: **That the . . . the hour** is a clause which refers back to, and means the same as, the subject **It**.   **(12)**

ANSWER 9.

A   REASON: **Condition** is used as an appositive which, in this case, means the same as the entire main clause that precedes it.   **(12)**

ANSWER 10.

C   REASON: **Death**, by its intonation in speech and its grammatically unrelated position in the sentence, is a nominative of direct address.   **(12e)**

ANSWER 11.

C   REASON: The sentence, in its active form, would read: "They unanimously elected Mr. Browne . . . chairman of the . . . county." In the passive form sentence given in the book, the object complement **chairman** is a retained object.   **(13c)**

ANSWER 12.

B REASON: **Unseaworthy** is an adjective used as an objective complement to complete the meaning of the direct object **ship**. **(13g)**

ANSWER 13.

D REASON: **Crystal** is the direct object of the participle **dripping**. **(13a)**

ANSWER 14.

D REASON: Since **His decision**... **made** is not related grammatically to the rest of the sentence, it is a nominative absolute. **(12f)**

ANSWER 15.

D REASON: **Color** is a noun which completes the meaning of the direct object (**backdrop**). **(13g)**

ANSWER 16.

D REASON: A cognate object is a noun which comes after an intransitive verb and which, through its similarity to the verb, completes the meaning of the verb. **Race** is a noun which completes the meaning of the intransitive verb **ran**. Note the similarity ("cognativeness") between **race** and **ran**. **(13j)**

ANSWER 17.

D REASON: **Harmony** is a noun which has a close relationship to the rest of the sentence. However, it is not related grammatically. **Harmony** is, therefore, a nominative by direct address (nominative of address). **(12e)**

ANSWER 18.

B REASON: **Spoils** (just as **victory**) is the direct object of the infinitive **to wrest**. **(13a)**

ANSWER 19.

D REASON: The sentence in its active form, would read: "The reporters asked him whether... Amendment." In the passive form sentence given in the book, the objective complement of the active sentence is retained. **(13i)**

ANSWER 20.

C REASON: **Him** is a pronoun used as the subject of the infinitive **to be**. Note the objective case form (**him**) since the subject of an infinitive is in the objective case. **(13d)**

ANSWER 21.

D REASON: **The ship**... **port** is not related grammatically to the rest of the sentence. The noun **ship** forms with the other words that are underlined, a virtual adverbial clause of which **ship** is the subject. We have, therefore, a nominative absolute. **(12f)**

ANSWER 22.

B REASON: **Counselor** is the object of the preposition **but**. **(13c)**

ANSWER 23.

B REASON: The sentence, in its active form, would read: "They awarded him the place I lost." In the passive form given in the book, the direct object **place** is retained. **(13i)**

ANSWER 24.

D REASON: Originally, the sentence could have read: "When he retired, they gave him a gold watch." **Watch**, here, is the direct object after the active verb **gave**. In the new sentence, **watch** is a retained object after the passive verb (**was given**). **(13i)**

ANSWER 25.

D REASON: **Angry** is an adjective used as an objective complement to complete the meaning of the direct object **him**. **(13g)**

ANSWER 26.

D REASON: **The series won** may be expanded to **The series having been won**, and further expanded to the clause, **Since the series had been won**. The first and second non-clause constructions are called nominative absolutes. **(12f)**

ANSWER 27.

A REASON: **Us** is the subject of the infinitive **(to) go**. Incidentally, the subject of an infinitive is in the objective case. **(13e)**

ANSWER 28.

C REASON: **Kings** is a noun which has no grammatical relationship to the rest of the sentence. However, it has a close thought relationship to the rest of the sentence. **Kings** is, therefore, a nominative by direct address. **(12e)**

ANSWER 29.

B REASON: **Officer** is an indirect object—the preposition **to** is understood—after the gerund **offering**. Incidentally, **bribe** is the direct object. **(13b)**

ANSWER 30.

A REASON: **Masterpiece** is a noun that completes the meaning of, and further describes, the direct object **painting**. **(14g)**

ANSWER 31.

B REASON: **Dr. Jones** is the subject of the infinitive **to be**. **(13e)**

ANSWER 32.

B REASON: **Her** is the subject of the infinitive **to be**. As such, the objective form (**her**) is used (not **she**). **(13d)**

ANSWER 33

D REASON: **Entertain** (really **to entertain**) is an infinitive used as the object of the preposition **but**. **(13c, 44a)**

ANSWER 34.

D REASON: In **Our job well done**, the nominative (**job**) can be understood to form with the words with which it is connected a clause in which **job** serves as a logical subject: "Since our job was well done." In view of the fact that **Our job well done** contains no finite verb, we call it a nominative absolute. **(12f, 44g)**

ANSWER 35.

A REASON: **Eavesdropping** is a gerund used as the predicate nominative after the copulative verb **was**. **(13a)**

III. AGREEMENT AND REFERENCE

15 Introduction

Agreement is the logical relationship between parts of speech in a sentence. There can be no good, clear sentences without agreement. Grammar starts here; for the parts of the sentence must be in harmony with one another (must *agree*) if they are to express a clear thought. In the first chapter we talked a little of the parts that make up a sentence. Now we will take a closer look at the way some of these parts fit together.

Agreement of subject and verb is the "heart" of the good sentence. For, stripped to its bare essentials, a sentence is simply a union of a *thing* (the subject) and an *action* (the verb). These two must agree; in fact, their agreement *is* the sentence.

Other parts of the sentence, of course, must also be in agreement. Perhaps next in importance to the agreement of subject and verb is the agreement of a pronoun with its antecedent. It is these two areas that we will discuss in this chapter, since there is a relationship between the principles governing each.

15a Agreement of subject and verb

The verb must agree with the subject in number and in person. If the subject is singular, the verb form must also be singular; if the subject is in the third person—*it, he*—the verb must also be in the third person.

The chief problem is identifying the true subject of the sentence and determining whether it is singular or plural.

15b Agreement of pronoun and antecedent

The pronoun must agree with its antecedent (the word to which it refers—sometimes called its "referent") in number, in person, and in gender. Of the three, gender causes the writer the least difficulty.

The chief problem is identifying the antecedent and determining its number, person, and gender.

15c Agreement of both verb and pronoun with subject-antecedent

Often the subject of the verb is also the antecedent of the pronoun. One might think that this would greatly simplify things. And to some extent it does; for once he has determined that the subject-antecedent is singular, he knows where he stands—both verb and pronoun must likewise be singular. But here a word of caution: be consistent; don't shift from a singular verb (which properly agrees with its singular subject) to a plural pronoun later in the sentence.

16 Subject Problems

The first step in making the parts of a sentence agree is to identify the subject. In this section, therefore, we will discuss only those subjects that may present special problems.

16a Collective words

A collective names a group of people or things. Although usually singular in form, it is treated as either singular or plural according to the sense of the sentence:

Singular when members of the group act, or are considered, as a *unit*:

> The Survey Committee *is visiting* the X District this week. The National Office Evaluation Team *has* five trips scheduled for this quarter.

Plural when the members act, or are considered, *individually*:

> The jury *are* unable to agree on a verdict.

> The National Office Evaluation Team *pool* the data *they* gather and *prepare their* report.

Common collectives

> assembly, association, audience, board, cabinet, class, commission, committee, company, corporation, council, counsel, couple, crowd, department, family, firm, group, jury, majority, minority, number, pair, press, public, staff, United States.

Company names as collectives

Company names also qualify as collectives and may be either singular or plural. Usually those ending with a singular sound are considered singular; those with a plural sound, plural.

> Flowers, Inc., *mails its* advertisements in envelopes with floral decorations.
> Jones Brothers *have sent their* representative to the conference.

A name ending in *Company* or *Corporation*, though usually considered singular, may—if the sense of the sentence requires—be used as a plural.

> The X Company *is* not on the list of tax-exempt organizations.
> The ABC Corporation *report* on the activities of *their* subsidiaries tomorrow morning.

(1) Short collectives

The following short words—though seldom listed as collectives—are governed by the rule for collectives. They are singular or plural according to the intended meaning of the sentence.

> *all, any, more, most, none, some, who, which*

When a prepositional phrase follows the word, the number of the noun in the phrase controls the number of the verb. When no such phrase follows, the writer signals his intended meaning by his choice of the singular or the plural verb.

> Some of the *work has been done.*
> Some of the *returns have been filed.*

> Most of the *correspondence is* routine.
> Most of the *letters are* acceptable.

> *Is* there *any* left? (any portion—any paper, any ink)
> *Are* there *any* left? (any individual items—any forms, any copies)

> *Which is* to be posted? (which one?)
> *Which are* to be posted? (which ones?)

> Either: None of the items *is* deductible.
> Or:　　None of the items *are* deductible.

NOTE: Many treat *none* as singular in every instance, since it is a compound of no one. This usage is correct. It is equally correct, however, to treat *none* as plural (meaning *not any*) when it is followed by a prepositional phrase which has a plural object. Those who want to emphasize the singular meaning often substitute *not one* for *none*:

> *Not one* of the applicants *is* eligible.

(2) Special collectives

Certain words—called "abstract collectives" by some grammarians—are also treated as collectives, even though they do not name a group of persons or things.

Their singular form is used when they refer to (1) qualities, emotions, or feelings common to a group of persons or things; or to (2) action common to such a group. Their plural form is used when this common or general idea is not present.

Use the singular under such circumstances as these:

attention   Supervisors have their *attention* called to the value of management training. (not *attentions*)

consent   Several gave their *consent* to the proposal.

failure   The taxpayers' *failure* to file amended returns delayed the processing of their claims for refund.

interest   Their *interest* was not so much in long-range self-development as in immediate advancement.

leaving   If the employees have legitimate reasons, the supervisor should not question their *leaving* the work area.

sense   Our interpretation is based on the *sense* of the amendment.

work   Attending the meeting will not interfere with their *work*.

Use either the singular or the plural:

opinion   The taxpayer and his counsel expressed their *opinion* (or *opinions*) on the matter.

time   The only *time* these restrictions are in order is when the taxpayer.... *OR*
The only *times* these restrictions are in order are when the taxpayer....

use   What *use* (or *uses*) can be made of the revised form?

16b   Units of measure

When a number is used with a plural noun to indicate a unit of measurement (money, time, fractions, portions, distance, weight, quantity, etc.), a singular verb is used. When the term is thought of as individual parts, a plural verb is used.

Twenty dollars is the amount of tax due.
Twenty dollars are in this stack.

Ten years seems like a long time.
Ten years have gone by since I last saw him.

Twenty-one pages is our quota for each day.
Twenty-one pages are needed to finish the job.

When fractions and expressions such as *the rest of, the remainder of, a part of, percent of,* etc., are followed by a prepositional phrase, the noun or pronoun in that phrase governs the number of the verb.

Four-fifths of the job *was* finished on time.
Four-fifths of the letters *were* finished on time.

The *rest* (or *remainder*) of the work *is* due Friday.
The *rest* (or *remainder*) of the letters *were* mailed today.

What *percent* of the information *is* available?
What *percent* of the items *were* lost?

16c   Confusing singular and plural forms

It is sometimes hard for us to tell by its form whether a word is singular or plural. Some words that end in *-s* may be singular, and some seemingly singular words may be plural.

These words are singular, though they are plural in form.

> *apparatus, news, summons, whereabouts*

The *news is* disturbing.
His *whereabouts has* not yet been determined.

These words are plural, though they are singular (or collective) in meaning.

> *assets, earnings, means* (income), *odds, premises, proceeds, quarters, savings, wages, winnings*

His *assets are* listed on the attached statement.
Earnings are up this quarter.
The *odds are* against our settling this case swiftly.
The *proceeds are* earmarked for the revolving fund.

These words may be either singular or plural, depending on their meaning, even though they are plural in form.

> *ethics, goods, gross, headquarters, mechanics, politics, series, species, statistics, tactics*

Ethics is a subject on which he is well qualified to speak.
His business *ethics are* above question.

Statistics is the only course I failed in school.
The *statistics prove* that I am right.

A *gross* of pencils *is* not enough.
A *gross* of pencils *are* being sent.

A *series* of errors *has* marked our attempt.
A *series* of lucky breaks *are* about all that will save us now.

These nouns are plural, though they may appear to be singular because they have foreign or unusual plural forms.

The *analyses have* been completed.
(*Analyses* is the plural of *analysis*.)
What *are* your *bases* for these conclusions?
(*Bases* is the plural of *basis*.)
Some interesting *phenomena are* disclosed in this report.
(*Phenomena* is the plural of *phenomenon*.)
His conclusion seems sound, but his *criteria are* not valid.
(*Criteria* is the plural of *criterion*.)

Hyphenated compound nouns usually take their pluralization on the important part.

editors-in-chief, daughters-in-law, mousetraps

Solid compound nouns always take their pluralization at the end of the word.

stepdaughters, spoonfuls, bookshelves

16d   Indefinite pronouns

These indefinite pronouns are singular. When they are used as subjects, they require singular verbs; when used as antecedents, they require singular pronouns.

anybody, anyone, any one (any one of a group), *anything, each, either, every, everybody, everyone, every one* (every one of a group), *everything, neither, nobody, no one, nothing, one, somebody, someone, some one* (some one of a group), *something*

Anyone is welcome, as long as *he* (not *they*) behaves himself.
*Any one of the men *is* capable of doing it.
Each of us *is* obliged to sign *his* own name.
Either of the alternatives *is* suitable.
Everyone must buy *his* book for the course.
*Every one of the employees *wishes* to sign the card.

Everything seems to be going smoothly now.
Neither of the plans *is* workable.
No one believes that our plan will work.
Someone has to finish this report.
*Some one of you *has* to be responsible for it.

*Written as two words when followed by a phrase.

Even when two indefinite pronouns are joined by *and*, they remain singular in meaning.

Anyone and *everyone is* invited.
Nothing and *no one escapes* her attention.

When *each* or *every* is used to modify a compound subject (subjects joined by *and*), the subject is considered singular.

Every regional commissioner and *district director has sent* in *his* report.

When *each* is inserted (as a parenthetic or explanatory element) between a plural or a compound subject and its plural verb, neither the plural form of the verb nor the plural form of the pronoun is affected.

Region A, Region B, and Region C *each expect* to increase *their* personnel ceilings.
The Directors *each want* the requirements changed.
The taxpayers *each have requested* permission to change *their* method of accounting.

Many a (unlike *many*) is singular in meaning and takes a singular verb and pronoun.

Many a new employee feels insecure during *his* first few weeks on the job.

But: *Many employees feel* insecure during *their* first few weeks on the job.

More than one, though its meaning is plural, is used in the singular.

More than one vacation plan *was* changed because of the new requirement.
More than one detail *is* needed to handle the additional workload.

These words are plural.

both, few, many, several, others

Both of us *have received* new assignments.
Few will be able to finish their work on time.
Many plan to work all weekend.
Several of the divisions *have submitted* their reports.
But *others have* not yet *finished theirs.*

16e Relative pronouns

The verb in a relative clause must agree in number and in person with the relative pronoun (*who, which, that, what*—see Section 11b) serving as the subject of the clause. The relative pronoun, in turn, must agree with its antecedent. Therefore, before we can make the verb agree with the relative pronoun, we must find the antecedent and determine its person and number.

Have you talked with the man *who was* waiting to see you?
(*Man* is the antecedent of the relative pronoun *who*, and the verb *was* must agree with this antecedent in person and number.)

Where are the books *that were* left on the table?
(The verb in the relative clause—*were*—must agree with the relative pronoun—*that*—which must agree with its antecedent—*books*.)

We *who have* met him do not doubt his ability.
(The relative pronoun is *who*; the verb in the relative clause is *have*; the antecedent of the relative pronoun is *we*.)

In sentences that contain the phrases *one of the* or *one of those*, the antecedent of the relative pronoun is not *one*, but the plural words that follow.

One of the letters *that were* on my desk has disappeared.
(*One has disappeared*, or *One of the letters has disappeared*, is the main thought of the sentence. *That were on my desk* is a clause modifying *letters*, not *one*; thus the relative pronoun *that* must agree with *letters*, its antecedent, making the verb in the relative clause, *were*, plural.)

Here is one of those men *who are* applying for the position.
(The antecedent of the relative pronoun *who* is the plural noun *men*, not the singular *one*.)

One of the men *who are* attending the meeting is wanted on the telephone.
(The antecedent of the relative pronoun *who* is the plural noun *men*, not the singular *one*.)

NOTE: An easy way to find the antecedent of the relative pronoun in this type of sentence, is to shift the sentence elements thus:

Of the letters *that were* on my desk, one has disappeared.
(It now becomes obvious that the antecedent of the relative pronoun *that* is *letters*.)

Of those men *who are* applying for the position, here is one.

Of the men *who are* attending the meeting, one is wanted on the telephone.

But when the word *only* precedes *one* in this type of sentence, the singular pronoun *one* is considered to be the antecedent of the relative pronoun.

He is *one* of the applicants *who are* eligible.

He is the *only one* of the applicants *who is* eligible.
(Notice the difference in number of the relative pronoun *who*—and its verb—in these two sentences.)

Robbins is the *only one* of the employees *who is* receiving an award.

This is the *only one* of the letters *that has* not yet been answered.

Who, that, or *which* may be used to refer to a collective noun. When the members of the group act, or are considered, as a unit, either *that* or *which* should be used—*that* is usually preferred if the group comprises persons rather than things. *Who* is used when the persons comprising a group act, or are considered, individually.

He reports that there *is a group* of citizens *that* is critical of the city's long-range plan.
(Acting as a unit—*that* is used because the group is composed of persons, not things.)

We have heard from an *association* of home-owners *who feel* strongly opposed to the present zoning regulations.

(Considered individually—*who* signals this point.)

16f Subjects joined by *and*

When two or more subjects are joined by *and*, whether the subjects are singular or plural, they form a compound subject, which is considered plural.

The *date and the time* of the meeting *have* not been decided.
The *director and his assistants are* holding *their* weekly staff meeting.
The *letters, reports and other papers are* on the table where you *left them*.
He and I will deliver *our* report in person.

Phrases or clauses serving as subjects follow the same rule: when two or more phrases or clauses serving as the subject of a sentence are joined by *and*, the resulting compound subject is considered plural.

Rising early in the morning and *taking a walk before breakfast make* a person feel invigorated all day.

That your work is usually done satisfactorily and *that you are usually prompt are* the factors I considered in excusing your recent conduct.

Exception: When the subjects joined by *and* refer to the same person or object or represent a single idea, the whole subject is considered singular.

Ham and eggs is the traditional American breakfast.
The *growth and development* of our country *is* described in this book.

We indicate to the reader, *by using the article or personal pronoun* before each member of the compound subject, whether we see the subject as a single idea or as different ideas.

My teacher and friend helps me with my problems.
(one person)
My teacher and *my friend help* me with my problems.
(two people)

The *secretary and treasurer* of the committee *has* arrived.
The *secretary* and *the treasurer* of the committee *have* arrived.

16g Subjects joined by *or* or *nor*

When singular subjects are joined by *or* or *nor*, the subject is considered singular.

Neither the *director nor* the *assistant director knows* that *he* is scheduled to attend the meeting.
One or the other of us *has* to go.
Neither *love nor money is* sufficient to buy such devotion.
Neither *heat nor cold nor sun nor wind affects* this material.

When one singular and one plural subject are joined by *or* or *nor*, the subject closer to the verb determines the number of the verb.

I believe that this *office or* the central *files have* the material you requested.
I believe that the central *files or* this *office has* the material you requested.

When one antecedent is singular and the other antecedent is plural, the pronoun agrees with the closer antecedent.

Is it Patton or the rebels who *merit* praise?
Is it the rebels or Patton who *merits* praise?

NOTE: Because your reader may be distracted by your use of a singular verb with a subject containing a plural element, place the plural element nearer the verb whenever possible.

Ask him whether the *memorandum or* the *letters have* been signed.
Neither the *equipment nor* the *employees are* capable of maintaining that pace.

When the subjects joined by *or* or *nor* are of different persons, the subject nearer the verb determines its person.

I was told that *she or you were* to be responsible.
I was told that *you or she was* to be responsible.

17 Shifts in Number or Person

Once you establish a word as either singular or plural, keep it the same throughout the sentence. Be sure that all verbs and all pronouns referring to that word agree with it in number.

Not: Because this *country* bases *its* economy on voluntary compliance with *its* tax laws, we must all pay our share if *they are* to carry out the necessary functions of government.
> (The first two pronouns refer to *country* as a singular noun; later the reference changes to plural. Use either *it* or *they* throughout the sentence.)

But: Because this *country* bases *its* economy on voluntary compliance with *its* tax laws, we must all pay our share if *it is* to carry out the necessary function of government.

Not: A *person needs* someone to turn to when *they are* in trouble.
> (*Person* is singular; therefore, the use of the plural pronoun *they* is an incorrect shift.)

But: A *person needs* someone to turn to when *he is* in trouble.

Not: When *one* has had a hard day at the office, it is important that *they* be able to relax in the evening.
> (*One* is singular; either of the singular pronouns *one* or *he* should be used to refer to it.)

But: When *one* has had a hard day at the office, it is important that *one* (or *he*) be able to relax in the evening.

Be consistent. If you decide that a collective is singular, keep it singular throughout the sentence—use a singular verb to agree with it and a singular pronoun to refer to it. If you establish the collective as plural, see that both the verb and the pronoun are plural.

The committee *has* announced *its* decision.
> (Singular—acting as a unit)

The committee *have* adjourned and gone to *their* homes.
> (Plural—acting individually)

Our staff *is* always glad to offer *its* advice and assistance.
> (Singular—acting as a unit)

Our staff *are* assigned as liaison *officers* to the several operating divisions.
> (Plural—acting individually)

The number of claims processed this year *is* larger than that processed last year.
> (Using "the" before "number" signals the reader that you consider the items as a unit.)

A number of claims *have* been processed this month.
> (Using "a" before "number" signals that you are referring to the items individually.)

17a Most indefinite pronouns are singular and require singular verbs and pronouns.

Not: *Has anyone* turned in *their* report?
> (The indefinite pronoun *anyone* takes both a singular verb and a singular pronoun.)

But: *Has anyone* turned in *his* report?

17b Do not apply a verb form from one part of the sentence to another (elliptically) unless the same form is grammatically correct in both parts.

Not: The *statistics were* checked and the report filed.
> (The *statistics were* checked and the *report* (*were*) filed.)

But: The *statistics were* checked and the *report was* filed.

17c Avoid shifting the person of pronouns referring to the same antecedent.

Not: When *one* is happy, it often seems as if everyone around *you* is happy, too.
> (*One* is third person; *you* is second person.)

But: When *one* is happy, it often seems as if everyone around *one* (or *him*) is happy, too.

Not: As the *ship* entered *her* berth, *its* huge gray shadow seemed to swallow us.

But: As the *ship* entered *its* berth, *its* huge gray shadow seemed to swallow us.

or: As the *ship* entered *her* berth, *her* huge gray shadow seemed to swallow us.

18 Structure Problems

Usually it's easy for us to identify the subject or antecedent and determine its number and person. But occasionally a puzzling sentence comes along. The subject is there, as clear as can be, but something in the structure of the sentence tries to make us believe that another word is the subject.

18a Verb precedes subject

When the verb precedes the subject in the sentence (either in a question or in a declarative sentence), locate the *true* subject and make the verb agree with it.

> *Are* the *file cabinet and the bookcase* in this room?
>> (The *file cabinet and the bookcase are*....)
>
> Walking down the hall *are* the *men* we are waiting for.
> Clearly visible on the desk *were* the *papers* he had asked us to file.
> From these books *come some* of our best *ideas*.
> To us *falls* the *task* of compiling the data.
> Among those attending *were* two former *presidents* of the organization.

Where, here, and *there,* when introducing a sentence, do not influence the number or person of the verb. In such sentences, find the real subject and make the verb agree with it.

> Where *are* the individual *sessions* to be held?
> Where *is* the *case* filed?
>
> Here *are* the *messages* for which we were waiting.
> Here *is* the *message* for which we were waiting.
>
> There *are* two *books* on the table.
> There *is* a *book* on the table.

What, who, which, the interrogative pronouns, do not affect the number of the verb. Again, find the subject of the sentence and make the verb agree with it.

What *is* the *status* of the Adams case?
What *are* your *recommendations* on this problem?

Who *is* going to accompany you to the meeting?
Who, in this group, *are* members of your staff?

Which *is* the *memo* that he means?
Which *are* the *standards* that we are to apply?

The expletive *it* or *there* introduces the verb and stands for the real subject, which comes later in the clause. The expletive *it* requires a singular verb, even when the real subject is plural. Following the expletive *there,* the verb is singular or plural according to the subject which follows it.

> It *is solutions* we are looking for, not problems.
>> (Even though the real subject, *solutions,* is plural, the verb is singular to agree with the expletive.)
>
> It is doubtful that he will start today.
>> (The clause *that he will start today* is the subject of the verb *is.*)
>
> There *are* enclosed five copies of the pamphlet you requested.
> There *is* attached a letter from District Director, Blankville, requesting additional copies of the book.

NOTE: Avoid confusing your reader by using the expletive *it* and the personal pronoun *it* in the same sentence.

Not: I haven't read the book yet; *it* has been hard for me to find time for *it.*
> (The first *it* is the expletive; the second *it* is a personal pronoun referring to *book.*)

But: I haven't read the *book* yet; I haven't been able to find time for *it.*

18b Words intervene between subject and verb

The presence of explanatory or parenthetical phrases, or other modifiers, between the subject and verb does not change the number or person of the subject. Locate the real subject of the sentence and make the verb agree with it.

> His sworn *statement*, together with copies of the testimony and statements from others connected with the case, *was* made a part of the file.
>
> The *amount* shown, plus interest, *is* due within 30 days.
>
> The *letter* with its several attachments *was* received this morning.
>
> Our *letters*, like our speech, *are* indications of our knowledge of English.
>
> The *supervisor*, instead of the agents who had been assigned the case, *is* scheduled to visit the office.
>
> His *appraisal*, including extensive notes on the furnishings of the office, *was* well received.
>
> That *fact*, in addition to our already large file on the case, *completes* the information we requested.
>
> *No one* but those present *knows* of this information.

18c Subject and predicate differ in number

After forms of the verb *to be* we often find a construction (called the *predicate nominative*) that means the same thing as the subject. When the predicate nominative differs in number from the subject, the verb must agree with the element that precedes it (the subject).

> Our main *problem is* writing complete reports and keeping them short enough for fast reading.
>
> Writing complete reports and keeping them short enough for fast reading *are* our main problems.
>
> As always, the *question was* sufficient funds.
> As always, *sufficient funds were* the question.
>
> The director said that an increasing *problem is* the required statistical surveys.
>
> The director said that the required statistical *surveys are* an increasing problem.

18d Construction shift and parallelism

Use the same grammatical construction for each of the words or ideas in a sentence if these two words or ideas require *balance* according to the meaning which the sentence is conveying.

> Not: *Singing* and *to dance* are not permitted here.
> But: *Singing* and *dancing* (or *To sing* and *to dance*) are not permitted here.

> Not: This term, the children are learning the value of *courtesy* and *being kind*.
> But: This term, the children are learning the value of *courtesy* and *kindness*.

19 Special Problems of Pronoun Reference

19a Ambiguous antecedents

Do not use forms of the same pronoun to refer to different antecedents.

> Not: The supervisor told Mr. Johnson that *he* thought *his* work was improving.
> (Does the supervisor think that his own work is improving, or that Mr. Johnson's work is improving?)
> But: Mr. Johnson was told by his supervisor that his work was improving.

When it seems that the pronoun can logically refer to either of two antecedents, be sure that the reference is obvious.

> Not: The director told Mr. Roberts that *he* would have to make *his* proposed trip to Boston in June.
> (The pronouns *he* and *his* can refer to either *director* or *Mr. Roberts*. The meaning may be apparent when this sentence is placed in context, but rephrasing will insure clarity.)

> Could mean: Although Mr. Roberts had planned to travel to Boston in May, the director asked *him* to postpone the trip until June.

or: Since the director is planning a trip to Boston in June, he was obliged to decline Mr. Roberts' invitation to speak at the June conference.

Place the pronoun as close as possible to its antecedent, to avoid ambiguity or confusion.

Not: A young woman can readily find a job *that* is skilled in shorthand.
>(Although the pronoun *that* refers to *woman*, its placement makes it appear to refer to *job*.)

But: A young *woman that* is skilled in shorthand can readily find a job.

Not: The letter is on the conference table *that* we received yesterday.
>(If we assume that it was the letter that was received yesterday, not the conference table, this sentence should read:
The *letter that* we received yesterday is on the conference table.)

19b Indefinite antecedents

Be sure that the reference to an antecedent is quite specific.

Not: The carbons of these letters were not initialed by the writers, so we are sending *them* back.
>(What are we sending back? The carbons, the letters, or the writers?)

But: We are sending back the carbons of the letters because *they* were not initialed by the writers.

Not: When you have finished the book and written your summary, please return *it* to the library.

But: When you have finished the book and written your summary, please return the book to the library.

19c Implied antecedents

As a general rule, the antecedent of a pronoun must appear in the sentence—not merely be implied. And the antecedent should be a specific word, not an idea expressed in a phrase or clause. *It, which, this,* and *that* are the pronouns that most often lead our meaning astray. Any of these pronouns may refer to an idea expressed in a preceding passage if the idea and the reference are *unmistakably clear.* But too often the idea that is unmistakably clear to the speaker or writer is nowhere to be found when the listener or reader looks for it.

Not: Although the doctor operated at once, *it* was not a success and the patient died.
>(The pronoun *it* refers to the idea of *operation*, which is implied but not expressed in the first part of the sentence.)

But: Although the doctor performed the *operation* at once, *it* was not a success and the patient died.

or: Although the doctor operated at once, the *operation* was not a success and the patient died.

Not: This matter has also been taken up with the General Accounting Office, Washington, D.C., a copy of *which* is attached.
>(In this sentence the antecedent of *which* is barely implied. We assume that the writer is attaching a copy of his letter to General Accounting Office, not a copy of General Accounting Office itself, as his sentence says.)

But: This matter has also been taken up with the General Accounting Office, Washington, D.C. A copy of our letter to them is attached.

Not: Mr. Roberts has recently been promoted. *This* brings him greater responsibility and will probably mean longer hours for him.
>(Although it is pretty obvious that *this* refers to Mr. Roberts' promotion, the word *promotion* does not appear in the sentence.)

But: Mr. Roberts has recently received a *promotion. This* brings him greater responsibility and will probably mean longer hours for him.

Not: Miss Jones computed her tax liability under the premise that she was entitled to use rates applicable to the head of the household, *which* is in error.

But: Miss Jones computed her tax liability under the premise that she was entitled to use rates applicable to the head of the household. *This premise* is in error.

19d Vague reference

The usage illustrated below — the impersonal use of *it*, *they*, and *you* — is not incorrect. But using these impersonal pronouns tends to produce vague, wordy sentences.

Not: In the Manual *it* says to make three copies.
(Who says?)
But: The Manual says to make three copies.

Not: In the letter *it* says he will be here on Thursday.

But: The letter says he will be here on Thursday.

or: He says, in his letter, that he will be here on Thursday.

Not: *They* say we are in for a cold, wet winter.

But: The almanac predicts a cold, wet winter.

Not: From this report *you* can easily recognize the cause of the accident.

But: From this report *one* can easily recognize the cause of the accident.
(The first example is correct if the writer is addressing his remarks to a specific person.)

or: The cause of the accident can be easily recognized from this report.

Now, push forward! Test yourself, and practice for your test with the carefully constructed quizzes that follow. Each one presents the kind of question you may expect on your test. And each question is at just the level of difficulty that may be expected. Don't try to take all the tests at one time. Rather, schedule yourself so that you take a few at each session, and spend approximately the same time on them at each session. Score yourself honestly, and date each test. You should be able to detect improvement in your performance on successive sessions.

TEST VIII. AGREEMENT AND REFERENCE

TIME: 25 Minutes

DIRECTIONS: In each of the following groups of sentences, select the one sentence that is grammatically INCORRECT. Mark the answer sheet with the letter of that incorrect sentence.

Explanations of the key points behind these questions appear with the answers at the end of this test. The explanatory answers provide the kind of background that will enable you to answer test questions with facility and confidence.

1

(A) The boy is a brilliant student; however, he is too lazy to earn good marks.
(B) If any person wants more information on this topic, they should write to the company.
(C) At the end of the meeting, it may be hard to tell whether a coat is yours or your neighbor's.
(D) It is irritating to work with a person who postpones final decisions.

2

(A) The emigration of large numbers of persons each year were gradually reducing the excess population.
(B) Much to our surprise, the boys' suits cost more than the men's.
(C) If you had gone into the hall, you would have met your friends.
(D) It is unnecessary to make a complete survey, for any sample test will serve our purpose.

3

(A) Granting this to be true, what would you infer from it?
(B) His hostility to the government of the United States and zeal for the mission of Nazi Germany has been overwhelmingly established.
(C) We objected to his scolding us for our good, especially when he said it hurt him more than us.
(D) I was disappointed in his words, for I had always treated him like a brother.

4

(A) You have three books and she has two, but hers costs more.
(B) Between you and me, the reason he is not going on a vacation is lack of money.
(C) He is my friend; nevertheless, I would not favor him in making my selection.
(D) The new battery of tests is designed to measure pupil achievement with greater accuracy.

5

(A) Generally, learning the correct pronunciation should precede any attempt to learn the correct spelling of a word.
(B) To make candles, you need at least the following: paraffin, wicks, and molds.
(C) The outcome of the conspiracy may be different from what its planners expect.
(D) Every student competing in the art contest wished that their painting would win a prize.

6

(A) Anyone interested in science can get a scholarship if they show aptitude.
(B) If you're sure of your facts, you should not hesitate to state your opinion.
(C) When the package is opened, I am sure than it will be found to contain gifts for John, Alice, and me.
(D) As I said, I have driven thousands of miles in New England and have found many places where I should be happy to live.

S1857

7

(A) His ambiguous remarks were inconsistent with his reputation for intelligence.
(B) The dialogue was so irreverent as to border on the sacrilegious.
(C) A fool and his gold is soon parted.
(D) We found no precedents for his outrageous rulings.

8

(A) As we entered the field, a flock of birds took off.
(B) The cattlemen's steers roamed the rich pastures.
(C) What had seemed like years was but five appalling minutes.
(D) My father, along with hundreds of other workers, have been on strike since New Year's Day.

9

(A) With all that make-up on her face, she looked as though she were a clown.
(B) Give the nomination to whoever has achieved the highest average.
(C) Acting on my instructions, the custodian locked every door in the building.
(D) We were only halfway through the discussion when somebody voiced their opinion that long and dignified masculine tradition demanded concealing all sentiments.

10

(A) He stayed inside the yard all day.
(B) The coal was put in under the stairs.
(C) These kind of apples are not grown in Ohio.
(D) It does look like rain, but all signs fail in dry weather.

11

(A) "Finding the kidnapper should supersede all other activities of the police," declared Councilman Crane.
(B) I think, Mr. Gordon, that you've misunderstood the question.
(C) As pleased as Punch, the boy showed us the three fish he had caught.
(D) The constant rise of prices and wages bring about inflation.

12

(A) Either the mayor or the aldermen are to blame.
(B) Unlike actual money, however, the value of trading stamps are only partly estimated on the basis of their buying power.
(C) Approximately ten miles is the distance between my home and his.
(D) One part of an animal which reveals his identity is his limbs.

13

(A) The place where I was born is still as attractive as ever.
(B) When songs are sung and bouquets are flung, will you be there to receive them?
(C) In the Brazilian forests, the rustle of the leaves blend with the shrill calls of the birds.
(D) A new president will be elected just as soon as last year's officers agree to resign.

14

(A) Everyone can have a wonderful time in London if they will just not try to see the entire city in one week.
(B) Being a stranger in town myself, I know how you feel.
(C) New York is a city of man-made wonders awe-inspiring as those found in nature.
(D) He felt deep despair (as who has not?) at the evidence of man's inhumanity to man.

15

(A) Although we were all ready to continue on our trip, our host at the hotel still expressed doubts about the ability of our guide.
(B) Neither of our contestants in the mile run has a chance to defeat the champion.
(C) Evidence to the contrary notwithstanding, I am sure that he will be found innocent.
(D) Television, along with other media of communication, help us to keep informed.

16

(A) The number of failures in the written test of the examination for the position of superintendent of the project were surprisingly low.
(B) I appreciate your helping me do the dishes, but I wish you would lay them down on the table.
(C) His understanding of the materials and processes involved is unrivalled in the industry.
(D) No sooner had he begun to speak than an ominous muttering arose from the audience.

17

(A) By the end of February, we were all completely exhausted.
(B) The translation of all the selections are by the editor.
(C) While in Europe, they visited Rome, Paris, Berlin and Copenhagen.
(D) We saw an old man beside the stage door.

18

(A) Each of the candidates in this election are expected to prepare their own speeches.
(B) Long as the play is—and it usually runs four hours—the actors never seem to become tired.
(C) While our cat has the habit of showing its claws, it has never scratched anybody.
(D) The stranger asked where the town hall was and whether it was open at that hour.

19

(A) Modern furniture may be used for many purposes for which period furniture cannot.
(B) I had but five minutes to catch the train.
(C) He told Marjorie and me that he would not come.
(D) Each of the wheels on those trucks have twelve spokes.

20

(A) I was embarrassed when the teacher singled me out for criticism.
(B) He had to travel a mile father than I.
(C) More than any other prose form, drama relies on dialogue.
(D) We must prepare for any emergency on our travels, whether they occur or not.

21

(A) He has two friends to help him now, John and me.
(B) The richness of his arms and apparel were conspicuous.
(C) It seems strange that some substances serve merely as catalysts in chemical reactions and are themselves virtually unchanged.
(D) If I were in your position, I should ask my friends to assist me.

22

(A) The possession of certain skills and abilities are necessary for that type of work.
(B) The beautiful elm trees are in danger of being killed by a disease which was brought here from Europe.
(C) When you're in doubt about your best friend's loyalty, you can't help being disappointed.
(D) Churchgoers are expected to observe the canons.

23

(A) How many school boys mouthed "to be or not to be' without having the slightest idea of the soliloquy's meaning!
(B) Phonetic spelling, with its upsetting of established conventions, has had rough going.
(C) The textbook can be an inspiration or a crutch; the best teachers and the poorest use them in different ways.
(D) He professed an abiding love for democracy, but his actions belied him.

24

(A) The deliberations were conducted with calm and openness.
(B) There were among the spectators at least one who was unaware of the undercurrent of feeling.
(C) The driver waited impatiently; the light was slow in changing.
(D) "What's the reason for such scurrilous remarks?" the chairman asked.

25

(A) The graduating class have all agreed to have their pictures taken in caps and gowns.
(B) The demand for good serious literature has seriously depreciated.
(C) Eighteen was the number of pages assigned for daily reading.
(D) I fear, James, that you are incorrigibly lazy. From now on I shall see that every one of your daily assigned exercises are completed.

26

(A) I recalled Sir Francis Bacon's astute maxim: "Some books are to be tasted, others to be swallowed, and some few to be chewed and digested."
(B) The color of his eyes are brown.
(C) I did not realize that the pen was hers.
(D) I'm sure it was she who sent the telegram.

27

(A) Everybody, bustling about, laughing, and even shrieking, gave himself up to unmitigated joy.
(B) He was failing rapidly; the interval between each breath seemed longer and longer.
(C) On this question, which harbors so much complexity, there are likely to be acute differences of opinion.
(D) What he saw was six elephants moving gravely in single file.

28

(A) My best friend has advised me to be unfailingly vigilant.
(B) The recurrence of identical sounds help to awaken the emotions.
(C) Along the water's edge there are found many wild flowers.
(D) He objected strenuously to Mary's accepting the position.

29

(A) The rotation of duties and responsibilities among the employees are highly desirable.
(B) You must remember to maintain contact with your friends and relatives.
(C) She could not operate the electric typewriter because she had not plugged it in.
(D) Eleanor utilized a postal scale to determine the cost of mailing the parcel.

30

(A) We dived into the cool, refreshing water.
(B) He insists that he be given an explanation.
(C) My brother, together with all of his fraternity brothers, are upstairs in the attic.
(D) In a loud voice, the sergeant ordered his platoon to march on.

(A) It is difficult to recollect what life was like before the war.
(B) Will each of the pupils please hand their homework in?
(C) There are fewer serious mistakes in this pamphlet than I had thought.
(D) "Leave Her To Heaven" is the title of a novel by Ben Ames Williams.

(A) The letter, mailed from abroad, bore a type of stamp that was unfamiliar to me.
(B) The inventor contributed many new ideas to his employers, which was very profitable to all concerned.
(C) In order to effect the reorganization you speak of, we must not dissipate our funds.
(D) Dr. R. B. Johnson will confer with Messrs. Greene and Williamson on Friday, June 14, at 2:00 P.M.

(A) The murderer failed to benefit from his crime.
(B) "My mother will be here," replied the little girl, "as soon as she finishes her shopping."
(C) Tired from so much walking, the girls asked permission to rest.
(D) A boy are really hundreds of different persons.

CONSOLIDATE YOUR KEY ANSWERS HERE

(answer grid, questions 1–40, columns A B C D E)

Correct Answers For The Foregoing Questions

(Check your answers with these that we provide. You should find considerable correspondence between them. If not, you'd better go back and find out why. On the next page we have provided concise clarifications of basic points behind the key answers. Please go over them carefully because they may be quite useful in helping you pick up extra points on the exam.)

1.B	6.A	11.D	16.A	21.B	26.B	31.B
2.A	7.C	12.B	17.B	22.A	27.D	32.B
3.B	8.D	13.C	18.A	23.C	28.B	33.D
4.A	9.D	14.A	19.D	24.B	29.A	
5.D	10.C	15.D	20.D	25.D	30.C	

TEST VIII. AGREEMENT AND REFERENCE

EXPLANATORY ANSWERS CLARIFYING CARDINAL POINTS

The core of the Question and Answer Method... getting help when and where you need it. Even if you were able to write correct key answers for the preceding questions, the following explanations illuminate fundamental facts, ideas, and principles which just might crop up in the form of questions on future tests.

Bold-face references in the following answers direct you to paragraphs in the Arco Grammar Text, where fuller explanations are provided.

ANSWER 1.

B   If any person wants more information on this topic, **he** should write to the company. REASON: **he** refers to a singular subject (**any person**). **(15b)**

ANSWER 2.

A   The emigration of large numbers of persons each year **was** gradually reducing the excess population. REASON: Since the subject (**emigration**) is singular, the verb must be singular (**was reducing**). **(15a)**

ANSWER 3.

B   His hostility to the government of the United States and zeal for the mission of Nazi Germany **have been** overwhelmingly established. REASON: The verb must agree with the two subjects (**hostility and zeal**) constituting a plural subject. **(15a)**

ANSWER 4.

A   You have three books and she has two, but hers cost more. REASON: **hers** refers to books which is plural. Therefore, the verb must be plural (**cost**). **(15a)**

ANSWER 5.

D   Every student competing in the art contest wished that **his** painting would win a prize. REASON: The singular possessive form (**his**) refers to the singular noun (**student**). **(15b)**

ANSWER 6.

A   Anyone interested in science can get a scholarship if **he shows** aptitude. REASON: The singular subject (**anyone**) requires a singular relative pronoun (**he**). **(15c)**

ANSWER 7.

C   A fool and his gold **are** soon parted. REASON: The subject, consisting of two words (**fool** and **gold**) is plural. The verb must, accordingly, be plural (**are parted**) **(15a)**

ANSWER 8.

D   My father, along with hundreds of other workers, **has been** on strike since New Year's Day. REASON: The subject is singular—therefore, the verb is singular (**has been**). **(15a)**

ANSWER 9.

D   We were only halfway through the discussion when somebody voiced **his** opinion that long and dignified masculine tradition demanded concealing all sentiments. REASON: **somebody**, being a singular antecedent, requires a singular possessive pronoun (**his**). **(15b)**

ANSWER 10.

C   **This kind** of apples **is** grown in Ohio. REASON: Since **kind** is a singular noun, its demonstrative adjective modifier (**this**) must be singular. Also, the verb must be singular (**is**) to agree with the singular subject. (**kind**). **(15a, 71)**

ANSWER 11.

D   The constant rise of prices and wages **brings** about inflation. REASON: The singular subject is rise—therefore, the verb must be singular (**brings**).   **(15a)**

ANSWER 12.

B   Unlike actual money, however, the value of trading stamps **is** only partly estimated on the basis of their buying power. REASON: The subject of the verb **is** is singular (**value**).   **(15a)**

ANSWER 13.

C   In the Brazilian forests, the rustle of the leaves **blends** with the shrill calls of the birds. REASON: The subject of the verb is a singular noun **rustle**—therefore, the verb must be singular (**blends**).   **(15a)**

ANSWER 14.

A   Everyone can have a wonderful time in London if **he** will just not try to see the entire city in one week. REASON: Since the subject of the main clause is singular (**everyone**), the personal pronoun referring to the subject must be singular.   **(15b)**

ANSWER 15.

D   Television, along with other media of communication, **helps** us to keep informed. REASON: The singular subject (**television**) takes a singular verb. **media** is not a subject—it is the object of a preposition.   **(15a)**

ANSWER 16.

A   The number of failures in the written test of the examination for the position as superintendent of the project **was** surprisingly low. REASON: The subject of **was** is the **number**. Since the latter is singular, the verb must be singular (**was**). **(15a, 16a)**

ANSWER 17.

B   The translation of all the selections **is** by the editor. REASON: The singular subject **translation** requires a singular verb (**is**).   **(15a)**

ANSWER 18.

A   Each of the candidates in this election **is** expected to prepare his own speech. REASON: The singular subject **each** requires a singular verb (**is expected**). Moreover, the possessive pronoun-adjective **his** is singular because it refers to **Each** which is singular.   **(15a, 17a)**

ANSWER 19.

D   Each of the wheels on those trucks **has** twelve spokes. REASON: The subject of the sentence (**each**) is singular. The verb, therefore, must be singular (**has**).   **(15a)**

ANSWER 20.

D   We must prepare for any emergency on our travels, whether **it** occurs or not. REASON: **it** refers to emergency.   **(15b)**

ANSWER 21.

B   The richness of his arms and apparel **was** conspicuous. REASON: The subject of the verb is singular (**richness**). Accordingly, the verb must be singular (**was**).   **(15a)**

ANSWER 22.

A   The possession of certain skills and abilities **is** necessary for that type of work. REASON: The subject of the sentence (**possession**) is singular—therefore, the verb must be singular.   **(15a)**

ANSWER 23.

C   The textbook can be an inspiration or a crutch; the best teachers and the poorest use **it** in different ways. REASON: **textbook** is a singular noun. The relative pronoun that relates to textbook must, therefore, be singular (**it**).   **(15b)**

ANSWER 24.

B   There **was** among the spectators at least one who was unaware of the undercurrent of feeling. REASON: The subject of the verb (**was**) is **one**.   **(15a)**

ANSWER 25.

D   I fear, James, that you are incorrigibly lazy. From now on I shall see that every one of your daily assigned exercises **is completed**. REASON: The subject **one** requires a singular verb (**is completed**). **(15a)**

ANSWER 26.

B   The color of his eyes **is** brown. REASON: The subject is singular (**color**) — therefore, the verb must be singular (**is**) **(15a)**

ANSWER 27.

D   What he saw **were six** elephants moving gravely in single file. REASON: The copulative verb (**were**) is in agreement in number with the plural subject (**six elephants**). **(15a)**

ANSWER 28.

B   The recurrence of identical sounds **helps** to awaken the emotions. REASON: Since the subject **recurrence** is singular, the verb (**helps**) must be singular. **(15a)**

ANSWER 29.

A   The rotation of duties and responsibilities among the employees **is** highly desirable. REASON: The subject (**rotation**) is singular. Therefore, the verb is singular (**is**). **(15a)**

ANSWER 30.

C   My brother, together with all of his fraternity brothers, **is** upstairs in the attic. REASON: The subject of the sentence is the singular noun **brother**. Accordingly, the verb (**is**) must be singular. **(15a)**

ANSWER 31.

B   Will each of the pupils please hand **his** homework in? REASON: The antecedent of the pronoun **his** is **each**. **Each** is singular. Therefore, the pronoun itself (**his**) must be singular. Incidentally, it would be more accurate to say that **his** or **her** is a pronoun-adjective since it does modify a noun (**homework**). **(15b)**

ANSWER 32.

B   The inventor contributed to his employers many new ideas which were very profitable to all concerned. REASON: First of all, the misplaced modifer (**which was . . . all concerned**) refers to **ideas** — not to **employers**. Secondly, since **ideas** is plural, the verb of the "which" clause must be plural (**were**). **(15b, 47)**

ANSWER 33.

D   A boy **is** really hundreds of different persons. REASON: The subject **boy** is singular; therefore, the verb must be singular (**is**). The plurality of the predicate noun **hundreds** does not affect the number of the verb. **(15a)**

TEST IX. AGREEMENT AND REFERENCE

TIME: 25 Minutes

DIRECTIONS: In each of the following groups of sentences, select the one sentence that is grammatically INCORRECT. Mark the answer sheet with the letter of that incorrect sentence.

Explanations of the key points behind these questions appear with the answers at the end of this test. The explanatory answers provide the kind of background that will enable you to answer test questions with facility and confidence.

1

(A) All I wish to say, in conclusion, is that the executives spoken of attest the weakness of their rule by breaking it themselves.
(B) You will come and see us, won't you?
(C) The success of a small business enterprise depends on hard work, good location, and factors beyond the full control of the owner.
(D) Gracious means pleasing, attractive, a person who practices the amenities naturally and easily.

2

(A) The lawyer who directed the investigation is the man whom we thought to be best qualified for the new post.
(B) Whether the report has been released or not will determine our action.
(C) The award will go to him who completes the course with the highest score.
(D) Proud of his skill in decanting, he poured some of the wine into his own glass first so that he would get the cork and not the lady.

3

(A) Instead of looking disdainfully at London grime, think of it as a mantle of tradition.
(B) Nobody but the pilot and the co-pilot was permitted to handle the mysterious package.
(C) Not only is industry anxious to hire all available engineers, but by the armed forces they are being offered commissions.
(D) For immediate service go direct to the store manager.

4

(A) Why don't you try to please the customers, Ted?
(B) The coach with his entire team are traveling by plane.
(C) Credulous as she usually is, even Mrs. Brown refused to believe such an implausible story.
(D) Three students—two girls and one boy—served on the committee.

5

(A) The teacher, together with the entire faculty, were bound by parliamentary procedure.
(B) The doctor decided that there was a definite separation in the shoulder area.
(C) He reacted indignantly, like the man of principle that he really was.
(D) An exquisite piece of jewelry hung from her neck in an ostentatious display of wealth.

6

(A) Two more dollars are missing from the drawer tonight.
(B) The conscientious nurse was extremely startled when she observed how the drug affected the patient.
(C) "The Lottery" is one of those stories that leaves you more puzzled when you finish than when you began.
(D) I think we should empower the nominating committee to name whoever, in its considered opinion, is best suited to direct the society.

7

(A) I have enjoyed the study of the Spanish language not only because of its beauty and the opportunity it offers to understand the Hispanic culture but also to make use of it in business associations.
(B) The opinions he expressed were decidely different from those he had held in his youth.
(C) Had he actually studied, he certainly would have passed.
(D) An executive should be patient and tactful.

8

(A) The children's determination to find their dog almost resulted in tragedy.
(B) They spent the first night in a house that was unlocked and with no one at home.
(C) "What he asked me," said the boy, "was, 'Where can I find your father?'"
(D) It was the whimpering of the younger child and the comforting words of her brother that a member of the search-party heard about ten feet off the road.

9

(A) Besides us, he can count upon few of his constituents.
(B) My first inclination—and I don't claim credit for originality—was to refuse.
(C) He had a chance to invest wisely, establish his position, and displaying his ability as an executive.
(D) Picnicking in these woods is one way to avoid the noise and crowds.

10

(A) He saw, facing him across the spring, a small man, his hands in his coat pockets, a cigarette in his mouth.
(B) You must pay the fine unless you can prove that no traffic law was violated.
(C) I would rather have been a French peasant and worn wooden shoes.
(D) If we here in America cannot live peaceably together, how can we and other nations live in peace?

11

(A) The wild game hunter stalked the tiger slowly, cautiously, and in a silent manner.
(B) A large number of students contributed gifts for the school bazaar.
(C) Every pupil understood the assignment except me.
(D) European film distributors originated the art of "dubbing."

12

(A) Even a connoisseur of fine wines would hesitate to predict that a certain wine will be popular in the future.
(B) Whether the book is Edward's or yours can be determined easily if you have written your name in your copy.
(C) Mr. Martin, together with all the members of his large family, are enjoying themselves in Europe.
(D) This technique may be usable in your business if you can adapt it to your particular situation.

13

(A) A torrential downpour, in addition to long stretches of road construction which made it necessary to slow down to fifteen miles an hour, have so delayed us that we shall not be able to be on hand for the ceremony.
(B) If I were rich, I should live in the suburbs.
(C) They took him to be me despite the fact that he is taller and heavier than I.
(D) The most important criterion in judging the performance of a violinist is not virtuosity but maturity of interpretation.

14

(A) He had better do as he is told unless he wants to get into trouble.
(B) Such a habit is not only dangerous to the individual's health but a man will find it a serious drain on his finances.
(C) After the mother had yelled at the child for spilling the milk, the father bade him leave the room.
(D) The saint is brushed in boldly in wide strokes, while the seraphim are traced in delicately in faint gray tones.

15

(A) Because the order was canceled, the money remained in the bank.
(B) When in the vicinity, don't hesitate to drop in.
(C) The colonel ordered six men from his battalion to make a reconnaissance of the area.
(D) I considered walking down to the station and to post my letter there.

16

(A) The questionnaires were sent to all superintendents.
(B) I prefer winter to summer.
(C) The boy, as well as his mother, needs help.
(D) Because he has always been popular and with abundant wealth, he thoroughly enjoyed his college years.

17

(A) The newly appointed member of the office staff was told that Miss Jones would tell her how to complete the report.
(B) If you follow these suggestions, they will teach you self-control and to be tactful.
(C) Observing the girl's difficulty in understanding the problem, her mother offered to assist her.
(D) She was most eager to learn the operation of the duplicating machine.

18

(A) He will not lend me the book; therefore, I shall have to consult it in his library.
(B) Clearning the garage and washing the car took John all of a Sunday morning.
(C) His reading included not only books and magazines, but also consulting newspapers and unpublished letters.
(D) This unabridged dictionary is useful to general readers, to college students, and to scholars.

19

(A) After this act, events moved rapidly toward a climax.
(B) A treaty promoting American interests was signed.
(C) The malefactor was quickly apprehended by the vigilant policeman.
(D) Mary would neither take part herself in the production nor allowed her sister to do so.

20

(A) His father was disturbed to find that the boy had lied rather than told the truth.
(B) I am depending on the medicine's being delivered immediately.
(C) For conscience's sake he gave himself up, though no suspicion had been directed toward him.
(D) The following description, together with the drawings, present a master plan for the development of an airport.

21

(A) Smith asserted that whatever fame he enjoyed was due rather to chance than to talent.
(B) The prize will be awarded to whomever the committee agrees to give it to.
(C) Nor has the writer even the satisfaction of calling his reader a fool for misunderstanding him, since he seldom, if ever, sees him.
(D) Struggling hard against almost insurmountable odds, he was unable to effect even a small change.

22

(A) The committee recommended that accommodations be sought at the Grand Hotel.
(B) "The Man with the Hoe" has a message of social significance, has it not?
(C) Characteristic of all primitive civilizations is dependence on the immediate environment.
(D) Tom spends his time fishing and bowling, which is why his friends are envious.

23

(A) Do you feel as well as you look?
(B) Drive slow; live long.
(C) None of the women brought her children to the performance.
(D) He has always admired dramatists, and he is going to make that his lifework.

24

(A) He became a lawyer because it is interesting work.
(B) Oh, that's what you said.
(C) Down from the hills came the outlaws to lay waste the countryside.
(D) We have rearranged the entire directory to make it easier to find people quickly.

25

(A) Which student asked, "Why?"
(B) He asked for information as to whom the report should be given.
(C) The results of the test given in October have not yet been released.
(D) Three o'clock is when the meeting will be held, according to an announcement published today.

26

(A) He always drinks mineral water when traveling abroad.
(B) His descent from orbit in the satellite was extraordinarily rapid.
(C) A student's normal equipment consists of a pen, a notebook, a compass, and a ruler.
(D) Messrs. Jameson and Curry will represent the firm of Coleman & Brothers, Inc.

27

(A) Whatever his philosophy may be, his speeches do not reveal it.
(B) That he had swum the length of the lake in less than one hour was behond our belief.
(C) By now, we know that this problem can never be solved.
(D) The result of the discussion was that we decided not to buy the car; which was just what I had advised at the beginning.

28

(A) The picture stood on the mantel, discolored, dusty, and forgotten.
(B) In the encyclopedia article it says that the tendency toward nationalism was clear by 1840.
(C) The miner could scarcely detect the gas emanating from the crevice.
(D) The horse that had won the race suddenly went limp and crumpled to the ground.

29

(A) Even his palatial home and fine family do not seem to give him happiness.
(B) Who has been given the special training for this position?
(C) At the end of the season, Jones had failed to win a single game, which was what you would expect of a pitcher like him.
(D) Nobody was surprised when Dr. Robert C. Williams was elected president of the association.

30

(A) Jimmy and Joe were orphans whom our neighbors adopted when they were two years old.
(B) However he attempted to solve the cryptogram, the result was always the same—negative.
(C) The strikers have repeatedly shown that a number of them are in favor of their receiving retroactive pay.
(D) The cession of a piece of territory could have prevented the war.

31

(A) Have you ever swum out to the breakwater?
(B) Because they were unaware of his interest in the building, they did not understand why he felt so bad about its being condemned.
(C) Most of us students work best when we work alone.
(D) My mother is making chicken for dinner, and I don't want to miss it.

(32)

(A) This is a book rich and subtle in its texture, fluent in its emotional undertones.
(B) To an American, education has long since ceased being a phenomenon.
(C) When my father was a young boy, he discussed with his father how he could be an influence in his life.
(D) Most baccalaureate degrees are awarded in the field of liberal arts.

(33)

(A) Please ask whether the agenda of the next meeting are ready for the printer.
(B) Haven't I asked you a dozen times to take the bicycle to the repair shop?
(C) The State Crime Commission is investigating the outrageous dock situation, which is good, even if long overdue.
(D) More than 50,000 Americans participated in the Poor People's Campaign march.

CONSOLIDATE YOUR KEY ANSWERS HERE

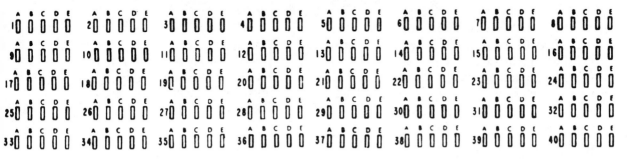

Correct Answers For The Foregoing Questions

(Check your answers with these that we provide. You should find considerable correspondence between them. If not, you'd better go back and find out why. On the next page we have provided concise clarifications of basic points behind the key answers. Please go over them carefully because they may be quite useful in helping you pick up extra points on the exam.)

1.D	6.C	11.A	16.D	21.C	26.A	31.D
2.D	7.A	12.C	17.B	22.D	27.D	32.C
3.C	8.B	13.A	18.C	23.D	28.B	33.C
4.B	9.C	14.B	19.D	24.A	29.C	
5.A	10.D	15.D	20.D	25.B	30.A	

TEST IX. AGREEMENT AND REFERENCE

EXPLANATORY ANSWERS CLARIFYING CARDINAL POINTS

The core of the Question and Answer Method . . . getting help when and where you need it. Even if you were able to write correct key answers for the preceding questions, the following explanations illuminate fundamental facts, ideas, and principles which just might crop up in the form of questions on future tests.

Bold-face references in the following answers direct you to paragraphs in the Arco Grammar Text, where fuller explanations are provided.

ANSWER 1.

D A person who practices the amenities naturally and easily is gracious, pleasing, and attractive. REASON: The word order is confusing and unbalanced in the original sentence. **(18d)**

ANSWER 2.

D Proud of his skill in decanting, he poured some of the wine into his own glass first so that he, not the lady, would get the cork. REASON: In the incorrect sentence, **cork** and **lady** are the direct objects of the verb **would get**. The word **lady** should be a subject along with **he**. **(18d)**

ANSWER 3.

C Not only is industry anxious to hire all available engineers, but the armed forces is offering them commissions. REASON: The original sentence is unbalanced and unclear. **(18d)**

ANSWER 4.

B The coach with his entire team **is traveling** by plane. REASON: The singular subject **coach** requires a singular verb. **(18b)**

ANSWER 5.

A The teacher, together with the entire faculty, **was bound** by parliamentary procedure. REASON: The subject of the sentence is the singular noun **teacher**. Therefore, the verb is singular (**was bound**). **(18b)**

ANSWER 6.

C "The Lottery" is one of those stories that leaves you more puzzled when you finish than when you **begin**. REASON: Parallel construction is necessary. Since **finish** is present tense, **begin** must also be present. **(18d)**

ANSWER 7.

A I have enjoyed the study of the Spanish language not only because of its beauty and the opportunity it offers to understand the Hispanic culture, but also because of its **usefulness** in business associations. REASON: Note that we now have consistency of construction. **(18d)**

ANSWER 8.

B They spent the first night in an **unlocked** and **unsupervised** house. REASON: The original sentence lacks unity of construction. **(18d)**

ANSWER 9.

C He had a chance to invest wisely, establish his position, and **display** his ability as an executive. REASON: The infinitive construction is used for parallelism. **(18d)**

ANSWER 10.

D If we here in America cannot live peaceably together, how can we expect to live peaceably with other nations? REASON: **live peaceably together** should parallel the structure of **live peaceably with other nations**. **(18d)**

ANSWER 11.

A   The wild game hunter stalked the tiger slowly, cautiously and **silently**. REASON: The modifiers of stalked should be consistent in form—all adverbs in this case (**slowly, cautiously, silently**).   **(18d)**

ANSWER 12.

C   Mr. Martin, together with all the other members of his large family, is enjoying himself in Europe. REASON: In the original sentence, **Mr. Martin**, as the subject, requires a singular verb.   **(18b)**

ANSWER 13.

A   A torrential downpour, in addition to long stretches of road construction which made it necessary to slow down to fifteen miles an hour, **has** so delayed us that we shall not be able to be on hand for the ceremony. REASON: The subject of the main clause (**downpour**) is singular. Therefore, its verb (**has delayed**) must be singular.   **(18b)**

ANSWER 14.

B   Such a habit is not only a danger to the individual's health but is also a serious drain on his finances. REASON: The original sentence does not have parallel structure.   **(18d)**

ANSWER 15.

D   I considered walking down to the station and posting my letter there. REASON: The gerund (**posting**) is used to parallel the other gerund (**walking**).   **(18d)**

ANSWER 16.

D   Because of his popularity and wealth, he thoroughly enjoyed his college years. REASON: The original sentence is awkward because of its lack of parallel structure.   **(18d)**

ANSWER 17.

B   If you follow these suggestions, they will teach you self-control and **tact**. REASON: For consistency and good style, we use two nouns.   **(18d)**

ANSWER 18.

C   His reading included not only books and magazines, but also newspapers and unpublished letters. REASON: The direct objects should all be nouns in order to have grammatical consistency. Moreover, it is unnecessary to use the word **consulting** since reading includes consulting.   **(18d)**

ANSWER 19.

D   Mary would neither take part herself in the production nor **allow** her sister to do so. REASON: The verb **allow** stands for **would allow** in this construction. Now we have verb balance.   **(18d)**

ANSWER 20.

D   The following description, together with the drawings, **presents** a master plan for the development of an airport. REASON: The subject **description** is singular—therefore, it takes a singular verb (**presents**). The word **drawings** is not part of the subject—it is the object of the compound preposition **together with**.   **(18b)**

ANSWER 21.

C   Nor has the writer even the satisfaction of calling his reader a fool for misunderstanding him, since the writer seldom, if ever, sees the reader. REASON: The pronouns (**he** and **it**) of the original sentence have indefinite antecedents.   **(19c)**

ANSWER 22.

D   Tom spends his time fishing bowling; therefore, his friends are envious. REASON: The relative pronoun **which** (in the original sentence) cannot be used because its antecedent is too indefinite.   **(19c)**

ANSWER 23.

D   He has always admired dramatists and he is going to make the **study of dramatists** his life work. REASON: In the original sentence, the antecedent of the pronoun **that** is dramatists. However, he is going to make the **study of dramatists** (not **dramatists**) his life work.   **(19c)**

ANSWER 24.

A He became a lawyer because **being a lawyer** is interesting work. REASON: A **lawyer**, itself, is not interesting work. **(19c)**

ANSWER 25.

B He asked for information as to **the one to whom** the report should be given. REASON: Grammatically, it is necessary to include the antecedent **the one**. **The one** is object of the compound preposition **as to; whom** is indirect object after the verb **should be given**. **(19c)**

ANSWER 26.

A He always drinks mineral water when he is traveling abroad. REASON: In the original sentence, the **water** could be traveling abroad. **(19c)**

ANSWER 27.

D The result of the discussion was that we decided not to buy the car. **This action** was just what I had advised at the beginning. REASON: In the original sentence, the relative pronoun **which** does not have a specific antecedent. **(19c)**

ANSWER 28.

B The encyclopedia article says that the tendency toward nationalism was clear by 1840. REASON: The roundabout usage in the original sentence is objectionable. **(19d)**

ANSWER 29.

C At the end of the season, Jones had failed to win a single game. This was a record you would expect of a pitcher like him. REASON: Two sentences are required to make the whole thought clear. **(19)**

ANSWER 30.

A When Jimmy and Joe, who were orphans, were two years old, our neighbors adopted them. REASON: As the original sentence stands, the neighbors could be two years old. **(19a)**

ANSWER 31.

D For dinner, my mother is making chicken, which I don't want to miss. REASON: In the original sentence, the antecedent of **it** is indefinite (maybe **chicken**—likely **dinner**, since it is closer to the pronoun). Note that in the revised sentence, the antecedent of the pronoun **which** is unquestionably **chicken**, because of the latter's proximity. **(19a)**

ANSWER 32.

C When my father was a young boy, he discussed with his father how the latter could be an influence in his life. REASON: **the latter** replaces **he** for the sake of clarity. **(19a)**

ANSWER 33.

C The State Crime Commission is investigating the outrageous dock situation. The Commission's effort, even if long overdue, is good. REASON: In the original sentence, **which** has an indefinite antecedent. The two sentences are necessary for clarity in this case. **(19c)**

TEST X. AGREEMENT, TENSE, AND MOOD

TIME: 14 Minutes

*DIRECTIONS: Most questions in this test begin with a sentence containing a word or expression in **boldface** type. Then follow four grammatical descriptions of the **boldface** type. They are lettered (A) (B) (C) (D). Choose the correct grammatical description, and mark your answer sheet with the letter of the correct answer.*

Explanations of the key points behind these questions appear with the answers at the end of this test. The explanatory answers provide the kind of background that will enable you to answer test questions with facility and confidence.

Those **who** want much are always much in need.

(A) adverbial accusative
(B) relative pronoun
(C) limiting adjective
(D) indefinite article

I shall give the paper to **whomever** you designate as your representative.

(A) object of **designate**
(B) object of **give**
(C) indirect object
(D) subject of **designate**

Since I have the same qualifications **as** he, why shouldn't I be eligible for the same promotion?

(A) relative pronoun
(B) conjunction
(C) conjunctive adverb
(D) demonstrative adjective

It was finally decided that it would be I who **was** to go.

(A) third person singular
(B) third person plural
(C) first person singular
(D) first person plural

That music is for such **as** like mere novelty.

(A) subordinating conjunction
(B) relative pronoun
(C) preposition introducing noun clause
(D) conjunctive adverb

Such a storm **as** he raised when he came home, we had not heard in many a month.

(A) modifies adjective
(B) modifies noun
(C) object of verb
(D) modifies verb

It was clear to all of us **that he was not telling the truth**.

(A) adjective clause
(B) participial phrase
(C) adverbial clause
(D) noun clause

8

It is not enough to be busy; so are the ants. The question is, what are we busy about?

(A) expletive pronoun
(B) object of preposition
(C) predicate noun
(D) interrogative pronoun

That **there** are threats to freedom in some types of planning cannot be gainsaid.

(A) subject of **are**   (C) adverb
(B) expletive   (D) none of these

Choose is an example of a (an)

(A) weak verb   (C) strong verb
(B) defective verb (D) anomalous verb

My homework **will have been completed** before you return.

(A) verb — active voice, future tense
(B) verb — active voice, future perfect tense
(C) verb — passive voice, future tense
(D) verb — passive voice, future perfect tense

The four basic forms of a verb are

(A) active, passive, indicative, subjunctive
(B) present, past, present participle, past participle
(C) tense, number, mood, condition
(D) present, past, perfect, future

If 'twere done when 'tis done,
Then 'twere well it **were** done quickly.

(A) poetic license
(B) the hortatory mood
(C) the subjunctive mood, past tense
(D) the future perfect tense

The new assistant was made **director** of visual aids.

(A) predicate noun   (C) objective complement
(B) retained object   (D) indirect object

For all his efforts, **he** was still considered a slothful **worker**.

(A) predicate nominative
(B) subject of **considered** in apposition with **he**
(C) objective complement
(D) cognate object

In accordance with custom, the barn had been painted **red**.

(A) indirect object
(B) predicate adjective
(C) in apposition with **barn**
(D) objective complement

He was heard **to stumble** as he entered the room.

(A) retained object infinitive
(B) an infinitive used as adverb
(C) direct object
(D) an infinitive used as adjective

Was McCarthy named the **candidate** on the first ballot?

(A) a direct object
(B) a predicate nominative
(C) an indirect object
(D) the real subject in an inverted sentence

He is considered an **authority** in the field.

(A) in apposition with **he**
(B) direct object
(C) objective complement
(D) predicate nominative

CONSOLIDATE YOUR KEY ANSWERS HERE

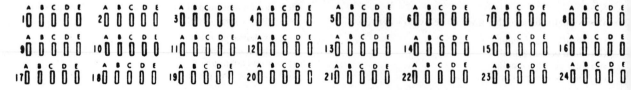

TEST X. AGREEMENT, TENSE, AND MOOD

KEY ANSWERS FOR THE FOREGOING QUESTIONS

1. B	4. C	7. D	10. C	13. C	16. B	19. D
2. A	5. B	8. A	11. D	14. A	17. A	
3. A	6. C	9. B	12. A	15. A	18. B	

EXPLANATORY ANSWERS CLARIFYING CARDINAL POINTS

The core of the Question and Answer Method . . . getting help when and where you need it. Even if you were able to write correct key answers for the preceding questions, the following explanations illuminate fundamental facts, ideas, and principles which just might crop up in the form of questions on future tests.

Bold-face references in the following answers direct you to paragraphs in the Arco Grammar Text, where fuller explanations are provided.

ANSWER 1.
B   REASON: **Who** is a relative pronoun whose antecedent is **Those**.   **(15b, 14d)**

ANSWER 2.
A   REASON: **Whomever** is a relative pronoun (antecedent is **one** understood). **Whomever** is the direct object of **designate**.   **(12, 16e)**

ANSWER 3.
A   REASON: The elliptical expression **as he** may be amplified to the clause **as he has**. In this clause, **as** means **which**. **As** is, therefore, a relative pronoun whose antecedent is **qualifications**.   **(16e)**

ANSWER 4.
C   REASON: In this type of relative clause construction, the number and person of the verb are determined by the number and person of the antecedent (**I**) of the relative pronoun (**who**).   **(16e)**

ANSWER 5.
B   REASON: **As** in the sentence given is used in place of **who** as a relative pronoun whose antecedent is the noun **such**.   **(12b, 16e)**

ANSWER 6.
C   REASON: **As** is a relative pronoun used in place of **which** as the direct object of the verb **raised**.   **(12b, 16e)**

ANSWER 7.
D   REASON: **That he was not telling the truth** is a noun clause which is the subject of the verb **were**. **It** is an expletive. **(18a)**

ANSWER 8.
A   REASON: The subject of the sentence is the infinitive phrase **to be busy**. **It** has no meaning and is, therefore, an expletive.   **(18a)**

ANSWER 9.

B REASON: **There** has no grammatical value but is used in an anticipating manner in preparing us for the subject **threats**. **(18a)**

ANSWER 10.

C REASON: There are two types of verb inflection—weak and strong. Strong verbs form the past tense by changing the root vowel: **choose, chose; know, knew; eat, ate.** **(21c)**

ANSWER 11.

D REASON: Since the subject is being acted upon, the verb is in the passive voice. When there are two future actions in a sentence—and one of the actions takes place before the other action—the action that takes place first is future perfect. **(22f, 33)**

ANSWER 12.

A REASON: A verb must be in either the active or the passive voice—in either the indicative or subjunctive mood (the imperative mood is little used). **(26, 33)**

ANSWER 13.

C REASON: In conditions which are contrary to fact, we use the simple past subjunctive in the condition, and in the conclusion we use **would, should, could,** or **might.** However, in poetry we sometimes use the old simple past subjunctive **were** in the conclusion. **(31)**

ANSWER 14.

A REASON: The passive verb in cases such as the following are regarded as copulative. He **is considered** a tyrant. The boy **is called** Adam. Lincoln **was elected** president. **Director,** after the passive verb **was made,** is a predicate noun referring to and meaning the same as the subject **assistant.** **(35)**

ANSWER 15.

A REASON: After a passive form **(was considered),** we have the predicate noun (or nominative) **worker.** The predicate noun always means the same as the subject **(he).** **(35)**

ANSWER 16.

B REASON: The passive verb **(had been painted)** has copulative force. The adjective **red** refers to the subject **barn. Red** is, therefore, a predicate adjective after the copulative verb. **(35)**

ANSWER 17.

A —REASON: In the active form, the sentence would read: "They heard him stumble." In this active form, **stumble (to stumble)** is an objective complement. In the passive form, **to stumble** is a retained object. **(13i)**

ANSWER 18.

B In the active declarative form, the sentence would read: "They named McCarthy the candidate..." In this active form, **candidate** is an objective complement. In the passive form, **candidate** means the same as the subject **McCarthy. Candidate** is, therefore, a predicate noun (or nominative). It could also be considered a retained object. **(13i)(35)**

ANSWER 19.

D REASON: In the active form, the sentence would read: "They considered him an authority in the field." In this active form, authority is an objective complement. In the passive form, authority means the same as the subject he. Authority is, therefore, a predicate nominative, but may also be thought of as a retained object. **(13i) (35)**

IV. TENSE OF VERBS AND VERBALS

20 Introduction

The verb is the backbone of the sentence. It is the word that tells what action is taking place or what condition exists. The verb puts life into the sentence; without it, there *is* no sentence—just a group of words lined up with nothing to do, with no place to go. Give such words a verb, and they spring into action.

Since verbs are so important, it is to our advantage to get as much use from them as we can—make them do our bidding. To do this, we must get better acquainted with them. We must learn enough about verbs, for example, to know what happens when we use an *active* instead of a *passive* verb. For when a verb is *active* the whole sentence takes on life and vigor—the subject is busy *doing something*; when a verb is *passive*, the movement of the sentence slows down—the subject isn't *doing* anything, simply waiting passively while something is *being done to it by someone.*

And we must learn more about *verbals*, those interesting but confusing words that come from verbs. They are interesting (and valuable) because they make writing and speaking more effective. They are confusing because, although they come from verbs and are like verbs in many ways, they can't do the work of verbs; instead, they function as other parts of speech—as nouns or as adjectives, for example.

Becoming more familiar with verbs and verbals will mean reviewing their peculiar characteristics (*properties*, the grammarians call them) and the way verbs change form to indicate these characteristics.

Two of the five properties of verbs—*number* and *person*—we discussed in the chapter on Agreement. Two others—*mood* and *voice*—we will discuss in the next chapter. In this chapter, we will discuss the most troublesome of all—*tense*.

21 Tenses of Verbs

21a Tense means time. We know that, as their main function, verbs describe an action or a state of being on the part of the subject. But verbs also tell *when* the action took place or *when* the state existed. This property of verbs is called tense.

Tense tells the time of the action from the point of view of the writer or speaker. Take the act of *walking* as an example.

> If we say, "I AM WALKING to work," we are looking, from the standpoint of the *present* time, at an action that is taking place now.

> If we say, "I WALKED to work last Tuesday," we are looking, again from the standpoint of the *present* time, at an action that happened in the past (last Tuesday).

> If we say, "If I walk to work tomorrow, I SHALL HAVE WALKED to work every day this week," we are placing ourselves in the future (tomorrow) and speaking from that point of view.

> If we say, "I told him yesterday that I HAD WALKED to work," we are speaking from the point of view of some time in the past (yesterday), of an action that was completed even before that "past time."

21b English has six tenses: three simple tenses (*present, past,* and *future*) in which an action may be considered as simply occurring; and three compound—called *perfect*—tenses in which an action may be considered as completed. (To be *perfected* means to be *completed*.)

Present Tense:	I walk, he walks
Present Perfect Tense:	I have walked, he has walked
Past Tense:	I walked, he walked
Past Perfect Tense:	I had walked, he had walked
Future Tense:	I shall walk, he will walk
Future Perfect Tense:	I shall have walked, he will have walked

Each of the six tenses has a companion form—the *progressive* form.

As its name indicates, the progressive says that the action named by the verb is a continued or progressive action. The progressive consists of the present participle (the *ing* form of the verb, that is, *walking*) plus the proper form of the verb *to be*. The progressive forms of the verb *to walk* are:

Present Tense:	I am walking, he is walking
Present Perfect Tense:	I have been walking, he has been walking
Past Tense:	I was walking, he was walking
Past Perfect Tense:	I had been walking, he had been walking
Future Tense:	I shall be walking, he will be walking
Future Perfect Tense:	I shall have been walking, he will have been walking

The present tense and the past tense also have an *emphatic* form which uses *do, does, did* as auxiliaries:

Present Tense:	I do understand, she does understand
Past Tense:	You did understand, they did understand

(See Section 22a.)

21c We indicate tense by changing the verb itself or by combining certain forms of the verb with auxiliary verbs. The verb tenses from which we derive every form of a verb are called the *principal parts*. The principal parts of a verb are:

The present tense:	*talk, write*
The past tense:	*talked, wrote*
The present perfect:	*have talked, has written*

Verbs are classified as *regular* (or *weak*) and *irregular* (or *strong*), according to the way in which their principal parts are formed. Regular verbs form their past tense and present perfect tense by the addition of *ed* to the infinitive:

Present Tense	*Past Tense*	*Present Perfect Tense*
talk	talked	has (have) talked
help	helped	has (have) helped
walk	walked	has (have) walked

The principal parts of irregular verbs are formed by changes in the verb itself:

Present Tense	*Past Tense*	*Present Perfect Tense*
see	saw	has (have) seen
say	said	has (have) said
go	went	has (have) gone

Consult a standard dictionary when you are not sure of the principal parts of a verb. This area of usage is changing, and a verb that was irregular yesterday may be regular (or both regular and irregular) today.

The following verbs illustrate this change:

Present Tense	*Past Tense*	*Present Perfect Tense*
dive	dived (formerly dove)	has dived
prove	proved	has proved (formerly proven)

The principal parts of a verb are given in a dictionary at the beginning of the listing for that particular verb. If no entry is given, the past tense and the present perfect tense are formed by the addition of *ed*. If the verb is irregular, or if it presents some difficulty of spelling, the past forms are given.

21d Principal parts give us all tense forms.

From the three principal parts, we get all parts of a verb. We repeat that the three principal parts of a verb consist of the following tenses:

1. *present tense*
2. *past tense*
3. *present perfect tense*

The other three tenses (there are six tenses in English) come from the principal parts. The future tense (*you will go*) is derived from the present tense (you *go*). The future perfect tense (you *will have gone*) and the past perfect tense (you *had gone*) are both derived from the present perfect tense (you *have gone*). It is clear, then, that if you learn the principal parts of the following irregular verbs, you will know every tense form of each of these commonly misused verbs.

21e Principal Parts of Troublesome Verbs

PRESENT TENSE	PAST TENSE	PRESENT PERFECT
abide	abode	has abode
arise	arose	has arisen
bear (carry)	bore	has borne
bear (bring forth)	bore	has borne
bid	bade	has bid, bidden
bide	bode, bided	has bode, bided
bleed	bled	has bled
broadcast	broadcast, broadcasted (radio and TV)	has broadcast (ed)
burst	burst	has burst
chide	chid, chidded	has chid, chidded, chidden
choose	chose	has chosen
cleave (adhere)	cleaved	has cleaved
cleave (split)	cleft, cleaved	has cleft, cleaved, cloven
cling	clung	has clung
drown	drowned	has drowned
drink	drank	has drunk
flee	fled	has fled
fling	flung	has flung
fly	flew	has flown
flow	flowed	has flowed
forsake	forsook	has forsaken
freeze	froze	has frozen
grind	ground	has ground
hang (a picture)	hung	has hung
hang (a person)	hanged	has hanged
lay (place)	laid	has laid
lead	led	has led
lend	lent	has lent
lie (rest)	lay	has lain
light	lit, lighted	has lit, lighted
raise	raised	has raised
rid	rid, ridded	has rid, ridded
ring	rang	has rung
set	set	has set

sew	sewed	has sewed, sewn
shrink	shrank or shrunk	has shrunk, shrunken
sink	sank, sunk	has sunk
sit	sat	has sat
ski	skied (rhymes with seed)	has skied
slay	slew	has slain
slide	slid	has slid or slidden
sling	slung	has slung
slink	slunk	has slunk
smite	smote	has smitten
spring	sprang or sprung	has sprung
steal	stole	has stolen
sting	stung	has stung
stink	stank, stunk	has stunk
stride	strode	has stridden
strive	strove	has striven
swim	swam	has swum
swing	swung	has swung
thrust	thrust	has thrust
weave	wove	has woven
wring	wrung	has wrung

22   Specific Use of Tenses

22a   Present tense

The present tense is used primarily to describe an action that is happening in the present—now—or a state that exists at the present time.

> I am a member of that club.
> I *am running* for the office of treasurer.

A special form of the present tense, called the *emphatic present*, uses *do* as an auxiliary verb. This tense form merely adds emphasis to a statement.

> Present: I may work slowly, but I *work* accurately.
> Emphatic: I may work slowly, but I *do work* accurately.

Some function of the present tense used less frequently require special mention:

(1) The present tense is used to indicate habitual or customary action, regardless of the tense of other verbs in the same sentence.

> Whenever he *makes* a mistake, he *blames* his secretary.

I always *eat* in the cafeteria.
He *leaves* the office promptly at 4:30 every day.

(2) The present tense may express a universal or relatively permanent truth, such as scientific or historical fact.

> I was taught that two and two *are* four.
> He reported that his client *is* dead.
> He said that Atlanta *is* the capital of Georgia.

(3) The present tense may be used to make more vivid the description of some past action. This usage is known as the *historical present*; it is more at home in informal than in business communication.

> As Bob *is leaving* the house the telephone *rings*. He *turns* back into the house and *picks* up the receiver. It *is* his sister calling.

Either the historical present tense or the past tense may be used to restate or summarize the facts from a book, report, letter, or similar document.

> The author *describes* (or *described*) the events leading him to his conclusion. He *begins* (or *begun*) with....

In his letter of January 24 Mr. Brown *states* (or *stated*) that he *is* (or *was*) unable to fill our order.

A word of caution: When you use the historical present, guard against unconsciously shifting to the past tense without cause.

Not: The author *describes* the events leading him to his conclusion. He *began* with....

But: ... He *begins* with....

(4) The present tense is often used to express future time:

(a) either with the help of a modifier fixing the time

Tomorrow I *go* (or *shall go*) to Chicago.
He *arrives* (or *will arrive*) Sunday for a week's visit.

(b) or in a subordinate clause introduced by *if, when, after, before, until, as soon as*, etc.

As soon as he *arrives*, we shall begin the meeting.
He will not be able to complete the report until I *give* him the figures.

22b Present perfect tense

The present perfect tense describes:

(1) an action just completed at the present time:

The president *has* just *arrived* at the meeting.
I *have worked* in the garden this afternoon.

(2) an action begun in the past and continuing into the present:

I *have been* with this company for seven years. (and still am)
He *has held* that job for three years. (and still does)

NOTE: In speaking, avoid the dialectal expression, "I *am* in Washington for 16 years," used instead of "I *have been* in Washington for 16 years.

22c Past tense

The past tense describes an action or state of being as having occurred some time in the past.

I *received* your letter this morning.
He *left* the office ten minutes ago.
I *was giving* the typists their instructions when he *entered*.

Like the present tense, the past tense has an emphatic form, formed by the auxiliary *did*.

Past tense: I *gave* him the letter, even though he says he can't find it.
Emphatic: I *did give* him the letter, even though he says he can't find it.

Past tense vs. past participle

The past tense form is used *only* for the past tense. Use the past participle, not the past tense, with auxiliaries to form other tenses. (The past tense and past participle forms of regular verbs are the same; it is the irregular verbs that cause trouble here.)

Not: I *have went* to the movies this afternoon.
But: I *went* to the movies this afternoon. (past tense)
or: I *have gone* to the movies.

Past tense vs. present perfect tense

Remember that the present perfect tense describes an action which may have started some time in the past but which continues up to, and perhaps through, the present.

I *worked* there for 15 years. (past tense)
I *have worked* there for 15 years. (present perfect tense)
(The first sentence, by the use of the past tense, implies that I no longer work there. The second sentence says that I still work there.)

I *lost* my notes of the meeting. (past tense)
(I lost them some time in the past; I may or may not have found them.)
I *have lost* my notes of the meeting. (present perfect tense)
(The use of the present perfect extends the action into the present; therefore, it is safe to assume that the notes are still missing.)

22d Past perfect tense

The past perfect tense indicates that the action or condition it described was completed (perfected) earlier than some other action that also occurred in the past. We use this tense when we need to show that two actions happened at different times in the past.

He *had finished* his breakfast before I *came*
    (past perfect)   (past)
downstairs.

I *had* mailed the letter when he *called*.
(past perfect)   (past)

Past tense vs. past perfect tense

Distinguish carefully between these two tenses. Remember that the past tense can describe an event that happened at any time in the past but that the past perfect tense must describe an event that happened *before* another event in the past. The sentences following may help clarify this usage.

When I *came* back from lunch, she *finished* the letter.
        (Both verbs are in the past tense; therefore, both actions happened at approximately the same time in the past.)
When I *came* back from lunch, she *had finished* the letter.
        (Again, both actions occurred in the past, but the use of the past perfect *had finished* tells us that this action was completed before the other action.)

We *discovered* that a detective *was following* us.
        (Both actions happened at the same time in the past.)
We *discovered* that a detective *had been following* us.
        (He had been following us some time before we discovered it.)

22e Future tense

The future tense is used to indicate that an action will take place some time in the future or that a state or condition will exist some time in the future.

I *shall not be* at the meeting Friday.
He *will be waiting* for me after work.

Distinction between SHALL—WILL *and* SHOULD—WOULD

In formal communication there is a distinction between these words. There, the simple future tense is formed by the use of *shall* (or *should*) in the first person and *will* (or *would*) in the second and third person.

Reversing this usage expresses the will or determination of the speaker that something is to be done.

(1) The office of origin *will* furnish this information.
        (A simple statement of fact.)
(2) The office of origin *shall* furnish this information.
        (This is mandatory; the office *must* furnish the information.)
(3) The Director *will* be responsible for complying with these regulations.
(4) The Director *shall* be held responsible for complying with these regulations.

In questions, *shall* is used in the first person; *will* is used in the second and third persons.

Simple future (expressing probable future action):

I shall	we shall	I should	we should
you will	you will	you would	you would
he will	they will	he would	they would

Emphatic future (expressing the determination or the will of the speaker):

I will	we will	I would	we would
you shall	you shall	you should	you should
he shall	they shall	he should	they should

This distinction is disappearing rapidly in both speech and writing. But a knowledge of this distinction is essential to anyone who writes or reads legal or procedural documents.

22f Future perfect tense

The future perfect tense names an action or condition that will be completed by some specified time in the future.

I *shall have been* with this company for 10 years on next Tuesday.
He *will have finished* that project by April 10.

23 Sequence of Tense

Knowing how *to form* the various tenses is not enough; we must also know how *to use* tense logically in our sentences. To do this, we must understand *sequence* of tense.

What is sequence of tense? It is the logical time relation (expressed by tense) between the verbs in a sentence or passage. It is the way we tell our reader in what order events occurred.

For sequence of tense in conditional statements, see Section 31.

23a Tense of verbs in principal clauses

The verbs in principal clauses should be in the same tense if they refer to the same time.

Be consistent in your point of view. When you describe a series of actions that occurred at the same time, keep the verbs in the same tense. But if you interrupt the series with an action that happened earlier or later, be sure to change tense to show the time relation of this new action.

> My new supervisor STRODE into the office. He SAT down at his desk and BEGAN to read the letters which the stenographer *had finished* typing just a few minutes before. As he read, she CROSSED her fingers, hoping he would find no errors.
>
> (The verbs in capitals are in the past tense, denoting that their actions happened at the same time. The italicized verb *had finished* is in the past perfect tense, indicating that this action took place before the others.)

23b Tense of verbs in subordinate clauses

The verb in the principal clause is taken as a starting point. The tenses of all verbs in subordinate clauses are determined by whether the action they describe takes place before, after, or at the same time as the action described by the verb in the principal clause.

(1) If the verb in the principal clause is in the present or future tense, the verbs in the subordinate clauses *are not restricted to* those two tenses but may be in any tense.

> I HOPE he *is* in his office.
> I HOPE he *was* in his office when you called.
> I HOPE he will be in his office when we arrive.

(2) If the verb in the principal clause is in the past or past perfect tense, the verbs in the subordinate clauses must be in some tense that denotes past time.

> I THOUGHT that they *were visiting* you this week.
> I THOUGHT that they *had been visiting* you all summer.
> I THOUGHT that they *had visited* you the previous year.

Exception: The present tense is preferred for the verb in a subordinate clause stating a universal truth, even if the verb in the principal clause is in some other tense.

> He TELLS me that Washington *is* the nation's capital.
> He TOLD me that Washington *is* the nation's capital.
> He DIDN'T BELIEVE that the world *is* round.

(3) In clauses of result or purpose (introduced by such conjunctions as *in order that, so that*) —

(a) if the verb in the principal clause is in the past or past perfect tense, use one of the past auxiliaries (*might, could, would*) in the subordinate clause.

> He GAVE (or HAD GIVEN) me a pass, so that I *could* enter the building on Saturdays.

(b) if the verb in the principal clause is in the present or the future tense, use a present auxiliary (*can, may*) in the subordinate clause.

> He WILL GIVE me a pass, so that I *can* enter the building on Saturdays.

(4) Often (particularly in correspondence), it is necessary that we refer to what someone else has said — indirect discourse.

If the verb in the introductory clause is past or past perfect, a present tense verb in the original wording becomes past tense.

Original: I am enclosing a copy of. . . .
Paraphrase: The attorney SAID that he *was enclosing* a copy. . . .

If the verb in the introductory clause is past or past perfect, a present perfect verb in the original wording becomes past perfect.

Original: I *have sent* a copy of. . . .
Paraphrase: He SAID that he *had sent* a copy of. . . .

If the historical present is used in the introductory clause, the verb in the original wording is unchanged in tense.

Original: I *am sending* a copy of. . . .
Paraphrase: He SAYS he *is sending* a copy of. . . .

If the verb in the introductory clause is past or past perfect, *shall* or *will* in the original wording becomes *would*.

Original: I *shall send* a copy of. . . .
Paraphrase: He SAID that he *would send* a copy of. . . .

24   Tenses of Verbals

In the previous sections we have been concerned with the tense of "finite" verbs—those verbs that perform the functions usually associated with verbs. But finite verbs are not the only verb forms involved in our use of tense. Verbals, too, need to be considered in any discussion of tense and tense sequence.

Even though the three kinds of verbals—gerunds, participles, and infinitives—do not function as verbs, they do retain some of the characteristics of verbs. One of these characteristics is "tense." Participles have three tenses; gerunds and infinitives, two.

24a   Gerunds

The gerund has two tense forms: present and perfect.

Present: *talking, writing*
Perfect: *having talked, having written*

WRITING *letters* is hard work.
(*Writing* is the gerund; *letters* is its object. The gerund phrase is the subject of the sentence.)

It is a treat to watch *his* SWIMMING.
(*His* is the subject of the gerund *swimming*.)

(The subject of a gerund should be in the possessive case. Notice this usage in the sentence above and in the two examples below.)

The *student's* WRITING won him first prize.
(The gerund *writing* and its subject *student's* form a gerund phrase which serves as the subject of the sentence.)

We will appreciate *your* FURNISHING *this information.*
(The gerund *furnishing*, its possessive subject *your*, and its object *information* form a gerund phrase which is the object of *appreciate*.)

Careful, courteous DRIVING is the trademark of a mature driver.
(The gerund and its two modifiers form a gerund phrase which is the subject of the sentence.)

He was honored for *his* HAVING DONE such an outstanding job.
(The perfect gerund *having done* and its subject *his* forms a gerund phrase which is the object of the preposition *for*.)

Our not HAVING ARRIVED *on time* meant that we missed the first half of the program.
(The gerund phrase is the subject of the sentence.)

24b   Participles

The participle has three tense forms: present, past, and perfect.

Present participle: *talking, writing*
Past participle: *talked, written*
Perfect participle: *having talked, having written*

The girl *talking* on the telephone is my secretary.
(The participle *talking* modifies *girl*.)

The article, *beautifully written*, appeared in last week's "Post."
> (The participle *written*, plus its modifier *beautifully*, modifies *article*.)

The letter, *having been typed* and *signed*, was ready for mailing.
> (The participles *having been typed* and *signed* modify *letter*.)

24c Infinitives

The infinitive has two tense forms: the present and the perfect.

> Present: *to talk, to write*
> Perfect: *to have talked, to have written*
> *To recognize* and *define* the problem is our first step.
> He is supposed to *have written* those letters.

24d Verbals in sentence fragments

Sentence fragments (or fragmentary sentences) are parts of sentences erroneously punctuated as complete sentences. A common type of fragmentary sentence is that containing one or more verbals but no finite verb in the main clause. Learn to distinguish between verbals and finite verbs, so that you can avoid writing this type of fragmentary sentence. Remember, mere length does not make a sentence — we need a verb.

> Fragment: Sentences of from 1 to 5 years in prison imposed upon six offenders arrested in connection with seizure of a large illicit distillery set up in a tobacco barn in southern Maryland.
> Corrected: Sentences of from 1 to 5 years in prison WERE IMPOSED....

> Fragment: Your memorandum dated March 4, 1969, requesting information about the availability of certain training materials and about the plans for distribution of these materials.
> Corrected: Your memorandum dated March 4, 1969, REQUESTED....

25 Tense Sequence With Verbals

Verbals cannot by themselves indicate the exact time of an action. They can express time only in relation to the time of the main verb in the sentence. Verbals show that an action happened at the same time as the action of the main verb or that it happened at an earlier time.

25a Participles

Only two forms of the participle — the present and the perfect — are of interest to us here, since the past participle is usually used as part of a verb phrase.

The present participle refers to action happening at the same time as the action of the main verb.

> ENTERING the office he *confirms* his appointment.
> > (The main verb is in the present tense; therefore the present participle *entering* carries the idea of present time.)
> ENTERING the office he *confirmed* his appointment.
> > (With the change in the tense of the main verb to the past, we also change the time of the participle.)

The perfect participle refers to action occurring *before* the action of the main verb.

> HAVING FINISHED the repairs, the plumber *is preparing* to leave.
> HAVING FINISHED the repairs, the plumber *was preparing* to leave.

Study the following pairs of sentences for the use of the present and perfect participles. Remember, the present participle names action occurring at the same time as the action of the main verb; the perfect participle names action occurring before that of the main verb.

> BEING late for work, I ran up the stairs.
> HAVING BEEN late for work, I decided to stay and finish the report after hours.

> INTENDING to return immediately, I left the door open when I went out.
> HAVING INTENDED to return immediately, I was disappointed at having to be away so long.

> SELLING their house, they prepared to move to Florida.
> HAVING SOLD their house, they were free to leave.

25b Infinitives

The present infinitive names an action occurring at the same time as the action of the main verb.

The sentences below all contain present infinitives. Notice that we must depend upon the tense of the main verb to tell us the time of the action of both the main verb and the infinitive.

I *am trying* TO FINISH this report today.
(Both actions are happening in the present.)
I *was trying* TO FINISH the report before he asked for it.
(Both actions happened at the same time in the past.)
I *shall try* TO FINISH the report by the end of the day.
(Both actions will happen at the same time in the future.)

I *am writing* TO REQUEST three copies of your latest publication.
(Both actions happen in the present.)
I *wrote* TO REQUEST three copies of their catalog.
(Both happened at the same time in the past.)
I *shall write* tomorrow TO REQUEST a copy of their brochure.
(Both actions will happen at the same future time.)

The present infinitive also expresses future time, sometimes with the help of a time modifier.

I *hope* TO ATTEND the meeting next Thursday.
(I *hope* NOW *to attend* IN THE FUTURE.)

I *plan* TO WRITE him about the luncheon.
(I *plan* NOW *to write* IN THE FUTURE.)

He *expected* TO BE here by today.
(He *expected* IN THE PAST *to be here* AT SOME FUTURE TIME)

He *had hoped* TO WIN the trophy.
(He *had hoped* IN THE PAST *to win* AT SOME FUTURE TIME)

The perfect infinitive expresses action occurring *before* that of the main verb.

I *am* glad TO HAVE BEEN of assistance.
(I *am* glad NOW *to have been* of assistance IN THE PAST)

I *am* honored TO HAVE KNOWN such a person.
(I *am* honored NOW *to have known* him IN THE PAST)

The sentences below contrast the use of the present and perfect infinitives.

He *appears* TO BE an Army officer.
(Present—he *appears* NOW *to be* an officer NOW)

He *appears* TO HAVE BEEN an Army officer.
(Perfect—he *appears* NOW *to have been* an officer IN THE PAST)

I *was* glad TO BE of service.
(Present—I *was* glad THEN *to be* of service AT THAT TIME)

I *am* glad TO HAVE BEEN of service.
(Perfect—I *am* glad NOW *to have been* of service IN THE PAST)

After a verb in the past or past perfect tense, the present infinitive will usually best express your meaning. Be especially cautious of sentences in which both the main verb and the infinitive are preceded by *has, have,* or *had.* These auxiliaries are rarely, if ever, needed in both constructions.

Not: I *should have liked* TO HAVE SEEN her when she was here.
But: I *should have liked* TO SEE her when she was here.

Not: I *had hoped* TO HAVE SHIPPED the order by now.
But: I *had hoped* TO SHIP the order by now.

25c Gerunds

The present tense of the gerund refers to an action happening at the present time:

Taking a review course will not solve your problems.

The perfect tense of the gerund refers to an action that was completed *before* the time of the main verb.

He attributes his success to *having studied* whenever possible.

TEST XI. TENSE OF VERBS AND VERBALS

TIME: 23 Minutes

DIRECTIONS: In each of the following groups of sentences, select the one sentence that is grammatically INCORRECT. Mark the answer sheet with the letter of that incorrect sentence.

Explanations of the key points behind these questions appear with the answers at the end of this test. The explanatory answers provide the kind of background that will enable you to answer test questions with facility and confidence.

1

(A) We will notify whomever you wish.
(B) I expect him this morning.
(C) If he lays down on the job, he will regret it.
(D) In the old records was found a queer mistake.

2

(A) In today's market, five dollars doesn't go very far.
(B) Mary is just the kind of girl who everyone hopes will be the life of the party.
(C) Ruthless, overbearing, and twisted mentally, the gangster proved a difficult witness before the committee.
(D) The underdogs rallied bravely after their burly opponents scored three touchdowns.

3

(A) His study of Sanskrit grammar was both interesting and informative.
(B) He is living in that village for the past four years.
(C) There is strong support for the suggestion that all holidays be celebrated on Mondays.
(D) The manager of the store asked why he had not been told about the robbery.

4

(A) "Who are these critics?" Mr. Hamilton demanded.
(B) We have not yet received a confirmation of our hotel reservations in Rome.
(C) I am concerned about his excessive absences.
(D) He laid on the bed for several hours before regaining consciousness.

5

(A) You will have gone by the time he arrives.
(B) Although I have attended college until recently, I left without getting my degree.
(C) I lived in Chicago for many years, but New York City has been my home for the past six months.
(D) I should not have gone before knowing what had to be done.

6

(A) The committee has chosen Jones unanimously.
(B) He walks up and said "Hello."
(C) I intend to go to the theatre tonight.
(D) I wish I were going, too.

7

(A) Do you believe that 15 bushels is enough of a load?
(B) At last it was Janet and Mary's turn to demonstrate their talents as dishwashers.
(C) How much happier my life could have been if I had had that kind of friends years ago.
(D) After I listened to the violinist and cellist, and enjoyed their interpretations, I hurried home to practice.

8

(A) The crew did its best to complete the job on time.
(B) They have already went home.
(C) The children drank some lemonade.
(D) The girl has written her composition.

9

(A) I regret the loss caused by the error.
(B) The students will have a new teacher.
(C) I believe it shall rain before the afternoon is over.
(D) They swore to bring out all the facts.

10

(A) If you are tired when you arrive home each day, you should lay down for a short time before dinner.
(B) It was you, my friend, who encouraged me when I thought my property was irretrievably lost.
(C) If any man here does not agree with me, he should set forth his own plan for ameliorating the conditions under which these people live.
(D) The effects of a nuclear war may well be cataclysmic for all on earth.

S1857

11

(A) By his perseverance, he succeeded in overcoming the apathy of his pupils.
(B) Having finished his homework, he listened to his new records.
(C) He replied, when she asked him about the project, that he hoped to have finished it soon.
(D) "We were never formally introduced," she answered gaily.

12

(A) When the really hot days of summer have come and everybody is thinking of the fine vacation that he is about to enjoy.
(B) Almost every member of the team has played in every game this season.
(C) "Please direct me to the corner of Smith Street and Baker Avenue," said the stranger.
(D) Mary is the tallest girl in her class, but she is shorter than one of the boys.

13

(A) Neither speech is to exceed fifteen minutes.
(B) A number of assemblages that are essentially alike is called a culture.
(C) Like one man, for example, who sent in a portfolio of 31 different stocks worth less than $20,000 all told.
(D) I thought it all right to excuse them from class to watch the telecast of Senator Kennedy's funeral.

14

(A) The manager's statement relating to the two letters was without doubt correct.
(B) Either you are the winner or I am.
(C) The mother knew where the little boy had hidden his toys.
(D) He has forgot where they bought the equipment.

15

(A) In "Stopping by Woods on a Snowy Evening," Frost deals with one of life's paradoxes.
(B) Let us not confuse the real with the apparent.
(C) They were exuberant when the end of the strike was announced.
(D) He laid down, closed his eyes, and promptly fell asleep.

16

(A) By the time you arrive in London, we shall be in Europe for two weeks.
(B) The judge proceeded to overrule the prosecutor, regardless of all protests.
(C) Appearance, vitality, and intelligence — these factors will be paramount in the contest.
(D) Trembling without cause may be a sign of emotional immaturity.

17

(A) He welcomed the glass of cold lemonade on that hot day.
(B) After seeing his work, I think he deserves the name of a genius.
(C) This book is better than any other I have read this year.
(D) "Is David's father an actuary, too?" asked Mr. Greene.

18

(A) Many children adopt the beliefs of their parents.
(B) He is addicted to drugs.
(C) I didn't eat yet, although I am hungry.
(D) He adhered to his principles.

19

(A) Nancy confided to Jane that she liked Fred more than me.
(B) Western powers have unsuccessfully tried to alleviate tension in the Far East.
(C) Two astronauts were disappointed because they had hoped to have made the first trip into space.
(D) Won't you agree that victory is ours?

20

(A) The committee are arguing among themselves.
(B) I have finished my studying many years ago and I do not now intend to enroll in any school for further study.
(C) Denny yelled "hi" as he entered.
(D) Michael's and Jean's bicycles are both broken.

21

(A) The quantity of sugar lost must be small, for the bag still weighs almost five pounds.
(B) These three things I can swear to: the question I put to him, the answer he gave me, and the decision we reached.
(C) When the trial was over and everybody knew the verdict, an outcome that should have been obvious to anybody who heard the testimony.
(D) We came to the real business of the convention.

22

(A) We should go some place to eat.
(B) Several persons have swam the English Channel.
(C) He was angry with his father.
(D) Certainly, I would have been sorry to miss him.

23

(A) Since he needed the money so badly, he regarded it as fortunate that he won the cash prize.
(B) Do you think it will be all right for me to apply for the position.
(C) A great deal of confusion, distrust, and resentment is evident every time the subject somes up for discussion.
(D) Since a stay of execution has not been granted, the prisoner will be hanged at midnight.

24

(A) Eloise carefully computed the diameter of the circle.
(B) The women wore their new hats to church on Easter Sunday.
(C) How to meet all their current bills is their problem.
(D) As soon as we raised the alarm, he comes racing around the corner.

25

(A) The girl swum the Mississippi River.
(B) Price levels rose ten points last year.
(C) The freshmen were forbidden to speak to the sophomores.
(D) He was here when the boy brought the news.

26

(A) Owing to the ravages of the icy storm, communications within the area were practically obliterated.
(B) Much crime goes unreported.
(C) The wing of the plane collapsing under the impact, the fliers plunged to their death.
(D) The detective, together with several of the uniformed men, was decorated for outstanding bravery.

27

(A) The children's plans for a surprise party had been made very quietly, but John's suspicions had been aroused.
(B) There must be some faraway place where one can spend a quiet holiday.
(C) Rather than crowd the page, it is preferable to skip a line between each sentence.
(D) I have never understood why a good facsimile should not be so valuable as an original.

28

(A) Outflanked by the enemy fleet, ten of our ships were sunk, two were blown out of water, and five were towed into port.
(B) He has torn himself away from human society, worn borrowed robes, and stole the possessions of others.
(C) Chosen for destruction and driven to the wall, I still shrank from a test of strength.
(D) Broken in mind and body, he swore he would rise once more to the challenge.

29

(A) Five yards of ribbon is sufficient.
(B) They acted as if they didn't know the route.
(C) Although they intended to have stayed only a week at Cannes, they remained there the entire summer.
(D) Economies were being effected throughout the studios, but, like Paramount and Fox, R.K.O. was soon to go bankrupt.

30

(A) If it were within my authority to overlook this offense, I should be glad to make allowance for the unusual circumstances.
(B) In order to calculate the percentage of gain on an investment, we must know the principal.
(C) This remarkable donation has been given to our society for charitable purposes.
(D) After the defendant was acquitted by the jury, the judge stated that a miscarriage of justice had taken place.

31

(A) If he had lain quietly as instructed, he might not have had a second heart attack.
(B) Shall you have cocktails served before dinner?
(C) John is likely to resent our refusal to accede to his demands.
(D) She saw that there was nothing else she could do; the room was as clean as it ever had been.

CONSOLIDATE YOUR KEY ANSWERS HERE

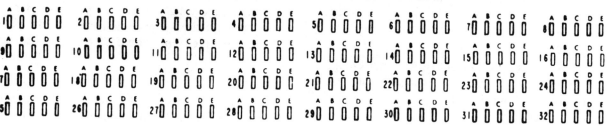

TEST XI. TENSE OF VERBS AND VERBALS

KEY ANSWERS FOR THE FOREGOING QUESTIONS

1.C	6.B	11.C	16.A	21.C	26.C	31.B
2.D	7.D	12.A	17.B	22.B	27.A	
3.B	8.B	13.C	18.C	23.A	28.B	
4.D	9.C	14.D	19.C	24.D	29.C	
5.B	10.A	15.D	20.B	25.A	30.D	

EXPLANATORY ANSWERS CLARIFYING CARDINAL POINTS

The core of the Question and Answer Method . . . getting help when and where you need it. Even if you were able to write correct key answers for the preceding questions, the following explanations illuminate fundamental facts, ideas, and principles which just might crop up in the form of questions on future tests.

Bold-face *references in the following answers direct you to paragraphs in the Arco Grammar Text, where fuller explanations are provided.*

ANSWER 1.

C   If he **lies** down on the job, he will regret it. REASON: The present tense of **to lie** is **lies**. **(21e)**

ANSWER 2.

D   The underdogs rallied bravely after their burly opponents **had scored** three touchdowns. REASON: The past perfect (**had scored**) is required to express the earlier of the two past actions. **(22d)**

ANSWER 3.

B   He **has been living** in that village for the past four years. REASON: The present perfect tense (**has been living**) ties up the past with the present. **(22b)**

ANSWER 4.

D   He **lay** on the bed for several hours before regaining consciousness. REASON: **lay** means reclined. **(21e)**

ANSWER 5.

B   Although I **attended** college until recently, I left without getting my **degree**. REASON: The past tense (**attended**) is correct here to express a completed action in the past. **(22c)**

ANSWER 6.

B   He walked up and said "Hello." REASON: The time of each reaction (**walked** and **said**) occurs at approximately the same time. Accordingly, since the past tense (**said**) is used in the second main clause, the past tense (**walked**) must be used in the first main clause. **(23b)**

ANSWER 7.

D   After I had listened to the violinist and cellist, and **had enjoyed** their interpretations, I hurried home to practice. REASON: When we have two past actions, one of which occurs before the other, the one that happens first must have a past perfect verb (**had enjoyed**). **(22d)**

ANSWER 8.

B   They have already **gone** home. REASON: The present perfect tense of **to go** is **have gone**.   **(21c)**

ANSWER 9.

C   I believe it **will rain** before the afternoon is over. REASON: The **will** form is used in the simple third person future indicative.   **(22e)**

ANSWER 10.

A   If you are tired when you arrive home each day, you **should lie** down for a short time before dinner. REASON: The future subjunctive of **to lie** is **should lie**.   **(21e)**

ANSWER 11.

C   He replied, when she asked him about the project, that he hoped **to finish** it soon. REASON: The present infinitive is required for tense sequence after **hoped**. The present tense of an infinitive is used to indicate that the infinitive has the same time or a future time with relation to the time of the main verb.   **(25b)**

ANSWER 12.

A   Just before the really hot days of summer come, everybody is thinking of the fine vacation that he is about to enjoy. REASON: The original sentence is incomplete.   **(24d)**

ANSWER 13.

C   One man, for example, sent in a portfolio of 31 different stocks worth less than $20,000 all told. REASON: The original sentence, which started with the preposition **like,** was incomplete.   **(24d)**

ANSWER 14.

D   He **has forgotten** where they bought the equipment. REASON: **forgotten** is the principal form of the present perfect verb.   **(21c)**

ANSWER 15.

D   He **lay** down, closed his eyes, and promptly feel asleep. REASON: The past tense of **to lie** is **lay**.   **(21e)**

ANSWER 16.

A   By the time you arrive in London, we **shall have been** in Europe for two weeks. REASON: The future perfect tense (**shall have been**) is required in the main clause to indicate future action that occurs before the future action (**arrive**) of the dependent clause.   **(22f)**

ANSWER 17.

B   After **having seen** his work, I think he deserves the name of a genius. REASON: The past participle (**having seen**) is required since its action takes place before that of the main verb (**think**).   **(25a)**

ANSWER 18.

C   I **haven't eaten** yet, although I am hungry. REASON: The present perfect form of the verb (**haven't eaten**) is needed here since it ties up with the present tense verb (**am**).   **(22b)**

ANSWER 19.

C   Two astronauts were disappointed because they had hoped **to make** the first trip into space. REASON: Sequence of tenses requires the present infinitive (**to make**).   **(23, 24c)**

ANSWER 20.

B   I **finished** my studying many years ago and I do not now intend to enroll in any school for further learning. REASON: The present perfect (**have finished**) refers to a past action that relates to the present.   **(22c)**

ANSWER 21.

C   When the trial was over, everybody knew the verdict, an outcome that should have been obvious to anybody who heard the testimony. REASON: **and** is to be eliminated since it is unnecessary and renders the sentence incomplete.   **(24d)**

ANSWER 22.

B   Several persons **have swum** the English Channel. REASON: The present perfect of **to swim** is **have swum**.   **(21e)**

ANSWER 23.

A Since he needed the money so badly, he regarded it as fortunate that he **had won** the cash prize. REASON: The past perfect tense (**had won**) is needed to indicate the earlier of the two past actions. **(22d)**

ANSWER 24.

D As soon as we raised the alarm, he **came** racing around the corner. REASON: The past tense is used for proper sequence of tenses. **(22c)**

ANSWER 25.

A The girl **swam** the Mississippi River. REASON: The past tense of **to swim** is **swam**. **(21c)**

ANSWER 26.

C The wing of the plane **having collapsed** under the impact, the fliers plunged to their death. REASON: The participle of the nominative absolute construction should be a past participle since the action occurs before the action of the main clause verb (**plunged**). **(25a)**

ANSWER 27.

A The children's plans for a surprise party had been made very quietly, but John's suspicions **were aroused**. REASON: Sequence of tenses here demands that we have a past tense (**were aroused**) to tie up with the past perfect form (**had been made**). **(22c)**

ANSWER 28.

B He has torn himself away from human society, worn borrowed robes, and **stolen** the possessions of others. REASON: The present perfect form is **has stolen**. **(21e)**

ANSWER 29.

C Although they intended **to stay** only a week at Cannes, they remained there the entire summer. REASON: Sequence of tenses requires the present infinitive **to stay** since it is concurrent with the verb **intended**. **(25b)**

ANSWER 30.

D After the defendant **had been acquitted** by the jury, the judge stated that a miscarriage of justice had taken place. REASON: When there are two past actions, the one that occurs first is in the past perfect tense. **(23b)**

ANSWER 31.

B **Will** you have cocktails served before dinner? REASON: In questions, **will** is used in the second person. **(22e)**

TEST XII. TENSE OF VERBS AND VERBALS

TIME: 23 Minutes

DIRECTIONS: In each of the following groups of sentences, select the one sentence that is grammatically INCORRECT. Mark the answer sheet with the letter of that incorrect sentence.

Explanations of the key points behind these questions appear with the answers at the end of this test. The explanatory answers provide the kind of background that will enable you to answer test questions with facility and confidence.

(1)

(A) "Although I have lived here for many years," said Mrs. Brown, "I still find New York City interesting and exhilarating."
(B) The pretensions of the old charlatan were so absurd that they amused his host.
(C) The ten-foot pole was just what the carpenter needed.
(D) The snow fell during the night so that it was laying in big drifts on the highway the next morning.

(2)

(A) To think coherently, to write with clarity and with style, and to speak clearly are worthy goals for a student.
(B) Business was proceeding quietly in the bank when suddenly a masked man comes in and says, "Hands up!"
(C) Adulatory speeches cannot convince us that we are better than we really are.
(D) The wearing of trousers by women is accepted.

(3)

(A) The game over, the spectators rushed out on the field and tore down the goal posts.
(B) The situation was aggravated by disputes over the captaincy of the team.
(C) Yesterday they lay their uniforms aside with the usual end-of-the-season regret.
(D) It is sometimes thought that politics is not for the high-minded.

(4)

(A) The treasurer and historian were absent from today's crucial session.
(B) He is a leading member of that group of English intellectuals which believes that society is growing increasingly blind, mad, and barbarous.
(C) The book has laid untouched on the shelves for years.
(D) By the time the news story is made public, he will, no doubt, already have been elected.

(5)

(A) She saw the letter laying here this morning.
(B) They gave the poor man some food when he knocked on the door.
(C) The plans were drawn before the fight started.
(D) He was here when the messenger brought the news.

(6)

(A) "Ten, nine, eight, seven...,"intoned the lieutenant.
(B) The experiment was a complete success.
(C) The surveyor's instruments had been lying behind a tree.
(D) After he had finished, he holds up his ink-stained right hand.

(7)

(A) Are you much taller than I?
(B) She lived in the city for three years before she visited her aunt.
(C) He lay the book down on the table and angrily stalked out of the room.
(D) He read excerpts from his new novel to John and me.

(8)

(A) Though Larry had awakened before the birds began to twitter, he lay in bed until long after the sun had risen.
(B) As Percy dived off the springboard, he was horrified to see that the water had been drained from the pool the night before.
(C) When he wrapped and addressed the package, he took it to the post office.
(D) There are still people who say that it has never really been proved that the earth is round.

9

(A) The taxpayer declared that he is ready to file a complaint.
(B) We have but to say the word and we can have our every wish fulfilled.
(C) All his 7's looked like 1's; it was almost impossible to check his addition.
(D) In my opinion, no permanent solution will be effected by this dubious course of action.

10

(A) It did not take him long to develop an interest in the great American pastime – baseball.
(B) While most New York schools were strikebound, classes went on uninterrupted in Ocean Hill.
(C) How I should have liked to have spent a few more days in Paris!
(D) Neither baseball pools nor any other form of gambling is allowed in or near the school.

11

(A) We have spoken to him about the promotion, but he does not wish to accept the position.
(B) There is more to this problem than you realize.
(C) The only uniform he has been issued was in camp last August.
(D) Look at the misspelled words in that letter!

12

(A) The secret is to be kept strictly between you and me.
(B) I planned to have gone to Canada during July and August.
(C) The group accepted Ted's suggestions with most of which we had all agreed.
(D) I objected strenuously (for who could be still?) to the plan proposed.

13

(A) I am sure that I have met you some time ago.
(B) He came a while ago.
(C) I have already seen the play.
(D) I'd as leave go as not.

14

(A) If he expected to be graduated in June, he ought to of tried harder.
(B) The game having been completed, the two teams gave each other cheers.
(C) There are certainly several reasons for his wanting to resign.
(D) Asking a person to help is kinder than making a peremptory demand for service.

15

(A) When he had carefully reviewed the work for the next day and planned his itinerary.
(B) Charles chose the lesser of the two evils.
(C) His verse had a Byronic quality.
(D) Impromptu speeches are often very effective.

16

(A) Charles would have liked to have been present at the party.
(B) Every informed person should know who the governor of his state is.
(C) If you say that you never received my letter, then I believe you.
(D) The more he shouts, the less his audience pays attention.

17

(A) The boy's clothing was still laying on the ground where he had carelessly thrown it the previous night.
(B) The astrologer was careful to study all the signs of the zodiac before making his predictions.
(C) All expect the winning team to accept the invitation to play a post-season game.
(D) If every unit does its duty, the drive will be successful.

18

(A) I wrote first and telephoned later.
(B) He should of taken the order.
(C) All our offices close on Saturday.
(D) Our principal business is selling.

19

(A) Why the long delay in trying the Kennedy and King assassins?
(B) The new waitress lay the fork to the right of the plate.
(C) Wallace was far behind Nixon and Humphrey.
(D) "Stop that thief!" he cried.

20

(A) He hoped that the members of the class did their homework in preparation for the test.
(B) "Peace on earth" – how often through the centuries have men responded to the words' appeal!
(C) Even when a little girl, she would go to the library every Saturday.
(D) Had you made up your mind by three o'clock, you could have come with us.

21

(A) Truthfully, now isn't this the house you have been looking for?
(B) When a hydrogen bomb is detonated, and you see the familiar mushroom cloud form in what was once a calm, blue sky.
(C) Since you have already read this book, please substitute another of the same type for the current book report.
(D) All freshmen must study mathematics, science, English, history, and French or Latin.

22

(A) The manager told me he would have my car ready for me as soon as he can get the service department on the telephone.
(B) I come from a state that raises corn and cotton and cockleburs and democrats, and frothy eloquence neither convinces nor satisfies me.
(C) It recedes as fast on one side as it gains on the other.
(D) He acquired a sound knowledge of Latin, French and Italian.

23

(A) It is interesting to study the lives of men who were contemporaries but who lived in different countries.
(B) He was one of those men who like to have others obey them.
(C) We were searching for our friend when suddenly a cry comes out of the darkness.
(D) "I am going to the library," said John. "Would you like to walk with me?"

24

(A) The parents taught brother and sister to help each other.
(B) Were anyone else's possessions lost in the hotel fire?
(C) Arthur has laid on the couch all morning.
(D) These kinds of remarks do little to bring about good will.

25

(A) I have learned many lessons when I worked for you.
(B) The jury are divided in their opinions.
(C) Neither of the teams was on the field at the scheduled game time.
(D) "Please take this report to the office," the man said, "and give it to Mr. Jones' secretary."

26

(A) I cannot but help admiring you for your dedication to your job.
(B) Because they had insisted upon showing us films of their travels, we have lost many friends whom we once cherished.
(C) I am constrained to admit that your remarks made me feel bad.
(D) My brother having been notified of his acceptance by the university, my father immediately made plans.

27

(A) I had expected to see my brother.
(B) He expected to have seen his brother.
(C) I hoped to see you do better.
(D) It was his duty to assist our friend.

28

(A) Amiable persons make amicable adjustments.
(B) Being unable to hear the speaker, we fell asleep.
(C) When Peter reached home, he found he lost his wallet.
(D) It had lain there for many days.

29

(A) They let him lie where he had laid.
(B) He borrowed a dollar from me today.
(C) After taking an apple from the table, he slipped out the back door.
(D) She made a loan of one hundred dollars.

30

(A) The child is able to shape the clay easily.
(B) I intended to go to the store.
(C) He is reported to be killed.
(D) I feel well again.

CONSOLIDATE YOUR KEY ANSWERS HERE

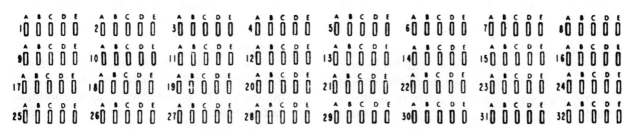

TEST XII. TENSE OF VERBS AND VERBALS

KEY ANSWERS FOR THE FOREGOING QUESTIONS

1.D	6.D	11.C	16.A	21.B	26.B
2.B	7.C	12.B	17.A	22.A	27.B
3.C	8.C	13.A	18.B	23.C	28.C
4.C	9.A	14.A	19.B	24.C	29.A
5.A	10.C	15.A	20.A	25.A	30.C

EXPLANATORY ANSWERS CLARIFYING CARDINAL POINTS

The core of the Question and Answer Method . . . getting help when and where you need it. Even if you were able to write correct key answers for the preceding questions, the following explanations illuminate fundamental facts, ideas, and principles which just might crop up in the form of questions on future tests.

Bold-face *references in the following answers direct you to paragraphs in the Arco Grammar Text, where fuller explanations are provided.*

ANSWER 1.

D The snow fell during the night so that it **was lying** in big drifts on the highway the next morning. REASON: **was lying** is the correct form of the verb **to lie — was laying** is incorrect. **(21e)**

ANSWER 2.

B Business was proceeding quietly in the bank when suddenly a masked man **came** in and said, "Hands up!" REASON: The past tense (**came**) must be used in sequence with the past tense of the verb (**was proceeding**) of the main clause. **(23b)**

ANSWER 3.

C Yesterday they **laid** their uniforms aside with the usual end-of-the-season regret. REASON: The past tense of **to lay** is **laid**. **(21e)**

ANSWER 4.

C The book **has lain** untouched on the shelves for years. REASON: **The present perfect of to lie is has lain.** **(21e)**

ANSWER 5.

A She saw the letter **lying** here this morning. REASON: The present participle of **to lie** is **lying**. **(21e)**

ANSWER 6.

D After he had finished, he **held** up his inkstained right hand. REASON: With the past perfect tense (**had finished**), we use the past tense (**held**) to indicate sequence of action. **(22d)**

ANSWER 7.

C He **laid** the book down on the table and angrily stalked out of the room. REASON: The past tense of **lay** (meaning **to place**) is **laid**. **(21e)**

ANSWER 8.

C After he **had wrapped** and addressed the package, he took it to the post office. REASON: The past perfect verb is required for an action that takes place before another past action. Also, note that the conjunction "After" is more logical than "When" in this case. **(22d)**

ANSWER 9.

A The taxpayer declared that he **was ready** to file a complaint. REASON: The past tense is used for sequence of tenses. **(23b)**

ANSWER 10.

C How I should have liked **to spend** a few more days in Paris! REASON: The tense sequence requires a present infinitive **(to spend)**. **(25b)**

ANSWER 11.

C The only uniform he **was issued** was in camp last August. REASON: The past tense **(was issued)** is correct here—the present perfect tense **(has been issued)** refers to the present. **(22b, c)**

ANSWER 12.

B I planned **to go** to Canada during **July and August.** REASON: The present infinitive is required. **(25b)**

ANSWER 13.

A I am sure that I **met** you some time ago. REASON: The past **(met)** is used for an action completed in the past. **(22c)**

ANSWER 14.

A If he expected to be graduated in June, he ought to have tried harder. REASON: Of is a preposition, not an auxiliary verb. **(24c)**

ANSWER 15.

A After carefully reviewing the work for the next day, he planned his itinerary. REASON: The original sentence is incomplete. **(24d)**

ANSWER 16.

A Charles would have liked **to be present** at the party. REASON: Since the infinitive action seems to be coincident with the **would have liked** action, the present infinitive should be used. The perfect infinitive **(to have been present)** indicates time prior to that of the principal verb. **(25b)**

ANSWER 17.

A The boy's clothing was still **lying** on the ground where he had carelessly thrown it the previous night. REASON: The progressive past tense of **to lie** is **was lying**. **(21e)**

ANSWER 18.

B He should **have taken** the order. REASON: In this sentence, **should** is synonymous with **ought** and is followed by the perfect infinitive **(to) have taken**. **(25b)**

ANSWER 19.

B The new waitress **laid** the fork to the right of the plate. REASON: The past tense of **to lay** is **laid**. **(21e)**

ANSWER 20.

A He hoped that the members of the class **had done** their homework in preparation for the test. REASON: When there are two past actions, one of which occurs before the other, the action occurring first is expressed by a past perfect tense **(had done)**. **(22d)**

ANSWER 21.

B When a hydrogen bomb is detonated, you see the familiar mushroom cloud form in what was once a calm, blue sky. REASON: The use of **and** is redundant and makes the sentence not only awkward but incomplete. **(24d)**

ANSWER 22.

A The manager told me he would have my car ready for me as soon as he **could get** the service department on the telephone. REASON: Sequence of tenses requires the past tense **(could)**. **(23b)**

ANSWER 23.

C   We were searching for our friend when suddenly a cry **came out** of the darkness. REASON: The past tense **(came out)** is in accordance with the natural sequence of tenses.   **(23b)**

ANSWER 24.

C   Arthur **has lain** on the couch all morning. REASON: The present perfect of **to lie** is **has lain**.   **(21e)**

ANSWER 25.

A   **I learned** many lessons when I worked for you. REASON: The past tense — not the present perfect tense — is proper here.   **(22b, c)**

ANSWER 26.

B   Because they had insisted upon showing us films of their travels, we **lost** many friends whom we once cherished. REASON: The past perfect tense **(had insisted)** requires a past tense **(lost)** in proper sequence of tenses.   **(22d)**

ANSWER 27.

B   He expected **to see** my brother. REASON: The present infinitive is used to indicate time that is the same as, or after, the principal verb **(expected)**.   **(25b)**

ANSWER 28.

C   When Peter reached home, he found he **had lost** his wallet. REASON: The past perfect **(had lost)** is needed to express a past action that occurs before the other past action **(reached)**.   **(22d)**

ANSWER 29.

A   The let him lie where he **had lain**. REASON: The past perfect of **to lie** is **had lain**.   **(21e)**

ANSWER 30.

C   He is reported **to have been killed**. REASON: Since the time of the infinitive is prior to that of the main verb **(reported)**, we use the past infinitive **(to have been killed)**.   **(25b)**

V. MOOD AND VOICE

We have seen in earlier chapters that, by its properties, a verb can tell the reader more than just the *name* of an action or a condition. By its *tense*, you remember, it tells the reader the *time* of an action and, by *sequence of tense*, the time-order of several actions.

In this chapter we will discuss two more properties of the verb which one can use to make his meaning clear. These properties are MOOD and VOICE.

26 Mood

Mood (sometimes written "mode") means *manner*. Mood tells the manner, or way, in which a statement is made—that is, whether it is a simple statement, a command, a wish, a statement contrary to fact, or a statement having a high degree of improbability.

One may use any one of three moods—

the *indicative*—to make a statement or to ask a question
the *imperative*—to give a command, make a request, or make a suggestion
the *subjunctive*—to express a wish, a possibility, a statement of doubt

27 The Indicative Mood

The *indicative mood*—used to make a statement or ask a question—is used in almost all our writing and speaking.

> The conference *was scheduled* for May 15.
> What *is* the correct form to be used?
> From the evidence submitted, it *seems* that he withheld information during the conference.

28 The Imperative Mood

The *imperative mood* expresses a command, a request, or a suggestion. The subject of an imperative sentence is ordinarily the pronoun *you* (not expressed, simply understood).

> *Lock* the safe before you leave the office.
> *Let* us help you start this program in your organization.
> Please *sign* the affidavit before returning it to us.
> > (Note that the word *please* may be inserted with no effect on the use of the imperative, but often with a desirable effect on the listener or reader.)

Probably the greatest mistake we make in using the imperative mood is in *not using it enough*. An order or a request stated in the imperative is usually not only more emphatic but much more quickly and easily understood.

> Indicative: It would be appreciated if you would forward this information promptly.
> Imperative: Please forward (send) this information promptly.

The use of the imperative instead of the indicative wipes out two problems: (1) deciding *when* to use *shall, should, will,* and *may* in such constructions as, "The employee *shall* (or *may*) submit a report"; and (2) avoiding a shift from one to the other of these forms within the same procedure. Using the imperative, the speaker or writer avoids these problems by simply instructing the employee to "submit a report."

The use of the imperative helps the listener and reader, too; for it results in sentences that are shorter, crisper, and easier to understand than those written in the indicative. Compare the following:

Indicative mood predominates:

> The address should be typed in block form, even with the left margin; single-space typing and open punctuation should be used. When letterhead bearing a printed typing dot is used, the address should be started one space below and in line with this typing dot.

Imperative mood substituted:

> Type the address in block form, even with the left margin; use single space and open punctuation. When using letterhead bearing a printed typing dot, start the address one space below and in line with the dot.

Indicative mood predominates:

> Vouchers should be prepared by typewriter with carbon duplicates whenever practicable. Otherwise, ink of a permanent nature should be used.

Imperative mood substituted:

> Whenever practicable, prepare vouchers by typewriter with carbon duplicates. Otherwise, use permanent ink.

29 The Subjunctive Mood

The *subjunctive mood* is used most often to express a condition contrary to fact, a wish, a supposition, or an indirect command.

Grammarians seem to agree that the subjunctive is going out of use. Be that as it may, the subjunctive is still being used in a number of instances; and one should know enough about its use and abuse so that he can use good judgment in determining when to use it.

29a Forms of the subjunctive

The only recognizable forms of the subjunctive (and consequently the only ones to be discussed in this chapter) are —

(1) the form of the third person singular present (which in the indicative has an -*s* and in the subjunctive has none):

Indicative: The detective PREPARES his report as soon as he completes the case.

Subjunctive: We suggested that the detective PREPARE his report immediately.

Indicative: The plane usually ARRIVES on schedule.

Subjunctive: Should the plane ARRIVE on schedule, we will be able to make our connection.

(2) forms of the verb *be*, which show the following differences between the indicative and the subjunctive:

Indicative: *I* AM, *you* ARE, *he* IS; *we, you, they* ARE

Subjunctive: If *I* BE   and Should *we* BE
             If *you* BE   Should *you* BE
             If *he* BE   Should *they* BE
             (Both *if* and *should* frequently introduce the subjunctive)

Indicative: *I* WAS, *you* WERE, *he* WAS; *we* WERE, *you* WERE, *they* WERE

Subjunctive: If *I* WERE (difference)
             If *you* WERE (no change)
             If *he* WERE (difference)

             If *we* WERE (no change)
             If *you* WERE (no change)
             If *they* WERE (no change)

Though *were* is the past form in the indicative, it is used as PRESENT or FUTURE in the subjunctive. Either *had* or *had been* is used to express PAST time in the subjunctive.

Present subjunctive: If the memorandum *were* available (NOW), we could finish the report.

Past subjunctive: If the memorandum *had been* available (IN THE PAST), we could have finished the report.

or: *Had* the memorandum been available, we could have finished the report.

Present: If he *were* able to do it, I am sure he would.

Past: *Had* he been able to do it, I am sure he would.

30 Uses of the Subjunctive

Most uses of the subjunctive have become so natural that they cause little trouble. However, there are some that require one to weigh the *degree of probability* of his statement before he uses the subjunctive instead of the indicative.

In the following sections, we shall list first those about which there is little question and then, in section 30e, those that cause confusion or concern.

30a   To express a wish not likely to be fulfilled or impossible of being realized

> I wish it *were* possible for us to approve his transfer at this time. (It is *not* possible.)
> I wish he *were* here to hear your praise of his work. (He is *not* here.)
> Would that I *were* able to take this trip in your place. (I am *not* able to go.)
> I wish I *were* able to help you.

30b   To express a parliamentary motion

> I move that the meeting *be* adjourned.
> *Resolved*, that a committee *be* appointed to study this matter.

30c   In a subordinate clause after a verb that expresses a command, a request, or a suggestion

> He asked *that* the report *be* submitted in duplicate.
> It is recommended *that* this office *be* responsible for preparing the statements.
> We suggest *that* he *be* relieved of the assignment.
> We ask *that* he *consider* the possibility of an adjustment.
> It is highly desirable *that* they *be* given the authority to sign these documents.

30d   To express a condition easily recognized as being contrary to fact

> If I *were* in St. Louis, I should be glad to attend.
> If this *were* a simple case, we would easily agree on a solution.
> If I *were* you, I should not mind the assignment.

30e   To express a condition or supposition which the speaker or writer believes to be contrary to fact or highly improbable, as contrasted with a condition or supposition which the speaker or writer considers to be within the realm of possibility.

This is the trouble area. Here, the speaker or writer has the obligation to tell the listener or reader which way he sees the situation: highly improbable or within the realm of possibility. He does this by his choice of the subjunctive or the indicative.

> Subjunctive: If his statement *be* true, this is a case of fraud.
> (The speaker or writer indicates that he thinks it is highly improbable that the statement is true.)

> Indicative: If his statement *is* true, this may be a case of fraud.
> (The speaker or writer indicates that it is quite possible that the statement may be true.)

> Subjunctive: If he *were* at the meeting, he would speak to the point. (or, *were* he at the meeting, he would . . .)
> (The speaker or writer tells his reader that the man is not at the meeting.)

> Indicative: If he *was* at the meeting, he would have been able to speak to the point.
> (Perhaps the man *was* at the meeting; the speaker or writer doesn't know.)

> Subjunctive: *Had* the first payment been made in April, the second would be due in September.
> (The speaker or writer tells his listener or reader that the payment was *not* made in April.)

Indicative: If the first payment *was* made in April, the second will be due in September.
(Perhaps it was made; perhaps not—the speaker or writer doesn't know.)

Subjunctive: If he *were* able to forecast the degree of interest in the program, he could be more specific in his budget requests.
(The speaker or writer considers it highly improbable — unlikely — that the man can forecast the degree of interest.)

Indicative: If he *is* able to forecast the degree of interest in the program, he can be more specific in his budget requests.

(Here, the speaker or writer thinks it is *possible* that the man can forecast the degree of interest.)

30f   After as if or as though

In formal writing and speech, *as if* and *as though* are followed by the subjunctive, since they introduce as supposition something not factual. In informal writing and speaking, the indicative is sometimes used.

He talked *as if* he *were* an expert on taxation. (He's not.)
This report looks *as though* it *were* the work of a college freshman.

31   Tense Sequence in Conditional Statements

The following table should clarify which tense to use in the main clause and in the "if" clause of a conditional statement.

	Capable of Fulfillment	Contrary to Fact
PRESENT	PRESENT INDICATIVE If you *are* grateful, PRESENT INDICATIVE so *am* I.	PAST SUBJUNCTIVE If you *were* tired, FUTURE SUBJUNCTIVE you *would rest*.
PAST	PAST SUBJUNCTIVE If they *complained,* FUTURE SUBJUNCTIVE they *would receive* no food.	PAST PERFECT SUBJUNCTIVE If they *had complained,* FUTURE PERFECT SUBJUNCTIVE they *would have received* no food.
FUTURE	**[more likely]** PRESENT INDICATIVE FUTURE INDICATIVE If she *studied (will study)* FUTURE INDICATIVE tonight, she *will pass.* - **[less likely]** FUTURE SUBJUNCTIVE If she *would study* tonight, FUTURE SUBJUNCTIVE she *would pass.*	If she PAST SUBJUNCTIVE + INFINITIVE *were to study* tonight, FUTURE SUBJUNCTIVE she *would pass.*

If-clauses are, of course, *conditional* clauses; that's what the writer tells his reader by his choice of the subordinate conjunction *if.* But not all *if*-clauses express thoughts that are suppositions or that are contrary to fact.

Simply conditional:	If it *is* assigned to me, I shall do it. (Perhaps it *will be* assigned to me.)
Contrary to fact:	If it *were* assigned to me, I would do it. (It has already been assigned to someone else; or it is highly improbable that it will ever be assigned to me.)
Simply conditional:	If the taxpayer *was* married on that date, he is entitled to . . . (Perhaps he was.)
Contrary to fact:	If the taxpayer *were* married . . . (He is not.)

32 Shifts in Mood

Be consistent in your point of view. Once you have decided on the mood that expresses the way you regard the message, use that mood throughout the sentence or the paragraph. A shift in mood is confusing to the listener or reader, because it indicates that the speaker or writer himself has changed his way of looking at the conditions.

Not: It is requested that a report of the proceedings *be* prepared and copies *should be* distributed to all members.
(*Be* is subjunctive; *should be,* indicative.)

But: It is requested that a report of the proceedings *be* prepared and that copies *be* distributed to all members.

33 Voice

Voice indicates whether the subject of the verb is performing or receiving the action described by the verb. There are two voices: active and passive.

If the subject is performing the action, the verb is in the active voice.

The *Director* APPROVED our time card.
The *report* SUMMARIZES the committee recommendations.
The *agent* ASKED the taxpayer to bring his receipts.

If the subject is being acted upon, the verb is in the passive voice. (The passive form always consists of some form of *be* plus the past participle.)

Our *time card* WAS APPROVED by the Director.
The committee *recommendations* ARE SUMMARIZED in the report.
The *taxpayer* WAS ASKED by the agent to bring his receipts.

34 Uses of the Active and Passive Voices

We need to use both the active and passive voice. In the past, the tendency has been to use the passive voice as much as possible, probably in the belief that the resulting sentences sound "more official." Lately, in an effort to put more life into expression, some grammarians have been stressing the use of the active voice, almost to the extent of advising us to avoid the passive voice at all costs. But one extreme is as bad as the other. We need both the active and the passive voice for emphasis and for exact expression.

If you want to emphasize *who* performed an action, let your subject be the person or thing that performed the action and put your verb in the active voice. If it is relatively unimportant *who* performed the action and you want to stress instead *what action* was performed or *who was affected* by the action performed, let your subject be the person or thing "acted upon" (the receiver of the action) and put the verb in the passive voice.

All supervisors attended the meeting.
(*Supervisors* is being emphasized.)
The meeting was attended by all supervisors.
(Here the *meeting* is being emphasized.)

The Blank Instrument Co. employs Mr. Johnson.
(This form emphasizes the company.)
Mr. Johnson is employed by the Blank Instrument Co.
(This form emphasizes Mr. Johnson, not the company.)

The Division Director himself checked the figures in the statistical report.
> (Here we want to emphasize *who* checked the figures.)

The figures in the statistical report were thoroughly checked by a proofreader.
> (In this sentence the important idea is that the figures were checked; by whom is relatively unimportant.)

NOTE: We can't say that one voice is "correct" in certain instances and "incorrect" in others. The decision of which voice to use rests with the speaker or writer; he is the only one who can say which voice better suits his purpose.

The active voice is, however, simpler and more direct; therefore, if either the active or the passive will serve your purpose, use the active.

35 A Passive Verb as Copulative

A passive verb may sometimes act as a copulative verb.

> He *is considered* a genius.
> (*genius* is a predicate nominative.)

> The lady *was made* ill by the pill.
> (*ill* is a predicate adjective.)

36 Shifts in Voice

Like the shift in mood, which we have discussed, a shift in voice is confusing. Even when it does not confuse, it may distract momentarily.

Shifts in voice—often accompanied by shifts in subject—usually occur in compound or complex sentences. Although it is not essential that all clauses in a sentence be the same in structure, any unnecessary shifts result in a disorganized sentence. Therefore, unless you have a good reason for changing, use the same subject and voice in the second clause that you used in the first.

Not: As I SEARCHED through the files for the memorandum, the missing REPORT WAS FOUND.
> (The first subject is *I*—its verb is active; the second subject is *report*—its verb is passive.)

But: As I SEARCHED through the files for the memorandum, I FOUND the missing report.
> (Subject is *I* in both clauses; both verbs are active.)

Not: As soon as WE RECEIVE his signed contract, ARRANGEMENTS CAN BE MADE to pay him.
> (*We* is the first subject—its verb is active; *arrangements* is the second subject—its verb is passive.)

But: As soon as his CONTRACT IS RECEIVED, ARRANGEMENTS CAN BE MADE to pay him.
> (Both verbs are in the passive voice, but we still have different subjects.)

or: As soon as WE RECEIVE his signed contract, WE CAN MAKE arrangements to pay him.
> (Now both verbs are in the active voice and the subjects are the same.)

Now, push forward! Test yourself and practice for your test with the carefully constructed quizzes that follow. Each one presents the kind of question you may expect on your test. And each question is at just the level of difficulty that may be expected. Don't try to take all the tests at one time. Rather, schedule yourself so that you take a few at each session, and spend approximately the same time on them at each session. Score yourself honestly, and date each test. You should be able to detect improvement in your performance on successive sessions.

TEST XIII. MOOD AND VOICE

TIME: 21 Minutes

DIRECTIONS: In each of the following groups of sentences, select the one sentence that is grammatically INCORRECT. Mark the answer sheet with the letter of that incorrect sentence.

Explanations of the key points behind these questions appear with the answers at the end of this test. The explanatory answers provide the kind of background that will enable you to answer test questions with facility and confidence.

1

(A) The helicopter stayed over my house for fully ten minutes.
(B) It was my earnest desire that an accord may be reached.
(C) The trio of sophomores looked good out on the court.
(D) How many poets laureate have you known?

2

(A) He could easily have won a scholarship if he would have devoted more time to his school work.
(B) The new handbook supersedes all earlier bulletins.
(C) It is a rare person who does not experience many vicissitudes in the course of his life.
(D) The Reverend Arthur Williams will speak at the next meeting of the Writers' Club in the local high school.

3

(A) If you would have been prompt, we might have arrived in time for the first act.
(B) The first two innings of the game were very exciting.
(C) Herbert will try to get the boat started.
(D) Reading, writing, and revising seem to be the principal activities of the graduate student.

4

(A) He will continue his good work, providing we show appreciation.
(B) I cannot drive somebody else's car.
(C) He has but one aim, to succeed.
(D) Everything would have turned out right if she waited.

5

(A) These transactions require your close attention.
(B) He is one of the men who were being considered for the position.
(C) Senator Brooke is not willing to take the assignment.
(D) If she would have learned that to have a friend one must be a friend, she would not now be friendless.

6

(A) If I were you, I would enter the swimming meet.
(B) The accident would not have happened if Father had driven the car.
(C) You may sneer if you wish, but if it weren't for movies, there would be few television sponsors today.
(D) Byron always walks as if he was in a hurry.

7

(A) Whether what they see is always worthwhile is of course debatable.
(B) Man has spun mythical genealogies and embroidered those that were actual.
(C) The doctor lost no time in telling him that he would have felt better if he would have taken his medicine on time.
(D) For all that he dislikes me, I still like him.

8

(A) Your employer would have been inclined to favor your request if you would have waited for an occasion when he was less busy.
(B) The fewer the chances for error, the less likely does error become.
(C) He has never stayed at the same hotel longer than two weeks.
(D) Though the world may blame us, neither he nor I am guilty of the crime.

9

(A) Before we could proceed to summarize the lesson, the bell rang, ending the period.
(B) Shakespeare's historical plays present a distorted picture of history; nevertheless, critics feel that they are worthy of study.
(C) If you would have waited for me, I could have helped you move your furniture to your new room.
(D) Not only did he fail to profit from his stock transactions but he also lost all that he had invested.

(10)

(A) In the recipe for custard, two cupfuls of milk will be enough.

(B) In the home economics classroom two tubs full of clothes showed that it was not a day for cooking.

(C) It was 4:00 p.m. before the dishes were cleared away, washed, and put back into the closet.

(D) If only I would have a fairy godmother like Cinderella!

(11)

(A) Although he looked as if he was tired, he refused steadfastly to let me help him.

(B) Every morning at nine the professor entered the room, a book under his arm.

(C) The mayor expressed concern about the large number of people injured at street crossings.

(D) We are studying English, mathematics, history, and French.

(12)

(A) His whereabouts has not yet been determined, though the police of several countries have been asked to look for him.

(B) Anyone and everyone is invited to the annual charity ball given for the benefit of orphaned children.

(C) If I were in your position and was offered a trip to Europe, I'd certainly go.

(D) More than one vacation plan was changed because of the new requirement.

(13)

(A) The most scientifically minded students do not always become the most successful scientists.

(B) Everyone but the author and us was unusually late, and for this we were duly praised.

(C) What he drank was three glasses of milk, two cups of coffee and one ounce of medicine.

(D) The senator, considered a "hawk," believed that if the U.S.S.R's policy was not one of constant aggression, we could probably reach some peaceful understanding with her.

(14)

(A) I inferred from what you said that you did not want me to stay for the meeting.

(B) If he would have come when I asked him, he might not have made the error.

(C) The reason he could not finish the work is that he ran out of material.

(D) He is one of those people who do their best work alone.

(15)

(A) There is no objection to his joining the party if he is willing to fit in with the plans of the group.

(B) If you had seen the number of pancakes he consumed at breakfast this morning, you might understand why he is so overweight.

(C) At five o'clock, this meeting will adjourn to the room next door.

(D) Ceremonies were opened by a drum and bugle corps of Chinese school children parading up Mott Street.

(16)

(A) Today's **Times** has headlines about another girl who has just swum the English Channel.

(B) If you ever visit Paris, you would sense for yourself the grace and charm of an old-world city that is forever new.

(C) Placing his longbow on the grass beside him, Robin Hood, who had had an exciting day, lay down to rest and soon fell sound asleep.

(D) I was not at all surprised to hear of Jim's success.

(17)

(A) The jury are still arguing over the credibility of one of the witnesses.

(B) If you would have considered all the alternatives logically, you would have chosen another course of action.

(C) He is different, in many respects, from his predecessor in the office of dean.

(D) Coming in on the bus, we can see the new atomic reactor plant.

(18)

(A) Because of his natural diffidence, he thought it would be presumptuous of him to ask for an increase.

(B) If he were there on time, all this trouble could have been avoided.

(C) Did he really say, "I don't intend to give you any information"?

(D) If these bricks had not been laid by an amateur, the wall would not now be toppling.

(19)

(A) Unlike you and me, Gwendolyn looks good in slacks.

(B) The reason the U. N. was established was that the people wanted peace.

(C) If you follow this path, you finally reach a hill from which you could overlook the whole valley.

(D) There was only one chance of our solving the mystery: we had to find the missing letter.

20

(A) Almost every alumna of this college has indicated her desire to teach.
(B) We must find out whether anybody has ever patented a machine of this type.
(C) The president of the advertising agency has indicated his dissatisfaction with the questionnaires prepared by the research department.
(D) If the manager would have planned more carefully, bankruptcy might have been avoided.

21

(A) The poem is somewhat longer than a sonnet; its rhythm is fittingly sedate.
(B) If they would have considered all the suggestions carefully, they would have come to a different conclusion.
(C) Among the plans submitted were many up-to-date ideas, some of which were adopted.
(D) When the toy balloon burst, the child screamed with fright.

22

(A) Adults having a sense of wonder share a certain joy in life with children.
(B) I would gladly have attended your wedding if you invited me.
(C) Tokyo has a larger population than any other city in the world.
(D) Natives of California attribute their superior height to the healthful climate of their state.

23

(A) Fighting diseases in the steaming jungles, as some doctors do, does not appeal to the average person.
(B) If I wasn't dressed in this uniform, I wouldn't feel so conspicuous.
(C) Nothing will satisfy him but that I go along.
(D) This vase is a memento of our trip to the Orient.

24

(A) All your arguments notwithstanding, I am convinced that I should invest in the stocks of this company.
(B) If I would have had more time, I could have written a better answer.

(C) "Girls and boys," cried the teacher, "do you realize what an exciting age you live in?"
(D) In spite of the great advances of modern science there are still numerous phenomena that we cannot explain.

25

(A) Then Jim Hawkins began to listen in earnest and . . .but you know the rest of the story.
(B) At this very moment the group are disagreeing about the interpretation of the new law.
(C) New Yorkers speak somewhat differently from their neighbors across the Hudson.
(D) He would have been much happier if he would have followed his own precepts.

26

(A) He could but surmise that all had gone well.
(B) Treat me as if I was your brother.
(C) It is the oldest society in the city, having been organized in 1712.
(D) Thinking of the course of German military history, von Moltke determined to put his reflections in writing.

27

(A) If the police arrived earlier, there would not have been such confusion.
(B) The Parks Commissioner should provide closer surveillance of the parks in the city.
(C) We came to a wide river, on the banks of which several rotted trees could be glimpsed.
(D) Whether you like it or not, the lessons of history cannot be ignored.

28

(A) No one but her could have recognized him.
(B) She knew the stranger to be him whom she had given up as lost.
(C) He looked like he had been in some strange land where age advanced at a double pace.
(D) It is impossible to include that item; the agenda has already been mimeographed.

CONSOLIDATE YOUR KEY ANSWERS HERE

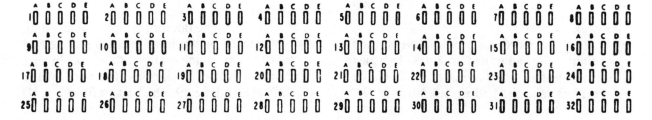

TEST XIII. MOOD AND VOICE

KEY ANSWERS FOR THE FOREGOING QUESTIONS

1.B	5.D	9.C	13.D	17.B	21.B	25.D
2.A	6.D	10.D	14.B	18.B	22.B	26.B
3.A	7.C	11.A	15.B	19.C	23.B	27.A
4.D	8.A	12.C	16.B	20.D	24.B	28.C

EXPLANATORY ANSWERS CLARIFYING CARDINAL POINTS

The core of the Question and Answer Method . . . getting help when and where you need it. Even if you were able to write correct key answers for the preceding questions, the following explanations illuminate fundamental facts, ideas, and principles which just might crop up in the form of questions on future tests.

***Bold-face** references in the following answers direct you to paragraphs in the Arco Grammar Text, where fuller explanations are provided.*

ANSWER 1.

B It was my earnest desire that an accord be reached. REASON: The desire was **that an accord be reached** — not **that an accord may be reached**. **(30c)**

ANSWER 2.

A He could easily have won a scholarship if he **had devoted** more time to his school work. REASON: The contrary-to-fact past condition requires the **had devoted** verb form in the "if" clause. **(31)**

ANSWER 3.

A If you **had been** prompt, we might have arrived in time for the first act. REASON: In a past contrary-to-fact condition, the "if" clause verb must have the **had** form. **(31)**

ANSWER 4.

D Everything would have turned out right if she **had waited**. REASON: In a past contrary-to-fact condition, the "if" clause verb must take the **had waited** form. **(31)**

ANSWER 5.

D If she **had learned** that to have a friend one must be a friend, she would not now be friendless. REASON: The verb in the "if" clause of a past contrary-to-fact condition must have the **had learned** form. **(31)**

ANSWER 6.

D Byron always walks as if he **were** in a hurry. REASON: In a contrary to fact condition, the verb in the "if" clause must take the subjunctive form **(were) (31)**

ANSWER 7.

C The doctor lost no time in telling him that he would have felt better if he **had taken** his medicine on time. REASON: In past contrary-to-fact conditions, the verb of the "if" clause takes the **had taken** form. **(31)**

ANSWER 8.

A Your employer would have been inclined to favor your request if you **had waited** for an occasion when he was less busy. REASON: In a contrary-to-fact clause, the "if" verb should have the **had waited** form. **(31)**

ANSWER 9.

C If you **had waited** for me, I could have helped you move your furniture to your new room. REASON: The past contrary-to-fact condition requires the **had waited** form in the "if" clause. **(31)**

ANSWER 10.

D If only **I had** a fairy godmother like Cinderella! REASON: The "if" clause of the contrary-to-fact condition must have the **had** verb form in this case. **(31)**

ANSWER 11.

A Although he looked as if he **were** tired, he refused steadfastly to let me help him. REASON: In the contrary-to-fact clause, the verb form is **were**—not **was**. **(31)**

ANSWER 12.

C If I were in your position and **were offered** a trip to Europe, I'd certainly go. REASON: After if, expressing a contrary-to-fact condition, the subjunctive form of the verb is used (**were**). **(31)**

ANSWER 13.

D The senator, considered a "hawk," believed that if the U.S.S.R.'s policy **were** not one of constant aggression, we could probably reach some peaceful understanding with her. REASON: The verb of the "if" clause of a contrary-to-fact condition must take a **were** form. **(31)**

ANSWER 14.

B If he **had come** when I asked him, he might not have made the error. REASON: The **would have come** verb form is incorrect in the "if clause" of a contrary-to-fact condition. **(31)**

ANSWER 15.

B If you had seen the number of pancakes he consumed at breakfast this morning, you **might have understood** why he is so overweight. REASON: In a contrary-to-fact condition in past tense, the conclusion verb should be past (**might have understood**)—not present. **(31)**

ANSWER 16.

B If you ever visit Paris, you will sense for yourself the grace and charm of an old-world city that is forever new. REASON: In a future condition which is capable of fulfillment, the principal clause has a verb which is future indicative (**will sense**). **(31)**

ANSWER 17.

B If you **had considered** all the alternatives logically, you would have chosen another course of action. REASON: In a past contrary-to-fact statement, the verb of the "if" clause takes the **had considered** form. **(31)**

ANSWER 18.

B If he **had been** there on time, all this trouble could have been avoided. REASON: The verb in the "if" clause of the past contrary-to-fact condition must be **had been**—not **were**. **(31)**

ANSWER 19.

C If you follow this path, you finally reach a hill from which you **can** overlook the whole valley. REASON: The indicative mood verb (**can**) not the subjunctive mood verb (**could**) is correct here. **(31)**

ANSWER 20.

D If the manager **had planned** more carefully, bankruptcy might have been avoided. REASON: The "if" clause of a past contrary-to-fact condition requires the **had planned** form. **(31)**

ANSWER 21.

B   If they **had considered** all the suggestions carefully, they would have come to a different conclusion. REASON: In a past contrary-to-fact condition, the verb of the "if" clause must be past perfect subjunctive (**had considered**).   **(31)**

ANSWER 22.

B   I would gladly have attended your wedding if you **had invited** me. REASON: The verb of the "if" clause in a past contrary-to-fact condition must take the **had invited** form.   **(31)**

ANSWER 23.

B   If I **weren't** dressed in this uniform, I wouldn't feel so conspicuous. REASON: The "if" clause of a present contrary-to-fact condition requires the **were** form. **(31)**

ANSWER 24.

B   If I **had had** more time, I could have written a better answer. REASON: The verb in the "if" clause of a past contrary-to-fact condition must have the **had had** form.   **(31)**

ANSWER 25.

D   He would have been much happier if he **had followed** his own precepts. REASON: A past contrary-to-fact condition necessitates the **had followed** form in the "if" clause.   **(31)**

ANSWER 26.

B   Treat me as if I **were** your brother. REASON: The present tense contrary-to-fact verb takes the **were** form in the "as if" clause.   **(31)**

ANSWER 27.

A   If the police **had arrived** earlier, there would not have been such confusion. REASON: The verb in the "if" clause of a past contrary-to-fact condition must have the **had arrived** form.   **(31)**

ANSWER 28.

C   He looked as if he had been in some strange land where age advanced at a double pace. REASON: The conjunction **as if** must be used here instead of the preposition **like**. Moreover, the expression **as if** requires a following verb (**had been**).   **(31, 71)**

VI. MODIFIERS

37 Introduction

37a Importance of modifiers

Why are modifiers important? For one thing, they form a part of almost every sentence. Important though the subject and the verb are (and this was stressed in preceding chapters), few sentences consist solely of these words. The sentence "Honesty pays" best illustrates the sentence that has only a subject and a verb, but how unusual such a sentence is.

Even a simple sentence like, "*The new* treasurer submitted *a timely* report" contains four modifiers—*the* and *a* as articles, *new* modifying *treasurer*, and *timely* modifying *report*. And the more complex the thought becomes, the more relationships are shown between the ideas it contains—the more modifiers one must use. Modifiers are important, then, because they make our meaning clear and exact.

37b Purpose of this chapter

What, then, must the speaker or writer know about modifiers if he is to choose them wisely and use them effectively?

As a minimum, he must know:

(1) that in choosing his modifiers—

    (a) he may use a single word, a phrase, or a clause

    (b) he may modify a subject, a verb, a complement, or another modifier

    (c) he must use adjective modifiers (whether words, phrases or clauses) to modify subjects, objects, and predicate nominatives

    (a) he must place them as closely as possible to the word(s) being modified

(2) that in using his modifiers—

    (a) he must place them as close by as possible to the word(s) being modified

    (b) he must not misuse modifiers lest he cause confusion

    (c) he must not overuse modifiers lest he ruin the conciseness of his writing

37c Classification of modifiers

Modifiers fall generally into two categories: *adjectives* and phrases or clauses used as adjectives; *adverbs* and phrases or clauses used as adverbs. Sometimes the form of the modifier clearly shows whether it is an adjective or an adverb; sometimes the form is the same for both.

Adjectives describe, limit, or make more exact the meaning of a noun or pronoun (any substantive).

Adverbs describe, limit, or make more exact the meaning of a verb, an adjective, or another adverb.

38 Types of Adjectives

All adjectives are divided into two classes— *limiting* and *descriptive*.

Limiting: *many* people, *much* work
Descriptive: *accurate* description, *long-term* gain

Following are the important types of adjectives:

Demonstrative: *that* book, *those* apples (see Section 11e)
Possessive: *my* car, *their* home
Relative: *which* road, *what* decision
Interrogative: Which road? What decision?
Proper: *American* flag, *Russian* embassy

38a Articles

The definite articles are *a, an,* and the indefinite article is *the.* Use *a* before words beginning with a consonant sound, *an* before those beginning with a vowel sound.

a desk, *a* book
an agent, *an* error, *an* LWOP case (el-W-O-P)

The article used before each of two connected nouns or adjectives signals that the words refer to different people or things.

We elected *a* secretary and *a* treasurer (two persons).
She uses *a* tan and green typewriter (one machine, two colors).

Do not use *a* or *an* after *sort of, kind of, manner of, style of,* or *type of.*

Not: What *kind of a* book do you want?
But: What *kind of* book do you want?

Do not use *the* before *both.*

Not: We'll buy *the both* of them.
But: We'll buy *both* of them.

39 Types of Adverbs

Adverbs may be classified according to the questions they answer; in general, there are five types:

Adverbs of manner: run *swiftly,* write *legibly,* compute *accurately*
Adverbs of place and direction: *above, before, below, here, out*
Adverbs of time and succession: *immediately, today, ago, lately*

Adverbs of degree and measure: *almost, enough, far, little, much*
Adverbs of cause, reason, or purpose: *why, hence, therefore*

40 Identifying Adjectives and Adverbs

Sometimes one has difficulty distinguishing between adjectives and adverbs. Here are a few helps.

40a The *ly* ending

Some adverbs, chiefly the adverbs of manner, are formed by adding -*ly* to the adjective or participle form. However, not all adverbs end in *ly*; and some adjectives end in *ly.* The writer cannot, then, look upon the *ly ending* as a means of distinguishing between adjectives and adverbs.

Adjectives that end in *ly*:

cleanly, deadly, friendly, likely, lively, lonely, lovely, kindly, orderly, timely

a *friendly* discussion, an *orderly* arrangement, a *timely* return

Adverbs that do not end in *ly*:

soon, often, around, down, very, now, yet

write *soon,* call *often, very* high production

40b Words that are both adjectives and adverbs

The following words may be either adjectives or adverbs, depending on their use:

above, bad, better, cheap, close, deep, early, fast, first, hard, late, long, loud, much, only, quick, slow, very, well

Mary types *better* than Joan does. (adverb)
The chief had a cold, but he is *better* now. (adjective)

We climbed a *very* high hill. (adverb)
That is the *very* return I was looking for. (adjective)

If you must use the detour, drive *slow* (or slowly). (adverb)
A *slow* driver is often a hazard on the highway. (adjective)

40c Adverbs with two forms

Some adverbs have two forms—one ending in *ly*, the other not. The longer form is nearly always correct and is preferable in formal writing. The short form is properly used in brief, forceful sentences (in commands—such as the road sign "Drive Slow") and may be used informally. The *ly* form should, however, always be used to modify an adjective.

Following are examples of adverbs having two forms:

slow, slowly	clear, clearly	quick, quickly
cheap, cheaply	sharp, sharply	loud, loudly
soft, softly	deep, deeply	direct, directly

Sometimes the meaning desired will determine which form should be used. Notice that either *direct* or *directly* may be used when the meaning is "in a straight line," but *directly* is the only choice when *soon* is meant.

NOTE: In informal speech, we sometimes drop the *ly* ending from some often-used adverbs. This practice is incorrect and, even though we occasionally let it slip by in our speech, we must not allow it in our writing.

Correct usage:

I am *really* glad you could come. (Not, *real* glad)
I'm feeling *considerably* better. (Not *considerable*)
He *surely* is lucky. (Not, *sure*)

40d Distinguishing between a predicate adjective and an adverb

A predicate adjective is, as its name implies, an adjective appearing in the predicate and modifying the subject.

The following categories of verbs (called *copulative* or *linking verbs*) are usually followed by a predicate adjective rather than by an adverb. A predicate adjective can occur only after these verbs:

(1) Forms of the verb *to be*

That man IS *old*.   (old man)
The report WAS *accurate*. (accurate report)

(2) Other no-action verbs, such as *become, appear, seem*

The town APPEARS *deserted*. (deserted town)
The air SEEMS *humid*.   (humid air)

(3) Verbs pertaining to the senses

The reports SOUND *exaggerated*. (exaggerated reports)
The peach TASTES *sweet*.   (sweet peach)
The work LOOKS *hard*.   (hard work)

NOTE: Be sure to distinguish between the predicate adjective and the adverb when the sense verbs are used. Usually these verbs are followed by adjectives, but they may be modified by adverbs.

She LOOKS *bad*. (She doesn't appear to be healthy.)
She LOOKS *badly*. (An awkward construction, which could mean that, having lost something, she is doing a poor job of looking for it.)

The steak LOOKS *tender*. (Has the appearance of *tender* steak)
The woman LOOKED *tenderly* at the child. (Tells "how" she *looked* at the child.)

The child LOOKS *wistful*. (Has a wistful look)
The child LOOKED *wistfully* at the candy. (Tells how the child *looked* at the candy.)

To determine whether the modifier following a sense verb modifies the subject or the verb, substitute *is* or *are* for the sense verb. If, after this substitution, the sentence is logical, you can be sure your choice (whether of a predicate adjective or of an adverb) is correct.

The steak IS *tender*. (Logical)
The woman IS *tenderly* at the child. (Illogical)

41 Compound Modifiers (With and Without Hyphens)

41a Modifiers preceding a noun

Two or more words serving as a single adjective are called a compound adjective. When these modifiers *precede* a noun, they are joined by a hyphen.

> Have you an *up-to-date* REPORT on that subject?
> Please submit the *above-mentioned* FORM in duplicate.
> That is a *well-written* DOCUMENT.
> Ours is a *well-equipped* OFFICE.

41b   Modifiers following a noun

When the modifying words *follow* a noun, do not use a hyphen unless the words are listed as hyphenated compounds in the dictionary.

> This REPORT is *up to date*.
> The FORM *mentioned above* must be submitted in duplicate.
> That DOCUMENT is *well written*.
> Our OFFICE is *well equipped*.
> This MOTOR is *self-starting*.

NOTE: Since usage is constantly changing, it is best to consult a recent dictionary when in doubt about hyphenated words. Notice that, in the last example above, *self-starting* is hyphenated, even though it follows the noun. The dictionary gives all "self" words except *selfsame, selfish, selfhood*, and *selfless* as hyphenated compounds.

41c   Suspending hyphens

In a series of hyphenated adjective-noun words having a common ending, suspending hyphens are used to carry the force of the modifier over to a later noun.

> Is he looking for a two- or three-bedroom apartment?
> It is a 4- or 5-page report.

41d   Two-word proper adjectives

Compound adjectives consisting of two-word proper adjectives are *not* hyphenated.

> He is vacationing at a *New Jersey* beach.
> It was a *Comptroller General* decision.

41e   Separate modifiers preceding a noun

Do not hyphenate two or more adjectives that precede the noun *if they do not act jointly* to modify the noun. Note, however, the correct punctuation of such constructions.

> He wore a *white* FLANNEL SUIT.   (a flannel suit that was white)
> Give me a *current* STATISTICAL REPORT. (a statistical report that is current)

> It was a *long, hard* JOB.   (a long job *and* a hard one)
> It was an *involved, difficult* CASE.   (an involved case *and* a difficult one)

NOTE: One suggestion to help you determine whether to put a comma between the two adjectives: If you can insert the word *and* between the two adjectives without destroying the meaning of the sentence, use a comma; otherwise, do not.

41f   Adverb ending in *ly* with adjective

Do not use a hyphen between an adverb ending in *ly* and an adjective or participle.

> This is a *carefully written* REPORT.
> That is a *frequently quoted* PASSAGE.

42   Comparison of Adjectives and Adverbs

42a   Degrees of comparison

Adjectives and adverbs change form to show a greater or lesser degree of the characteristic named by the simple word. There are three degrees of comparison.

Positive degree. — The positive degree names the *quality* expressed by the adjective or adverb. It does not imply a comparison with, or a relation to, a similar quality in any other thing.

> *high* morale, a *dependable* worker, work *fast*, prepared *carefully*

Comparative degree.—The comparative degree indicates that the quality described by the modifier exists to a greater or lesser degree in one thing than in another. It is formed by adding *er* to the positive degree or by inserting *more* or *less* before the positive form.

> Our organization has *higher* morale now than ever before.
> He is a *more dependable* worker than she.
> She can work *faster* than I.
> This plan was prepared *more carefully* than the one he submitted last month.

Superlative degree.—The superlative degree denotes the greatest or least amount of the quality named. It is formed by adding *est* to the positive degree of the adjective or adverb or by inserting *most* or *least* before the positive form.

> That organization has the *highest* morale of any Government agency.
> He is the *most dependable* worker in the office.
> This is the *most carefully* prepared report I have found.

The comparative degree is used to refer to only two things; the superlative to more than two.

> This book is the *longer* of the two.
> This book is the *longest* of the three.

42b Using -*er* and -*est* vs. *more* and *most*

There is no difference in meaning between -*er* and *more* or between -*est* and *most*. Either method may be used with some modifiers. However, most adjectives of three syllables or more and almost all adverbs are compared by the use of *more* and *most* (or *less* and *least*) rather than by the endings -*er* and -*est*. In choosing which method should be used with the modifiers that may take either method, you may base your choice on emphasis. By adding -*er* or -*est* to the root word you emphasize the *quality*, while by using *more* or *most* you stress the *degree* of comparison.

> Should I have been *kinder* or *harsher* in handling that call?
> That report is the *longest* of the three.

Should I have been *more firm* or *less firm* in handling that caller?
Of all the forms, this one is the *most simple* and that one is the *least simple* to fill out.

42c Irregular comparisons

Some modifiers are compared by changes in the words themselves. A few of these irregular comparisons are given below; consult your dictionary whenever you are in doubt about the comparison of any adjective or adverb.

Positive	*Comparative*	*Superlative*
good	better	best
well	better	best
bad (evil, ill)	worse	worst
badly (ill)	worse	worst
far	farther, further	farthest, furthest
late	later, latter	latest, last
little	less, lesser	least
many, much	more	most

43 Problems With Comparison

43a Adjectives and adverbs that cannot be compared

Some adjectives and adverbs express qualities that do not admit freely of comparison. They represent the highest degree of a quality and, as a result, cannot be improved. Some of these words are listed below.

complete	infinitely	square
correct	perfect	squarely
dead	perfectly	supreme
deadly	perpendicularly	totally
exact	preferable	unique
horizontally	round	uniquely
immortally	secondly	universally

However, there may be times when the comparison of these words is justified. If we use these modifiers in a relative or approximate sense, they may be compared. But proceed with care. It is usually better, for example, to say *more nearly round or more nearly perfect* than *rounder* or *more perfect*.

43b Comparison with *other* or *else*

When we use the comparative in such an expression as *This thing is better than any other,* we imply that *this thing* is separate from the group or class to which it is being compared. In these expressions we must use a word such as *other* or *else* to separate the thing being compared from the rest of the group of which it is a part.

Not: Our house is cooler than any house on the block.
(The mistake here is not separating the item being compared (*house*) from the group to which it is being compared.)

But: Our house is cooler than any *other* house on the block.
(Our house is one of the houses on the block.)

Not: He has a better record than any salesman in our group.

But: He has a better record than any *other* salesman in the group.
(He himself is one of the salesmen in the group.)

43c Incomplete comparison — improper ellipsis

When you make a comparison between two items, be sure that both terms of the comparison are named. Violation of this rule places the burden on the listener or reader, who may or may not clearly understand which of two items you are comparing. Be sure the listener or reader knows exactly what you mean when you say —

There have been more successful prosecutions of tax fraud cases in the "X" district this year.

Do you mean *more than in any other district?* or *more than in any previous year?*

Whenever a comparison is not completed, the meaning of the sentence is obscured. This is one form of the incomplete comparison. Here are a few more.

(1) Incomplete comparison — with possessive:

Obscure: Joe's letter states the problem better than John.
(We cannot tell whether it is *John* or *John's letter* that is stating the problem.)
Improved: Joe's letter states the problem better than *John's.*

Ambiguous: John's proposed form is less complicated than management.
Improved: John's proposed form is less complicated than management's.
(Or: than the one proposed by management.)

(2) Incomplete comparison — with conjunction:

Obscure: This text is as good, if not better than that one.
(Because of the omission of the second *as* after *good,* this sentence reads — "as good *than.*")
Improved: This text is as good *as,* if not better than, that one.
or: This text is as good as that one, if not better.

Obscure: This book is shorter, but just as comprehensive as that one.
Improved: This book is shorter *than,* but just as comprehensive as, that one.
or: This book is shorter than that one, but just as comprehensive.

(3) Incomplete comparison — with verb:

Ambiguous: I enjoy this kind of work more than John.
(This could be interpreted — I enjoy this kind of work more than I enjoy *John.*)
Improved: I enjoy this kind of work more than John *does.*

Obscure: I have known him longer than John.
Could mean: I have known him longer than John *has.*
or: I have known him longer than *I have known* John.

44 Verbals and Verbal Phrases as Modifiers

Verbals, words derived from verbs, are sometimes used as modifiers, either singly or in phrases.

44a Infinitive

The infinitive, as a modifier, may serve either as an adjective or as an adverb.

As an adjective:

> On a plane trip, I always carry SOMETHING *to chew*.
> The LETTER *to be rewritten* is on my desk.

As an adverb:

> I am READY *to write* the letter now.
> I am UNABLE *to speak* on that subject.
> We WROTE this letter *to explain* our policy.

NOTE: Much has been written on whether it is good usage to split an infinitive – that is, whether to insert a modifying word between the *to* and the rest of the infinitive (*to carefully consider* instead of *to consider carefully*). The problem most often arises when a modified infinitive follows another verb construction.

Take, for example, the problem of inserting the adverb *completely* in this sentence, "He wished to forget the controversy with his staff."

Placed before the infinitive – "He wished *completely* TO FORGET the controversy with his staff" – *completely* becomes a squinting modifier; it could modify either the infinitive or the verb *wished*.

Placed after the infinitive – "He wished TO FORGET *completely* the controversy with his staff" – *completely* interferes with the rhythm of the sentence by coming between the verb and its object.

Placed at the end of the sentence – "He wished TO FORGET the controversy with his staff *completely*" – *completely* loses most of its force because it is so far removed from the infinitive it is modifying.

Now, let's split the infinitive – "He wished TO *completely* FORGET the controversy with his staff." Despite the split infinitive, this construction seems the smoothest and most desirable of the four.

As you can see from this illustration, it is unwise to make the flat statement that an infinitive must *never* be split. Most grammarians recommend that writers avoid splitting an infinitive whenever possible (even if recasting the sentence is necessary), but they endorse the split infinitive if avoiding it would result in an awkward or ambiguous sentence.

44b Infinitive phrase

An infinitive phrase (an infinitive plus the words modifying it or completing it) may also be used as a modifier.

> *To get the most out of this course,* YOU must study regularly.
> The REQUEST, *to get favorable attention,* must reach us by May 15.
> *To complete the report on time,* KENNEDY should start gathering data now.

44c Participle

The participle, in all three forms (present, past, and perfect) is an adjective.

Present participle: ends in *ing*, as *talking, building, writing*

Past participle: verb form usually ending in *ed*, sometimes in *t*, and sometimes showing a vowel change, as *talked, built, written*

Perfect participle: verb form consisting of *having* or *having been* plus the past participle, as *having talked, having built, having written, having been written*

> *Rising*, the DIRECTOR greeted his caller.
> (*Rising* is a present participle modifying *director*)

> The LETTER, *typed* and *signed*, was mailed today.
> (*Typed* and *signed* are past participles modifying *letter*)

The LETTER, *having been corrected*, was ready for signature.

(*Having been corrected* is a perfect participle modifying *letter*)

44d Participial phrase

A participial phrase (a participle combined with its object or modifying words) functions as an adjective.

Leaving her desk, the TYPIST opened the file drawer.
Covering her typewriter, SHE prepared to leave the office.

The DRAFT, *typed hurriedly*, was on his desk.
The LETTER, *mailed in error*, could not be recovered.

The SUPERVISOR, *having called the meeting for 2 o'clock*, was waiting in his office.
The MEETING, *having been called for 2 o'clock*, had to be postponed.

44e Gerund phrase

The gerund phrase (composed of a gerund plus its subject, complement, or modifier), like the gerund itself, serves as a noun. But when this phrase becomes the object of a preposition, the resulting prepositional-gerund phrase may serve as an *adjective* or as an *adverb*. It is this use of the gerund phrase with which we are concerned in this chapter.

After meeting with representatives of the employee group, HE announced his decision.
(Serves as adjective; phrase modifies *he*.)

He ENDED his report *by summarizing his conclusions*.
(Serves as adverb; phrase modifies *ended*.)

44f Dangling verbal phrases

The term *dangling* is quite descriptive of what happens when an infinitive, participial, or prepositional-gerund phrase cannot refer, both logically and grammatically, to a noun or pronoun serving as the subject of the main clause of a sentence.

Corrective action may be taken in either of two ways: (1) by changing the subject of the main clause to one which the phrase may refer to, or (2) by changing the phrase itself into a dependent clause, so that it has a subject of its own.

(1) Dangling: *To get the most out of this course*, careful STUDY is necessary.
(The phrase cannot logically modify *study*; so it dangles.)

Corrected: *To get the most out of this course*, YOU must study it carefully.

or: If you are to get the most out of this course, you must study it carefully.

(2) Dangling: *To apply for this job*, a FORM 57 must be completed.
(Dangles; a *form* can't apply.)

Corrected: *To apply for this job*, the APPLICANT must complete a Form 57.

or: When the applicant applies for the job, a Form 57 must be completed.

(3) Dangling: *Rushing to meet the deadline for the project*, many ERRORS were made.
(Dangles; it wasn't the *errors* that were rushing to meet the deadline.)

Corrected: *Rushing to meet the deadline for the project*, THEY made many errors.

or: Because they rushed to meet the deadline for the project, many errors were made.

(4) Dangling: *By summarizing the information from the questionnaires*, a clear PICTURE of the situation was presented.

Corrected: *By summarizing the information from the questionnaires*, WE were able to present a clear picture of the situation.

or: After we had summarized the information from the questionnaires, a clear picture of the situation was presented.

NOTE: An infinitive or a participial phrase that modifies the whole sentence, designating general action rather than action by a specific agent, may be correctly used without relation to the subject of the main clause.

Generally speaking, these plants grow better in sunlight.
To summarize, the plan should be ready to put into effect next fall.

44g Nominative absolute—the sentence modifier

The *nominative absolute,* or simply *absolute,* modifies the whole sentence rather than a specific element in it. Unlike the participial phrase which it resembles, *the absolute has its own subject.* It therefore is grammatically independent of the rest of the sentence and does not dangle when it does not refer to the subject of the main clause.

All THINGS *considered,* you have done a fine job.
   (*Things* is the subject of the absolute phrase.)
The GAME *being over,* we went home.
Clear WEATHER *having been forecast,* we completed our plans for the office picnic.
The SUPERVISOR *having left the office,* his secretary took the call.

45 Prepositional Phrase as a Modifier

The prepositional phrase—composed of the preposition, its object, and any modifiers of the object—may serve as an adjective or as an adverb.

As an adjective:

The letter was addressed to the OFFICE *of the Director.*
   (modifies *office*)
I hope we don't have another CONFERENCE *like the one we had yesterday.*
   (Phrase modifies *conference. Like* is the preposition; *one* is its object; and the clause *(that) we had yesterday* modifies *one.*)

As an adverb:

They HAVE GONE *to the conference.*
   (The phrase modifies the verb *have gone.*)

GIVE it *to the person who answers the door.*
   (The phrase modifies the verb *give.* (Within the phrase, *to* is the preposition; *person* is its object; the clause *who answers the door* modifies the object.)

45a Dangling prepositional phrase

A prepositional phrase *dangles* when it does not, both logically and grammatically, refer to the subject of the main clause.

Dangling: With much effort, the REPORT was completed on time.
Corrected: *With much effort,* WE completed the report on time.

46 Dependent Clauses as Modifiers

Dependent clauses may serve as adjectives or as adverbs. The words that introduce them play a dual role—connecting (or linking) the clause with the rest of the sentence and showing the relationship between the dependent clause and the rest of the sentence. (Chapter 7 on Connectives discusses this topic more fully.)

46a Dependent clauses as adjectives

Dependent clauses that serve as adjectives may be introduced by either relative pronouns (*that, which, who, whom, whatever, whichever, whoever, whomever*) or relative adverbs (*where, when, while*).

By relative pronouns—

The MEMORANDUM *that is on your desk* has been revised.
The MAN *who called for an appointment* is here.
Your LETTER of May 15, *which called our attention to the error,* was answered yesterday.

By relative adverbs—

This is the BUILDING *where our office is located.*
We caught him at a TIME *when he was not busy.*

An adjective clause may be restrictive or nonrestrictive. Restrictive clauses cannot be omitted without changing the meaning of the sentence. They restrict or limit the word preceding them, and by answering the question, "Which one?" they also serve an identifying function. Because they are an essential part of the sentence, they are not set off by commas.

Nonrestrictive clauses, on the other hand, are not essential to the meaning of the sentence. They may add interesting or helpful information, but they are not necessary as restrictive clauses are. To show that they contain ideas of secondary importance, nonrestrictive clauses are set off by commas.

> The girl *who is sitting at the front desk* is his secretary.
> (Restrictive clause; essential to meaning of the sentence, answers question, "Which one?")

> Miss Martin, *who is sitting at the front desk*, is his secretary.
> (Nonrestrictive clause. Adds another thought, but is not essential to the meaning of the sentence.)

46b Dependent clauses as adverbs

Dependent clauses that serve as adverbs are introduced by subordinating conjunctions. A few of these conjunctions are: *as, because, since, although, if, provided, after.* (See Chapter 7, Connectives, for a longer list.)

> *While he was reviewing the letter,* he NO-TICED several errors in sentence construction.
> *Before he signed the letter,* he INSERTED a qualifying statement.

46c Elliptical clauses

Parts of a dependent clause are sometimes omitted because the missing elements can be easily supplied. These incomplete clauses are known as *elliptical clauses.* An elliptical clause must be able to modify, both logically and grammatically, the subject of the main clause. If it does not, it dangles.

To correct a dangling elliptical clause we may either (1) change the subject of the main clause to one which the elliptical clause can logically modify or (2) supply the missing elements in the elliptical clause.

> Dangling: *Unless compiled by early June,* we cannot include the figures in this year's annual report.
> Corrected: *Unless compiled by early June,* the figures cannot be included in this year's annual report.
> or: Unless *the figures are* compiled by early June, we cannot include them in this year's annual report.

> Dangling: *While making his periodic tour of the offices,* a few changes in procedure were recommended.
> Corrected: *While making his periodic tour of the offices,* he recommended a few changes in procedure.
> or: While *he was* making his periodic tour of the offices, a few changes in procedure were recommended.

46d Relative pronouns introducing clauses

Be careful to select the correct relative pronoun to introduce the adjective clause. *Who* refers to *persons; which* refers to *things; what (that which)* refers to *things; that* usually refers to *things,* but is sometimes used to refer to *persons.* (See Note.)

> The SECRETARY *who typed this letter* has had extensive experience.
> The monthly STATEMENT, *which is due tomorrow,* will contain that information.
> The statistical REPORT *that you have been submitting weekly* will be required once a month from now on.

Which may introduce either restrictive or nonrestrictive clauses. *That* introduces restrictive clauses only.

> The CASE *that* (or *which*) *Capt. Jones is working on* is a particularly complicated one.
> (Restrictive clause; necessary to identify the case.)

> The Adams Manufacturing Company CASE, *which Capt. Jones is working on,* is a particularly complicated one.
> (Nonrestrictive clause; the case is already identified by name.)

> The REPORT *that* (or *which*) *is on my desk* is ready to be typed.
> (Restrictive clause)

The monthly statistical REPORT, *which is on my desk*, is ready to be typed.
(Nonrestrictive clause; not essential to meaning.)

NOTE: We may use *that* in place of *who* to refer to persons if we mean *a class or type of person*, rather than an individual.

Any secretary *that works in the general office of the company* is eligible to attend this program.
(Refers to a class or type of employee.)

The secretary *who sits at that desk* is Miss Jones.
(Refers to a specific individual.)

Whose may be used as the possessive of any of these relative pronouns — *who, which, that.*

The staff member *whose job was abolished* has been reassigned.
This is the book *whose approach has been the subject of so much discussion.*
(This use of *whose* to refer to inanimate objects is acceptable in informal speaking and writing; the phrase "of which" is preferred in formal writing.)

47 Placement of Modifiers

Modifiers should be placed as closely as possible to the words they modify. This is true, whether the modifier is a single word, a phrase, or a clause. In English, the only way the reader can tell which word is being modified is by the location of the modifier. It's simply a matter of geography.

Many ambiguous (and unintentionally humorous) sentences result from the misplacement of modifiers.

47a Modifier between subject and verb

Wherever possible, avoid placing the modifier between subject and verb and between verb and object.

Not: The accountant, *to explain the difference between gross income and net income,* used several illustrations.
But: *To explain the difference between gross income and net income,* the accountant used several illustrations.

or: The accountant used several illustrations *to explain the difference between gross income and net income.*

47b Single adjectives

A single adjective is usually placed immediately *before* the word it modifies.

The taxpayer and his wife filed a *joint* return.
Send the return to your *local* office.

Not: I would like a *cold* GLASS of water.
But: I would like a glass of *cold* WATER.

47c Multiple adjectives

To make sure his sentences read more smoothly, the writer may also place immediately after the word —

(1) A modifier consisting of two or more adjectives.
(The report — *long, tedious,* and *involved* — was finally completed.)

(2) A modifier consisting of one or more adverbs plus an adjective.
(The report — *carefully written* and *well documented* — was submitted to the committee.)

47d Single adverbs

Some adverbs — *only, almost, nearly, also, quite, merely, actually* — are frequent troublemakers. Be sure they are placed as closely as possible to the words they modify.

Example: The problem can *only* be defined by this committee.
Could mean: *Only* this committee can define the problem.
or: This committee can *only define* the problem, not solve it.

Do not use *hardly, only, scarcely, barely* — so-called subtractive adverbs — together with a negative construction. If you do, you will have a *double negative.*

Not: They *haven't only* a single blanket.
But: They *have only* a single blanket.

Not: He *hasn't scarcely* done anything worthwhile.
But: He *has scarcely* done anything worthwhile.

47e Phrases and clauses

Phrases and clauses, like single-word modifiers, should be placed as closely as possible to the words they modify, so there will be no danger of their attaching themselves to the wrong sentence element.

Not: We need someone to audit ACCOUNTS *with statistical experience.*

But: We need SOMEONE *with statistical experience* to audit accounts.

Not: Mr. Dough has resigned from the presidency of the Club after HAVING SERVED four years *to the regret of all the members.*

But: *To the regret of all the members,* Mr. Dough HAS RESIGNED from the presidency of the Club after having served four years.

47f Relative clauses

Relative clauses should also be placed immediately after the word they modify, since they attach themselves to the sentence element nearest them.

Not: The man has an APPOINTMENT *who is waiting in my office.*

But: The MAN *who is waiting in my office* has an appointment.

Not: This refers to your memorandum regarding the number of cases closed by agents in the "X" group which are over a year old.

But: This refers to your memorandum regarding the number of cases over a year old which have been closed by agents in the "X" group.

47g Squinting constructions

Avoid *squinting constructions* — that is, modifiers that are so placed that one cannot tell whether they are modifying the words immediately preceding them or those immediately following them.

Obscure: The lawyer AGREED *after the papers were signed* TO TAKE the case.

Could mean: The lawyer agreed TO TAKE the case *after the papers were signed.*

or: *After the papers were signed,* the lawyer AGREED to take the case.

Obscure: He AGREED *that morning* TO SIGN the offer in compromise.

Could mean: He agreed TO SIGN the offer in compromise *that morning.*

or: *That morning,* he AGREED to sign the offer in compromise.

47h Adverb clauses

An adverb clause may be placed either at the beginning of a sentence or, in its natural order, after the main clause. There are two reasons why we might choose to place the adverb clause first: (1) to put greater emphasis on the main clause; (2) to avoid piling up modifying clauses after the main clause.

(An introductory adverb clause — sometimes called an "inverted clause," since it is out of its natural order — should usually be followed by a comma.)

Natural order: This report must contain information from all the offices in the region *if it is to reflect a true picture of our activities.*

Inverted order: *If the report is to reflect a true picture of our activities,* it must contain information from all the offices in the region. (*more emphatic.*)

47i Long modifying phrases

A long or complex modifying phrase at the end of the sentence has an anticlimactic effect. We strengthen our writing when we place such phrases before the main clause.

Weak: We have asked each region to tell us the number of copies it will need *in order to insure adequate distribution of this report.*

Stronger: *In order to insure adequate distribution of this* report, we have asked each region to tell us the number of copies it will need.

TEST XIV. MODIFIERS

TIME: 26 Minutes

DIRECTIONS: In each of the following groups of sentences, select the one sentence that is grammatically INCORRECT. Mark the answer sheet with the letter of that incorrect sentence.

Explanations of the key points behind these questions appear with the answers at the end of this test. The explanatory answers provide the kind of background that will enable you to answer test questions with facility and confidence.

1

(A) At the beginning of any campaign, there is a period when people are not really interested.
(B) We selected the simplest of the two schedules and proceeded with our plans.
(C) The name of Captain John Smith is familiar to all students of American history.
(D) If he were really interested in becoming a writer, he would try to write something every day.

2

(A) We expect help in providing adequate facilities and a well-stocked library from everyone.
(B) He spoke of history as the link between the past and the present.
(C) The hoboes testified that they had known the man well.
(D) The oldest sister is the prettiest of all.

3

(A) Instinctively afraid of her mother, she hesitated before going to the door.
(B) Every man, every woman, and every child was involved in the precautionary lifeboat drill.
(C) The soldiers were chagrined at having to give up positions in obedience to orders which the enemy couldn't possibly seize.
(D) Favored by a warm climate, Florida is a popular winter resort.

4

(A) The weather this month is like Alaska.
(B) The tackler lunged desperately after the runner's heels and barely got his man.
(C) The beggar could not stand the taunts of the passers-by.
(D) In town and hamlet, in field and prairie, on ridge and mountain, the flowers were in bloom.

5

(A) If you take too much time during the mid-morning break, you place an extra burden on the secretaries who remain in the office.
(B) Please edit and proofread all notices before duplicating them.
(C) I do not anticipate any difficulty in developing the touch needed for operation of the electric typewriter.
(D) In comparing the work done by the two secretaries, I must admit that Miss Smith is the fastest typist.

6

(A) At the end of this lake stands a reminder of his dreams, a deserted mansion.
(B) The entire matter can be settled between her and me.
(C) The climatic conditions in the Aleutian Islands were more depressing, in my opinion, than those in any other part of the world.
(D) Pupils today, some people say, don't scarcely know half of what their parents knew at the same age.

7

(A) Which of the two machines would be the most practical?
(B) All of us are entitled to a reply if we are to determine whether you should remain as a member of the club.
(C) Everyone who was listening got to his feet and applauded.
(D) There was no indication from his actions that he knew he was wrong.

8

(A) Her mien revealed her abhorrence of his actions.
(B) To tie the package, she used a great deal of rope so it would not come apart.
(C) After he had lived among them, he found much to admire in their way of life.
(D) He waited patiently for the fish to snatch at the bait.

9

(A) At first glance, the old man believed him to be me.
(B) His failure to complete his work in college last term might have been due to his child's illness.
(C) The scenery in Banff is somewhat like Switzerland, although Banff is much farther north.
(D) Whatever your decision may be will be quite satisfactory, I am sure.

10

(A) Jack is one of those boys who consistently rate high on standard achievement tests.
(B) Using pseudonyms, the two editors have almost written every article in the magazine.
(C) When the boys and girls went to Montauk Point, they took a picnic lunch.
(D) Intramural athletic competitions drew large crowds from every class in the school.

11

(A) The teacher spoke clearly and emphatically.
(B) He bought a red and green tie.
(C) She is the tallest of the two girls.
(D) We watched the plane soar high in the sky.

12

(A) The student demonstrations at Berkeley, to nobody's surprise, were not much different from those of any other large college.
(B) The heroine bore the unlikely name of Letitia Delacroix.
(C) Paddling doggedly against the current, we managed at length to reach the shore.
(D) According to Miss Dew, the electronic clothes will be absolutely safe; the lamps give off no perceptible heat.

13

(A) Alex is not so tall as his brother.
(B) The reason why I failed was that I had not studied my lesson.
(C) Their radio cost more than ours, but ours is equally good.
(D) The hostess only wanted five couples to come for a week.

14

(A) The child whom I supposed to be the leader saw me, a misfortune that I had not anticipated.
(B) Although no dangerous chemicals had been left lying around, an explosion occurred and the building was destroyed.
(C) How can you function with the committee when you have no belief in nor appreciation of the goals they have set up?
(D) Did you hear him say, "The end is near"?

15

(A) You are sure to enjoy the performance, if only for the brilliant settings executed by a new designer.
(B) The language in Faulkner is somewhat like Proust, although Faulkner is much more inclined to sesquipedalianism.
(C) He said he thought he would buy two pairs of shoes and save one pair for special occasions.
(D) By tomorrow the book will have lain on the shelf, unread for two centuries.

16

(A) Watching her thus, I could not but help reflect how greatly she had changed in my absence.
(B) Uninhibited by legal requirements to accept all applicants, colleges have gotten highly selective.
(C) He felt that his college's criterions for admission were vague and unfair.
(D) The award should go to the pupil whom we think the parents intended it for.

17

(A) Today, fewer pedestrians are guilty of jaywalking.
(B) You look well today, after this illness.
(C) The terrain of New Mexico is quite like Arizona.
(D) The amount of money in American banks is increasing.

18

(A) Investigation has shown that, as a rule, the man with a large number of words at his command is the one who becomes a leader and directs his fellows.
(B) A dictionary is reliable only to the extent that it is based on a scientific examination of usage.
(C) He ran swiftly, the dog in front of him, and plunged into the forest.
(D) We can't assist but one of you at a time, so try to be patient.

19

(A) Ninety men were assigned to guarantee the success of the entire exercise.
(B) Understanding how sensitive he is to criticism, all mention of his poor performance was avoided.
(C) For some time, the river has been frozen solid.
(D) We need further information before we can accede to your request.

20

(A) Although the salesman was very persuasive, I refused to let him see the boss while the latter was in conference.
(B) Don't you think that it would be worth your while to improve the speed and accuracy of your typing?
(C) If the manager has left for the day, be sure to have the administrative assistant check the form.
(D) We ordered the book before the special circular arrived describing the procedure to be followed.

21

(A) Sailing along New England's craggy coastline, you will relive a bygone era of far-roving whalers and graceful clipper ships.
(B) The march of history is reenacted in folk festivals, outdoor pageants, and fiestas — local in theme, but national in import.
(C) Visiting the scenes of the past, our interest in American history is renewed and enlivened.
(D) What remained were a few fragments.

22

(A) Because all members of the office staff pitched in and helped, the huge task was completed in an extraordinarily short period of time.
(B) "If it cannot be completed by three o'clock, I am willing to stay overtime," she said.
(C) Your typing has improved greatly both in accuracy and in speed.
(D) Turning the page, the buyer's eye was attracted to the advertisement for a time-stamping device.

23

(A) The proverb, so short yet so meaningful, became the slogan of the marchers.
(B) "What is the value of across-the-board increases?" asked the fireman.
(C) The young performer picked up his mandolin and strummed a tune.
(D) The next chapter treated the causes of the American Revolution.

24

(A) Thoreau maintained that the average man lives a life of quiet desperation.
(B) Journalese has unquestionably influenced Robertson's style — for the worse, alas!
(C) I wish that Jim might be here to listen to this stirring oration.
(D) Although the altitude of Mexico City is much higher, I found it less taxing than Acapulco.

25

(A) The work had been done long before the date specified in the original agreement.
(B) In some books printed years ago, the s's look like f's.
(C) "The Woodlanders" is seldom read today.
(D) To make sure your speech is audible, practice in an auditorium is helpful.

26

(A) Acting on His Majesty's orders, the Prime Minister's offices were invaded last night and ransacked.
(B) The answer, probably, is — nothing.
(C) Since the agenda has been approved by the executive committee, I cannot approve your request to add a new item.
(D) Indeed, we now expect that science will, on demand, routinely produce miracle drugs.

27

(A) The lawyers tried to settle the case out of court.
(B) "Get out of my life!" she cried.
(C) Walking down the road, the lake comes into view.
(D) The loan which I received from the bank helped me to keep the business going.

28

(A) None are so deaf as those that will not hear.
(B) If I had lent him that money, he would have gone free.
(C) England's small expanse necessitates many people's living close together.
(D) The hotel looked less dreary than the night before.

29

(A) Playing tennis, reading books, and hiking provide healthful recreation.
(B) People, who lightly accuse others, cause great harm.
(C) "Perhaps," he said, "you will believe me now."
(D) Mine is the one with the painted cover.

30

(A) Industry, as well as genius, was essential to the development of the automotive business.
(B) Go at once if you can; if not, as soon as possible.
(C) Why consult Harold, who knows nothing about the matter?
(D) We the people of the United States, do ordain and establish this Constitution.

31

(A) All have applied, Daniel and she included.
(B) The jurors agreed that the accident had been clearly due to negligence and that a settlement should be made.
(C) At 10:15 a.m. promptly, the professor stalked majestically into the room, a book under his left arm.
(D) Please do not present your plan until thoroughly worked out in advance.

32

(A) I cannot encourage you any.
(B) Don't blame me for that statement.
(C) The ball rolled under the stairs.
(D) It looks like rain.

33

(A) He asked whether he might write to his friends.
(B) There are many problems which must be solved before we can be assured of world peace.
(C) Each person with whom I talked expressed his opinion freely.
(D) Holding on to my saddle with all my strength, the horse galloped down the road at a terrifying pace.

(34)

(A) Atomic energy must be controlled internationally lest war annihilate our entire civilization.
(B) When walking along the bank of the river, the waterfall is clearly visible.
(C) Of all the candidates I've heard in the campaign, Mr. Wallace appears to be the least qualified.
(D) He had no choice but to enter the army.

(35)

(A) Ella's temperament will stand her in good stead not only as an actress but also as a musician.
(B) Neither of us is eager to do the research.
(C) Driving through the rain and fog, the Seminole reservation looked deserted.
(D) Whatever they may think to the contrary, I do plan to attend the banquet on Veterans' Day.

CONSOLIDATE YOUR KEY ANSWERS HERE

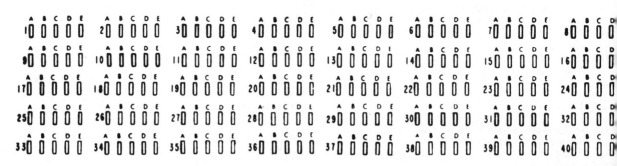

Correct Answers For The Foregoing Questions

(Check your answers with these that we provide. You should find considerable correspondence between them. If not, you'd better go back and find out why. On the next page we have provided concise clarifications of basic points behind the key answers. Please go over them carefully because they may be quite useful in helping you pick up extra points on the exam.)

1. B	6. D	11. C	16. A	21. C	26. A	31. D
2. A	7. A	12. A	17. C	22. D	27. C	32. A
3. C	8. B	13. D	18. D	23. C	28. D	33. D
4. A	9. C	14. A	19. B	24. D	29. B	34. B
5. D	10. B	15. B	20. D	25. D	30. B	35. C

TEST XIV. MODIFIERS

EXPLANATORY ANSWERS CLARIFYING CARDINAL POINTS

The core of the Question and Answer Method ... getting help when and where you need it. Even if you were able to write correct key answers for the preceding questions, the following explanations illuminate fundamental facts, ideas, and principles which just might crop up in the form of questions on future tests.

Bold-face references in the following answers direct you to paragraphs in the Arco Grammar Text, where fuller explanations are provided.

ANSWER 1.

B We selected the **simpler** of the two schedules and proceeded with our plans. REASON: The comparative form (**simpler**) refers to a choice between two. **(42a)**

ANSWER 2.

A We expect help **from everyone** providing adequate facilities and a well-stocked library. REASON: **from everyone** is misplaced in the original sentence. **(47)**

ANSWER 3.

C In their obedience to orders, the soldiers were chagrined at having to give up positions **which the enemy couldn't possibly seize**. REASON: The misplaced modifier (**which the enemy ... seize**) should be closer to the noun (**positions**) which it modifies. **(47)**

ANSWER 4.

A The weather this month is like **that** of Alaska. REASON: **that of** refers to **weather**. **(43c)**

ANSWER 5.

D In comparing the work done by the two secretaries, I must admit that Miss Smith is the **faster** typist. REASON: The comparative degree (**faster**) is used for two. The superlative degree (**fastest**) is used for three or more. **(42a)**

ANSWER 6.

D Pupils today, some people say, scarcely know half of what their parents knew at the same age. REASON: **Don't** is to be deleted. **(47d)**

ANSWER 7.

A Which of the two machines would be the **more** practical? REASON: The comparative degree (**two** items) is **more practical** — the superlative degree (**three or more** items) is **most practical**. **(42a)**

ANSWER 8.

B She used a great deal of rope **to tie the package** so it would not come apart. REASON: **to tie the package** should be placed so that the relative pronoun **it** is close to its antecedent (**package**). **(47e)**

ANSWER 9.

C The scenery in Banff is somewhat like **that of** Switzerland, although Banff is much farther north. REASON: The pronoun **that** is the object of the preposition **like**. The antecedent of **that** is **scenery**. **(43c)**

ANSWER 10.

B Using pseudonyms, the two editors have written almost every article in the magazine. REASON: **almost** is a misplaced modifier in the original sentence. **(47)**

ANSWER 11.

C She is the **taller** of the two girls. REASON: The comparative degree (**taller**) is used for two. The superlative degree (**tallest**) is used for three or more. **(42a)**

ANSWER 12.

A The student demonstrations at Berkeley were, to nobody's surprise, not much different from **those of** any other large college. REASON: The position of the "squinting" modifier (**to nobody's surprise**) must be changed for the sake of clarity. **(47g)**

ANSWER 13.

D   The hostess wanted only five couples to come for a week. REASON: The modifier **only** is misplaced in the original sentence.   **(47)**

ANSWER 14.

A   The fact that the child whom I supposed to be the leader saw me was a misfortune that I had not anticipated. REASON: The original sentence is unclear because the appositive (**a misfortune . . . not anticipated**) has no specific reference.   **(47)**

ANSWER 15.

B   The language in Faulkner is somewhat like **that of** Proust, although Faulkner is much more inclined to sesquipedalianism. REASON: The reference to **language** must be expressed by **that of**.   **(43c)**

ANSWER 16.

A   Watching her thus, I could not **help but** reflect how greatly she had changed in my absence. REASON: **help but reflect** is the correct expression.   **(47)**

ANSWER 17.

C   The terrain of New Mexico is quite like that of Arizona. REASON: There is no justification for omitting **that of** in the original sentence.   **(43c)**

ANSWER 18.

D   We can assist **but one** of you at a time, so try to be patient. REASON: Avoid the double negative (**can't** and **but**).   **(47d)**

ANSWER 19.

B   Understanding how sensitive he is to criticism, we feel that all mention of his poor performance should be avoided. REASON: The participle (**understanding**) of the original sentence must modify a noun (or pronoun — **we** in this case).   **(44f)**

ANSWER 20.

D   **Before the special circular arrived**, we ordered the book describing the procedure to be followed. REASON: The adverbial clause (**before . . . arrived**) was misplaced in the original sentence.   **(47)**

ANSWER 21.

C   Visiting the scenes of the past, we renewed and enlivened our interest in American history. REASON: **Visiting** is a participle dependent on a personal subject (**we**).   **(44f)**

ANSWER 22.

D   Turning the page, the buyer was attracted to the advertisement for a time-stamping device. REASON: The participle **turning** modifies the subject **buyer**. In the original sentence the **eye** was turning the page — of course, it is the **buyer** who should be turning the page.   **(44f)**

ANSWER 23.

C   The young performer picked up his mandolin **to strum** a tune. REASON: Purpose is expressed by using the infinitive.   **(44a)**

ANSWER 24.

D   Although the altitude of Mexico City is much higher, I found it less taxing than **that of** Acapulco. REASON: Reference to the **altitude** is clarified with **that of**.   **(43c)**

ANSWER 25.

D   To make sure your speech is audible, you are advised to practice in an auditorium. REASON: In the original sentence, the infinitive construction is dangling.   **(44f)**

ANSWER 26.

A   Acting on His Majesty's orders, they invaded and ransacked the Prime Minister's offices last night. REASON: The participle **acting** must refer to a personal subject (**they**).   **(44f)**

ANSWER 27.

C   Walking down the road, we see the lake comes into view. REASON: The participle (**walking**), being an adjective, must modify a noun or pronoun (**we**).   **(44f)**

ANSWER 28.

D   The hotel looked less dreary than **it looked** the night before. REASON: The ellipsis (omission) in the original sentence is not justified.   **(43c)**

ANSWER 29

B   People who lightly accuse others cause great harm. REASON: Commas are not used with a restrictive clause. A restrictive clause is one that is essential to the sentence. **(46a, 62)**

ANSWER 30.

B   Go at once if you can; if you cannot, go as soon as possible. REASON: Omitting the words **go** and **you can(not)** would be improper ellipsis. **(46c)**

ANSWER 31.

D   Please do not present your plan until **it is** thoroughly worked out in advance. REASON: There should be no ellipsis of the subject and complete verb in this case. **(46c)**

ANSWER 32.

A   I cannot encourage you **in any way.** REASON: The indefinite pronoun (**any**) cannot modify the verb (**cannot encourage**). The prepositional phrase (**in any way**) is used adverbially to modify the verb. **(45)**

ANSWER 33.

D   While I was holding on to my saddle with all my strength, the horse galloped down the road at a terrifying pace. REASON: In the original sentence, **the horse is holding on to the saddle.** **(44f)**

ANSWER 34.

B   When we walk along the bank of the river, the waterfall is clearly visible. REASON: In the original sentence, the **waterfall** is doing the walking. **(44f)**

ANSWER 35.

C   Driving through the rain and fog, **we noticed that** the Seminole reservation looked deserted. REASON: The participle (**Driving**) must refer to the personal subject (**we**). **(44f)**

VII. CONNECTIVES

Four kinds of words can serve as connectives—prepositions, conjunctions, relative pronouns, and relative adverbs. Each not only connects two sentence elements but also shows the relationship between them.

48 Prepositions

A preposition *connects* the word, phrase, or clause that follows it (its object) with some other element in the sentence *and shows the relationship* between them.

There are three kinds of prepositions:

48a Simple prepositions

> *at, but, by, down, for, from, in, like, of, off, on, out, over, per, through, till, to, up, via, with . . .*

48b Compound prepositions

> *about, above, across, after, against, along, among, around, before, behind, below, beneath, beside, besides, between, beyond, despite, except, inside, into, outside, toward(s), under, until, upon, within, without . . .*

48c Phrasal prepositions (two or more words that function as a single preposition)

> | | |
> |---|---|
> | *according to* | *contrary to* |
> | *because of* | *inasmuch as* |
> | *as well as* | |

49 Choice of Preposition

Choosing the preposition is usually either no problem at all or a problem that seems to defy a reasonable solution.

When the choice is simple, it is because prepositions have become such a basic part of our vocabularies that we choose them almost without being aware of making a choice. They seem to slip into our sentences of their own volition. In many constructions, one preposition just *seems right*; another *wrong*.

When the choice is difficult, it is because we lack this "sensing" of the essential rightness or wrongness of the preposition. Being unable to select the appropriate preposition, we look for a rule of grammar to help us make a choice (or to help us defend or explain the choice we have made). Then we find that there *is* no governing rule of grammar; *idiomatic usage* is the only key.

49a Idioms and idiomatic usage

Idiom is often quite different from grammar and often conflicts with it. When we say that something is *idiomatic usage*, we mean that usage has established it as correct and acceptable, whether or not it conflicts with grammar.

It is idiom that requires us to say—

able *to* work	but	capable of working
the way *to* cut	but	the way *of* cutting (method)
aim *at* getting	but	try to get

Grammar doesn't help us to make this choice. For, as far as grammar is concerned, in each of the three illustrations, *to, of, for,* and *at* are equally acceptable. But idiom says, "It doesn't *make sense* to say *aim to getting;* only *aim at getting* can get the idea across."

used. However, when we cannot make this instinctive choice, we must make it our business to find out what the idiomatic usage is.

Prepositional idioms outnumber most other idioms. For example, one reference book — the Standard Handbook of Prepositions, Conjunctions, Relative Pronouns and Relative Adverbs (Funk & Wagnalls, New York) — lists *more than 2,000 prepositional idioms.*

50 Prepositional Idioms

Fortunately, if English is our native language, most of these idiomatic expressions are so ingrained that we use them instinctively and cringe when we hear them mis-

Following is a list of commonly used (and misused) prepositional idioms:

PREPOSITIONAL IDIOMS

accede **to**	We cannot *accede to* the request for an extension of time.
accessory **of**	He was an accessory of the criminal.
accessory **to**	He was an *accessory to* the act.
accommodate **to**	He finds it hard to *accommodate* himself *to* new situations. (changed conditions)
accommodate **with**	We *accommodated* him *with* a loan of five dollars.
accompany **by**	He was *accompanied by* a counsel. (a person)
accompany **with**	The letter was *accompanied with* an affidavit. (a thing)
accountable **for**	The supervisor is *accountable for* my actions.
accountable **to**	I am *accountable to* the supervisor for my actions.
accused **by**	He was *accused by* the plaintiff of having filed a false statement.
accused **of**	He was *accused of* perjury.
acquiesce **in**	The Commissioner has *acquiesced in* the decision.
acquit **of**	He was *acquitted of* the crime.
acquit **with**	He acquitted himself *with* honor.
adapted **for**	The work simplification guide was *adapted for* our use.
adapted **from**	The movie was *adapted from* the book.
adapted **to**	He finds it difficult to *adapt to* new procedures.
adequate **for**	His salary was not *adequate for* his needs.
adequate **to**	His ability was *adequate to* the job.
averse **to**	He was not *averse to* hard work.
advise **of**	The employees were *advised of* the new regulations.

affix **to**	A stamp was *affixed to* the container.
agree **in**	We *agree in* principle with those who favor the plan.
agree **on**	They cannot *agree on* the delegation order.
agree **to**	They state that they *agree to* the compromise.
agree **with**	The defendant and his counsel *agree with* us that ....
amenable **to**	He was *amenable to* our argument.
analogous **to**	This situation is *analogous to* the one we faced last year.
annoy **by**	The clerk was *annoyed by* the frequent interruptions.
annoy **with**	The supervisor showed that he was *annoyed with* the recalcitrant employee.
apparent **in**	His attitude is *apparent in* his actions.
apparent **to**	The trouble is *apparent to* everyone in the office.
append **to**	A rider was *appended to* the bill.
appreciation **for**	The student had a real *appreciation for* the arts.
appreciation **of**	He expressed *appreciation of* their hard work.
appreciative **of**	We are *appreciative of* their efforts.
authority **in**	Dr. X is an *authority in* his field.
authority **on**	Mr. X is an *authority on* linear programming.
authority **to**	He has *authority to* sign this document.
basis **for**	They had a sound *basis for* agreement.
basis **in**	His argument has no *basis in* fact.
commensurate **with**	His salary was *commensurate with* his abilities.
comply **with**	We must *comply with* the request.
concur **in**	We *concur in* the decision of the survey committee.
concur **with**	One member did not *concur with* the others.
conform **to**	All employees must *conform to* the regulations.
consist **in**	His value *consists in* his ability to work with others.
consist **of**	The handbook *consists of* principles of supervision.
consistent **in**	We should be *consistent in* applying the law.
consistent **with**	His actions are not *consistent with* his statements.
correspond **to**	His description of the incident *corresponds to* what we believe to be the case.
correspond **with**	We have been *corresponding with* his counsel.
demand **from**	What did he *demand from* them in payment?
demand **of**	They had *demanded* an accounting *of* the company funds.

differ **from**	My estimate of the amount due *differs from* his.
differ **in**	We *differ in* our opinions on the matter.
differ **on**	They *differ on* the amount to be assessed.
differ **with**	I *differ with* him about the evaluation method to be used.
discrepancy **between**	There is a *discrepancy between* the two accounts.
discrepancy **in**	There is a *discrepancy in* his account.
displeased **at**	The supervisor was *displeased at* the employee's conduct.
displeased **with**	The supervisor was *displeased with* the employee.
eligible **for**	He is *eligible for* the job.
eligible **to**	Everyone is *eligible to* apply for the job.
equivalent **in**	His office and mine are *equivalent in* size.
equivalent **of**	This is the *equivalent of* a full payment.
equivalent **to**	Each payment is *equivalent to* a week's salary.
excepted **from**	He was *excepted from* further responsibility.
excluded **from**	This item may be *excluded from* gross income.
exempt **from**	This type of income is *exempt from* tax.
expect **from**	What return do you *expect from* your investment?
expect **of**	What does Bacon *expect of* his assistant?
familiar **to**	The name is *familiar to* me.
familiar **with**	He is quite *familiar with* the proceedings.
find **for**	The jury *found for* the defendant.
furnish **to**	Adequate supplies were *furnished to* them.
furnish **with**	Please *furnish* us *with* background information on this matter.
habit **of**	He made a *habit of* waiting until the report was due before he began writing it.
identical **with**	That case is *identical with* the one I am working on.
identify **by**	The witness was *identified by* the tattoo on his arm.
identify **with**	He was *identified with* the opposing members.
ignorant **of**	He was *ignorant of* his rights.
improvement **in**	The *improvement in* his writing was soon noted.
improvement **on**	His second draft was an *improvement on* the first.
inconsistent **in**	He was *inconsistent in* his review.
inconsistent **with**	This is *inconsistent with* established policy.
infer **from**	We *infer from* his statement that he plans to discuss the adjustment further.
influence **for**	His *influence* was always *for* harmony.
influence **by**	We were all *influenced by* the Director's statements.

influence **on** (upon)	The rumor of an organizational change had an *influence on (upon)* production.
influence **over**	The supervisor had a strong *influence over* his staff.
influence **with**	He referred frequently to his *influence with* those in authority.
inform **of**	Supervisors should keep their subordinates *informed of* any changes in procedure.
inherent **in**	A capacity for growth is *inherent in* all people.
insert **in**	This phrase should be *inserted in* the draft.
intercede **for**	My lawyer *interceded for* me.
intercede **with**	He *interceded with* the board in my behalf.
invest **in**	The owner said he had *invested* the money *in* stocks.
invest **with**	He was *invested with* full power to act.
irrelevant **to**	This statement is *irrelevant to* the matter under discussion.
irrespective **of**	They decided to appoint him *irrespective of* the criticism that might result.
liable **for**	He is *liable for* damages.
liable **to**	The employee is *liable to* his employer.
liberal **in**	He was very *liberal in* his views.
liberal **with**	He was *liberal with* praise.
necessity **for**	There is no *necessity for* a reduction in force.
necessity **of**	We are faced with the *necessity of* reducing travel expenses.
oblivious **of** (to)	He was *oblivious of* the effect that his remote manner had on his employees.
precedent **for**	Is there a *precedent for* this action?
precedent **in**	His decision established a *precedent in* law.
recompense **for**	He was fully *recompensed for* the time he spent on the work.
reconcile **to**	We have become *reconciled to* our fate.
reconcile **with**	Our views cannot be *reconciled with* his.
similarity **in**	I agree that there is much *similarity in* their appearance.
similarity **of**	The *similarity of* the cases caused confusion.
similarity **to**	This time-saving device shows a *similarity to* one I have.
talk **of**	The traveler *talked* long *of* his experiences.
talk **to**	The lecturer *talked to* a large audience.
talk **with**	The lawyer *talked with* his client.
transfer **from**	He has been *transferred from* his former position.
transfer **to**	They *transferred* him *to* another department.
unequal **in**	The contestants were *unequal in* strength.
unequal **to**	She was *unequal to* the demands placed on her.
use **for**	He had no *use for* the extra table.
use **of**	She made good *use of* her opportunity.
wait **at**	I will *wait at* the back of the conference room until I can talk with the conference leader.
wait **for**	He seemed to be *waiting for* someone.
wait **on** (upon)	This matter must *wait on (upon)* my leisure.

51 Placement of Preposition

The strong conviction that a sentence should not end with a preposition was, for a long time, shared by many people; but there is almost universal agreement now that one need no longer be bound by this restriction.

A studied effort to avoid ending a sentence with a preposition often results in a sentence that is unnatural, awkward, and sometimes confusing.

Consider these illustrations, which are much more natural than they would be if they were reconstructed to avoid the terminal preposition:

> What did you do that *for*?
> Here is the bill he sent *in*.
> We had many problems to talk *about*.
> Tell me what it is you object *to*.

52 Superfluous Prepositions

In talking, more than in writing, we tend to use double prepositions when only one is needed. But we should take care lest this informal colloquial use creep into our writing.

> Not: We will divide *up* the work.
> But: We will divide the work.

> Not: He is standing near *to* the door.
> But: He is standing near the door.

> Not: When are you going to start *in* to write that letter?
> But: When are you going to start to write that letter?

53 Faulty Omission of Prepositions

53a Especially in formal writing, repeat the preposition before the second of two connected elements.

> Not: He seemed interested in us and our problems.
> But: He seemed interested in us and *in* our problems.

> Not: He was able to complete the project by planning carefully and working diligently.

> But: He was able to complete the project by planning carefully and *by* working diligently.

53b In the so-called *split* (or *suspended*) construction, in which two words are completed by different prepositions, be especially careful to use both prepositions.

> Not: He has an interest and an aptitude *for* his work.
> But: He has an interest *in* and an aptitude *for* his work.
> > (Commas may be used in this construction: He has an interest in, and an aptitude for, his work.)

> Not: He was puzzled and concerned *about* her behavior.
> But: He was puzzled *by* and concerned *about* her behavior.

54 Prepositional Phrase

The prepositional phrase is the preposition plus its object plus any modifiers of the object. The object of the preposition may be a word, a phrase, or a clause; and the modifiers of the object may likewise be words, phrases, or clauses. (In Chapter 2 on Case we discussed the fact that a word used as the object of the preposition must be in the objective case.)

54a Function of the prepositional phrase

The prepositional phrase functions most often as an adjective or an adverb; occasionally it may also serve as a noun. In Chapter 6 on Modifiers we discussed the modifying function of the prepositional phrase.

55 Conjunctions, Relative Pronouns, and Relative Adverbs

These three types of connectives perform two distinctly different functions: some of them connect coordinate sentence elements (elements of equal grammatical rank); others both introduce a subordinate element and connect it with the rest of the sentence.

Three types of conjunctions connect coordinate elements:

Coordinate conjunctions — *and, but, or, for, so, yet, nor*

Correlative conjunctions (used in pairs) — *neither...nor, either...or, both...and, if...then, since...therefore, whether...or, not only...but also*

Conjunctive adverbs — *therefore, otherwise, hence, nevertheless, however, besides, accordingly.*

The function of the subordinating clause governs the type of connective to be used in introducing it:

Adverb clauses are introduced by SUBORDINATING CONJUNCTIONS — *as, since, because, if, provided, after, before, where*

Noun clauses are introduced by RELATIVE PRONOUNS — *that, whichever, whatever, whoever*

Adjective clauses are introduced by either RELATIVE ADVERBS (*where, when, while*) or RELATIVE PRONOUNS (*who, whom, which, that*)

56 Connecting Elements of Equal Rank (Coordinate Elements)

56a Use parallelism to show coordination

Sentence elements are said to be *coordinate* (or *parallel*) when they are of equal rank (of equal importance) both grammatically and logically.

Determining equal *grammatical* importance is relatively simple: words = words; phrases = phrases; subordinate clauses = subordinate clauses; principal clauses = principal clauses.

Elements not grammatically equal (not parallel):

His main virtues are *that he is sincere* and his *generosity.*
(a clause linked to a word)

Improved:

His main virtues are *that he is sincere* and *that he is generous.*
(two noun clauses, now parallel; noun clause = noun clause)

His main virtues are his *sincerity* and his *generosity.*
(two words)

56b Use coordinate conjunctions to show coordination (parallelism)

The coordinate conjunctions, including *and, but, or, nor, for, yet, moreover,* are the connectives most frequently used to show that two ideas are equal (are parallel). Notice in the following illustrations that the two ideas connected are parallel.

The *Director* AND the *Assistant Director* will attend.
(connecting a word with a word)

He is a man *of great capability* BUT *of little experience.*
(connecting a phrase with a phrase)

He said *that he had filed a claim for a refund* BUT *that he had not heard anything further from this office.*
(connecting a subordinate clause with a subordinate clause)

I was eager to attend the seminar; MOREOVER, *I knew that the exchange of ideas would be helpful.*
(connecting an independent clause with an independent clause)

NOTE: See section 58, Alphabetical List of Troublesome Conjunctions, for a discussion of common problems in the use of these coordinate conjunctions — such problems as the use of too many *and's,* the confusion of *and* with *but,* and the popular fallacy that a conjunction cannot be used to begin a sentence.

56c Use correlative conjunctions to show coordination (parallelism)

The correlative conjunctions — *either...or, neither...nor, not only...but also, both...and, if...then, since...therefore* — work in pairs to show that words and ideas are parallel (equal in importance).

EITHER the *Director* OR the *Assistant Director* must attend.

(connecting a word with a word)

The report is designed NOT ONLY *to present a list of the problems facing us* BUT ALSO *to recommend possible solutions to these problems.*

(connecting a phrase with a phrase)

The significant point in the use of pairs of correlatives is that each member of the pair must be followed by the same part of speech (same grammatical construction). That is, if NOT ONLY is followed by a verb, then BUT ALSO must be followed by a verb; if EITHER is followed by a phrase, OR must likewise be followed by a phrase.

> Not: EITHER *cases of this type* are much fewer in number OR *are not attended* by the same administrative difficulties.
> (*Either* is followed by a noun, *cases; or* is followed by a verb phrase.)
> But: Cases of this type EITHER *are much fewer* in number OR *are not attended* by the same administrative difficulties.

> Not: His reply NOT ONLY *was prompt* BUT ALSO *complete.*
> But: His reply was NOT ONLY *prompt* BUT ALSO *complete.*

> Not: One of the reporters who arrived shortly after the raids had started complimented the police NOT ONLY *on the systematic method in which the raids were conducted* BUT ALSO *with respect to their conduct while on the premises.*
> But: One of the reporters who arrived shortly after the raids had started complimented the police NOT ONLY *on the systematic method* in which the raids were conducted BUT ALSO *on their conduct* while on the premises.

When this plan is not followed, the result is "faulty parallelism." To turn faulty parallelism into effective parallelism, sometimes we need add only a word or two.

> Not: The project was a disappointment NOT ONLY *to me* BUT ALSO *my assistant.*
> (*Not only* is followed by the prepositional phrase *to me; but also* is followed by a noun.)
> But: The project was a disappointment NOT ONLY *to me* BUT ALSO *to my assistant.*

(Note that each of the correlative conjunctions is followed by a prepositional phrase.)

> Not: His assignment was BOTH *to conduct* the course AND *the evaluation* of it.
> But: His assignment was BOTH *to conduct* the course AND *to evaluate* it.

NOTE: The correlative *as . . . as* is used affirmatively while the correlative *so . . . as* is used negatively.

> This melon is *as* sweet *as* that one.
> This melon is not *so* sweet *as* that one.

56d Use conjunctive adverbs to show coordination

The conjunctive adverbs — *therefore, however, consequently, accordingly, furthermore, besides, moreover, neverthelsss, still* — serve the double purpose of connecting independent clauses and of showing relationship between the clauses. Although the clause introduced by a conjunctive adverb is *grammatically independent,* it is *logically dependent* on the preceding clause for its complete meaning.

The conjunctive adverb has more modifying force than the coordinate conjunction, but less connecting force. Therefore, the clauses joined by a conjunctive adverb are not so closely related as are those joined by a coordinate conjunction. Clauses joined by a conjunctive adverb must be separated by a semicolon or a period.

> The regulations have not yet been published; *nevertheless,* we must proceed with the preparation of our course.
> The special study committee has approved our program. *Moreover,* it has commended us on our proposed method.
> The meeting was held at 3 o'clock; *however,* I was not able to attend.

NOTE: Certain phrases — such as *on the contrary, on the other hand, in the first place, in fact, in addition, for this reason, for example, at the same time, in the interim* — have the same modifying and connective force as conjunctive adverbs.

The survey committee may propose a solution to our problem; *on the other hand*, it may only define the problem.

We discussed the items on the agenda. *In addition*, several members proposed new topics.

56e Use punctuation to show coordination

The semicolon may be substituted for the connective between coordinate elements.

I have almost finished these letters; there are only three more on my desk.

The reception of this course will be interesting to watch; it is the first of its kind to be offered.

57 Connecting Elements of Unequal Rank (Connecting Subordinate Elements With Principal Elements)

57a How to show subordination

In the previous section we discussed how to put ideas of equal importance into structures that show they are equal. But many of our sentences contain ideas that are not equal in importance and that should be expressed in a way that emphasizes their inequality. Weigh the ideas in your sentence to determine which are basic to the purpose of the sentence and to the goal of the whole writing, and which are less important. Then make this distinction clear to your reader by putting the less important ideas into subordinate constructions.

57b Use subordinating conjunctions to show subordination

Subordinating conjunctions—*as, because, since, as though, than, although, provided, if, unless, how, after, before, so that, in order that, when, while, until*—introduce adverb clauses and connect them to independent clauses. The subordinating conjunction shows a relationship between the clauses it connects.

I must miss that meeting, EVEN THOUGH I would like to attend.

WHILE he was reviewing the letter, he noticed several references to the manual.

IF the project is to be finished on time, we must have those figures by Friday.

He will check in at the office AFTER he returns from the meeting.

Section 58 discusses some problems in using subordinating conjunctions.

57c Use relative pronouns to show subordination

Some relative pronouns—*who, whom, which, that*—introduce adjective clauses. Others—primarily, the compound relative pronouns *whichever, whatever, whoever, whomever*—introduce noun clauses. Both types of relative pronouns connect the clause they introduce to the rest of the sentence.

The man WHO *called for an appointment* has arrived.

An electric typewriter THAT *is operating properly* is a great help to the typist.

The officer *to* WHOM *I wrote* has since left the company.

Give the package to WHOEVER *answers the door.*

He will tell us WHATEVER *we need to know* about the new system.

See Section 58, Alphabetical List of Troublesome Conjunctions, for a further discussion of relative pronouns.

57d Use relative adverbs to show subordination

The relative adverbs—*where, when, while*—introduce adjective clauses and connect them to the rest of the sentence.

This is the building WHERE *the office is located.*

This is the time of year WHEN *we are particularly busy.*

58 Alphabetical List of Troublesome Conjunctions

58a and vs. also

Also, a weak connective, should not be used in place of *and* in sentences such as:

> He writes letters, memorandums, *and* (not *also*) some procedures.

58b and etc.

The abbreviation *etc.* stands for the Latin *et cetera*, meaning *and so forth*. Obviously, then, an additional *and* is not only unnecessary but incorrect.

> Not: He requisitioned paper, pencils, pens, *and etc.*
> But: He requisitioned paper, pencils, pens, *etc.*

58c and which, and who, but which

Avoid using *and which, and who, but which, but that*, etc., when there is no preceding *who, which,* or *that* in the sentence to complete the parallel construction.

> Not: We are looking for a program more economical to operate *and which* will be easy to administer.
> But: We are looking for a program *which* will be more economical to operate *and which* will be easy to administer.

58d Too many and's

Avoid stringing together a group of sentence elements connected by *and's*.

> Not: The evaluation of the training program was planned and conducted and reported to the appropriate officials.
> But: The evaluation of the training program was planned and conducted; then it was reported to the appropriate officials.

58e and vs. but

Use *and* to show addition; use *but* to show contrast.

> Not: The Director and his assistant have been called to a meeting, *and* our supervisor will be in the office all afternoon.
> But: The Director and his assistant have been called to a meeting, *but* our supervisor will be in the office all afternoon.

58f and or but to begin a sentence

We may begin a sentence, or even a paragraph, with *and, but,* or any other coordinating conjunction. A coordinate conjunction or a conjunctive adverb at the beginning of a sentence is often a handy signpost for the reader, telling him in which direction this new sentence will carry him.

58g as, since, because

These conjunctions can be used interchangeably to introduce clauses of cause or reason.

> *Because* the book was due at the library, I returned it.
> *Since* the book was due at the library, I returned it.
> *As* the book was due at the library, I returned it.

However, *since* and *as* have another function — *since* introduces clauses of sequence of time, and *as* introduces clauses of duration of time. Because of the double function of these two words, we must be careful to use them only in sentences in which they cannot be misunderstood.

> Not: *Since* this report was prepared to analyze the effects of . . .
> (Could mean: *Since the time that* this report was prepared . . .)
> But: *Because* this report was prepared to analyze the effects of . . .

> Not: *As* I was typing the monthly report, he gave the assignment to Beth.
> (Could mean: *During the time that* I was typing the monthly report . . .)
> But: *Because* I was typing the monthly report . . .

NOTE: When an *as* or *since* clause comes last in the sentence, the meaning of the conjunction can be made clear by the punctuation of the clause. If *as* or *since* is used as a time indicator, the clause it introduces is not set off from the sentence. But if the conjunction introduces a clause of cause or reason, the clause is set off.

> There have been several changes in policy *since* the committee released its findings.
> (No punctuation; *since* means *since the time that*)

> There have been several changes in policy, *since* the committee released its findings.
> (... *because* the committee released its findings)

58h   as vs. that or whether

Avoid using *as* in place of *that* or *whether* to introduce clauses following such verbs as *say, think, know*.

> Not: I don't know *as* I believe you.

> But: I don't know *that* I believe you.
> or: I don't know *whether* I believe you.

58i   if vs. whether

If is used to introduce clauses of condition or supposition.

> We will go *if* the meeting is postponed.
> *If* you cannot answer the 'etter immediately, please send an acknow'.edgment.

Whether introduces clauses indicating an alternative. The alternative may be expressed in the sentence or understood.

> It will not make any difference *whether* John agrees or disagrees with the proposal.
> Please let me know *whether* you received the check.

Some grammarians endorse the use of either *if* or *whether* in such constructions as

> Please let me know *if* (or *whether*) you received the check.
> I wonder *if* (or *whether*) he will attend.
> I don't know *if* (or *whether*) he is qualified for that position.

Most grammarians, however, prefer *whether* when there is any danger that the reader may fail to understand the meaning.

58j   whether vs. whether or not

It is not essential that *or not* be used with *whether* to complete the alternative choice. These words may be added if they are needed for emphasis.

> Either: Please let me know *whether or not* you received our letter.
> Or: Please let me know *whether* you received our letter.

58k   that introducing parallel clauses

When either *that* or *which* introduces one of a series of parallel clauses, the same conjunction must introduce the other clauses in the series. Do not shift conjunctions or omit the conjunction in later clauses.

> Poor (conjunction omitted):
> He said *that* he would call me before noon and his secretary would deliver the papers by two o'clock.
> Improved (conjunction supplied):
> He said *that* he would call me before noon and *that* his secretary would deliver the papers by two o'clock.

> Shift in conjunction:
> The report *that* was written by Prof. Smith and *which* was the subject of so much discussion at the last meeting has been accepted.
> Improved:
> The report *that* was written by Prof. Smith and *that* was the subject of so much discussion at the last meeting has been accepted.

58l   Proper omission of that

That may be omitted in noun clauses (especially those following such verbs as *say, think, feel, believe, hope*), and in adjective clauses, if the meaning of the sentence is clear.

> Noun clauses:
> He said (*that*) he would call me before noon.
> I hope (*that*) we can finish this project today.

Adjective clauses:
> The report (*that*) I asked for is out on loan.
> The instructions (*that*) he gave were perfectly clear.

58m Faulty repetition of that

Do not use *that* twice to introduce the same noun clause. This error most often occurs in a long sentence in which a long interrupting expression occurs between the *that* and the rest of its clause.

Not: I am sure you can appreciate *that*, in order to protect the interests of all taxpayers as well as the interests of the Government, *that* we must establish whether the original remittances were correctly applied.

But: I am sure you can appreciate *that*, in order to protect the interests of all taxpayers as well as the interests of the Government, we must establish whether the original remittances were correctly applied.

58n when

Avoid using *when* to introduce a definition unless the definition pertains to time.

Not: Their first important step in the improvement of the conditions was *when* they thoroughly surveyed the situation. (The step was not "when.")

But: Their first important step in the improvement of the conditions was *the thorough survey* of the situation.

Correct usage:
> Three o'clock is *when* the meeting will be held.

58o where

Avoid using *where* to introduce a definition unless the definition pertains to place or location.

Not: A sentence is *where* you have a subject and a verb. (A sentence is not "where.")

But: A sentence is a group of words containing a subject and a verb.

Correct usage:
> The large conference room is *where* the meeting is being held.

Avoid substituting where for *that*.

Not: I saw in the bulletin *where* the new law has been put into effect.

But: I saw in the bulletin *that* the new law has been put into effect.

58p while vs. when

While indicates duration of time; *when* indicates a fixed or stated period of time.

> *When* I return to the office, I will call him.
> (At that fixed time)

> *While* I am at the office, I will look for that information.
> (During the time that I am at the office . . .)

58q while vs. though, although, and, but

While pertains to time and should not be substituted loosely for *though, although, whereas, and, but.*

Not: *While* I did not remember the applicant's name, I thought I could recognize her face.

But: *Although* I did not remember the applicant's name, I thought I could recognize her face.

Not: I assembled the material for the manual *while* he wrote the outline.
> (Could mean: *during the time that he* . . .)

But: I assembled the material for the manual, *but* he wrote the outline.

Now, push forward! Test yourself and practice for your test with the carefully constructed quizzes that follow. Each one presents the kind of question you may expect on your test. And each question is at just the level of difficulty that may be expected. Don't try to take all the tests at one time. Rather, schedule yourself so that you take a few at each session, and spend approximately the same time on them at each session. Score yourself honestly, and date each test. You should be able to detect improvement in your performance on successive sessions.

TEST XV. CONNECTIVES

TIME: 23 Minutes

DIRECTIONS: In each of the following groups of sentences, select the one sentence that is grammatically INCORRECT. Mark the answer sheet with the letter of that incorrect sentence.

Explanations of the key points behind these questions appear with the answers at the end of this test. The explanatory answers provide the kind of background that will enable you to answer test questions with facility and confidence.

(1)

(A) The Democrats chose Chicago for their 1968 convention – the Republicans, Miami Beach.
(B) I have always had a sincere interest and admiration for the important work of the teacher.
(C) He is one of the best pupils there are in our school.
(D) A predatory animal is voracious and rapacious.

(2)

(A) Can you imagine my dancing, singing, clowning, and doing other silly things?
(B) To lie, to falsify, and to commit perjury are tactics I must condemn.
(C) I spent the summer swimming, boating, fishing, and anything else I could find to do at the lake.
(D) A student teacher is to observe, teach, and counsel – in short, she is to do all that a regular teacher does.

(3)

(A) Everyone concurs with the judge's decision.
(B) The loss of their material proved s severe handicap.
(C) My principal objection to this plan is that it is impractical.
(D) The doll has lain in the rain all evening.

(4)

(A) John found that he enjoyed working in all these media.
(B) He says that he has no recollection or interest in his father.
(C) Sitting on that bench are a student who is majoring in English and one who is majoring in French.
(D) The chief attraction of the garden is the azaleas.

(5)

(A) How will this failure affect my final mark?
(B) Two qualities of a true gentlemen are respect and trust in his fellow men.
(C) He found the climate of Arizona very healthful.
(D) There are fewer serious errors in this essay than I had expected.

(6)

(A) He stoutly maintained that he was innocent.
(B) She was asked whether he was ill.
(C) Although I received an invitation, I don't know if I can go.
(D) Who is the author of "Gone With The Wind"?

(7)

(A) Whether or no the State Legislature shall pass laws permitting off-track betting is not for us to predict.
(B) Who wrote "There's not a joy the world can give like that it takes away"?
(C) The tense situation already existing in the classroom was aggravated by the rudeness of the new pupil.
(D) Their grandfather began the tremendous task of giving away the world's greatest fortune.

(8)

(A) You are entitled to take whichever appeals most to you.
(B) I cannot report anything as to his hunting luck.
(C) Give them several hours more, they will have the package ready for you.
(D) The insects annoyed the campers during July.

9

(A) American politics demands that we stage an exciting game of "Musical Chairs" every four years.
(B) Pericles' decision to fight rallied the Athenians to the common defense of the country.
(C) When you went into the dark office, whom were you looking for?
(D) In fact, Schultz also reportedly offered the officer a house in Westchester not to take him in as a racketeer.

10

(A) No one really desires fulsome praise.
(B) The children wanted to canvass the entire town for advertisements for the newspaper.
(C) Do you know by what route they're coming?
(D) My closest friend is studying for a French teacher.

11

(A) You have to read widely if you except to understand all the allusions in modern literature.
(B) In 1966, February 22 fell on a Tuesday, consequently, workers could not have a long weekend vacation.
(C) The town is prosperous, for many older persons have chosen to live there permanently.
(D) Although the school is small, many famous men and women have been graduated from it.

12

(A) He had to depend on his canoe to get him across the river.
(B) I bought this set off the dealer.
(C) No one was there except Charles.
(D) Your sample is the most satisfactory of all that I have seen.

13

(A) A kite must have a tail in order to fly.
(B) He placed the books upon the desk.
(C) Helen had a habit for postponing her homework.
(D) He had an amused look on his face.

14

(A) Commissioner Simpson's speech consisted in many remarks that were offensive.
(B) The new foreman tried to effect some changes in the established routines.
(C) No one, not even the agents of the F.B.I., knows how many Mafia members are in the United States.
(D) His antagonist accused him of willfully concealing evidence.

15

(A) However difficult the assignment may be, he will complete it satisfactorily.
(B) By next month, the organization will have worked well for fourteen years.
(C) He should have read either a great deal more or a great deal less.
(D) His mother forbade him from playing football until his marks improved.

16

(A) He has an interest and an aptitude for his work.
(B) I shall send him rather than her.
(C) I set the can of paint on the window sill.
(D) I had just lain down when the telephone rang.

17

(A) This is the report we were looking for and which documents the actions taken.
(B) Rover, a black Labrador retriever, won the blue ribbon.
(C) The moist, chilly climate aggravated her sinus condition.
(D) Many a student has been disappointed in his marks.

18

(A) The murderer suffered from a persistent and frightening hallucination.
(B) The college, therefore, is a combination of many factors.
(C) Dr. Arthur Jones, a Baptist minister, lectured on the tenets of Taoism.
(D) The play, for all its much-heralded novelty, was not near as challenging as we had expected it to be.

19

(A) Each applicant was required to give his name, age, and where he lived.
(B) Andrew has been away for months; hence his bewilderment at these new laws is understandable.
(C) Whether he be vagabond or courtier, he may enter through these portals.
(D) At the conference, it transpired that the president had absconded with the funds six months before.

20

(A) Jack liked all sports: tennis, basketball, football, and etc.
(B) The boy began his research by consulting the encyclopedia.
(C) The dull introduction was a poor prelude to the subsequent chapters.
(D) The waters began to recede when the wind died down.

(21)

(A) Her gown was of heavy green brocade, and which was most becoming to her.
(B) "She said that you wanted to see me," said Louise.
(C) I wish he were more like Joe, an honor student in high school and a good athlete.
(D) The study of grammar can be an exciting experience when the proper technique of instruction is used.

(22)

(A) Much to his surprise, his classmates agreed at the proposal to cancel the picnic.
(B) This is the more interesting of the two books.
(C) Between you and me, I am positive that Ellen is in error.
(D) The Misses Foley were invited to the party.

(23)

(A) He knew the woman to be her whom he had dreamed about only the previous night.
(B) The creatures looked as though they had come from outer space, goggle-eyed, squat, and thin.
(C) It is evident that they like nothing but dancing, racing around in hot-rod cars, and, hour after hour, to listen to the records of the Beatles.
(D) Twenty thousand dollars is really very little to pay for such a well-built house.

(24)

(A) The building superintendent had already determined that a local statute forbade the use of plastics in this area.
(B) My friend planned a trip to several countries, but which cost more than he could afford.
(C) Perhaps it was easier to discover the principles of atomic radiation than to invent the bomb that made use of these principles.
(D) Pencils, pens, and notebooks are the customary tools of the pupil.

(25)

(A) Neither the protests nor tears effected the least change in their parents' decision.
(B) We thought the author of the letter to be him.
(C) We are looking for a candidate with a knowledge of accounting and who is willing to accept assignment in Washington.
(D) The victim's mother, beside herself with grief, could give no coherent account of the accident.

(26)

(A) Who is the tallest boy in the class?
(B) Where shall I look to find a similar kind of stone?
(C) The horse took the jumps with a great deal of ease.
(D) He is as good, if not better than, any other jumper in the country.

(27)

(A) He had a large number of friends until he lost all his money.
(B) Neither John or I would join such an organization.
(C) I'd like to represent my colleague, Tom Rover, who helped me in all my research.
(D) Seldom have so many gathered to honor so few.

(28)

(A) To me, motion pictures are a waste of time; to my brother, they are fine entertainment.
(B) The teacher angrily insisted that a child so mischievous as William should be punished.
(C) Lifeguards have been known to effect rescues even during tumultuous storms.
(D) "If you wish to read on a particular topic," said the teacher, "the librarian is prepared to furnish you with a list of books."

(29)

(A) Participation in active sports produces both release from tension as well as physical well-being.
(B) The problem of a surtax was passed on by Johnson to Nixon.
(C) Every boy and every girl in the auditorium was thrilled when the color guard appeared.
(D) At length our club decided to send two representatives.

(30)

(A) The machine is not easy to fool, or is it entirely foolproof.
(B) For all practical purposes history is, for us and for the time being, what we know it to be.
(C) All words are pegs to hang ideas on.
(D) He told an incredible story of an encounter with a creature from outer space.

TEST XV. CONNECTIVES

CONSOLIDATE YOUR KEY ANSWERS HERE

	A	B	C	D	E
1	〇	〇	〇	〇	〇
2	〇	〇	〇	〇	〇
3	〇	〇	〇	〇	〇
4	〇	〇	〇	〇	〇
5	〇	〇	〇	〇	〇
6	〇	〇	〇	〇	〇
7	〇	〇	〇	〇	〇
8	〇	〇	〇	〇	〇
9	〇	〇	〇	〇	〇
10	〇	〇	〇	〇	〇
11	〇	〇	〇	〇	〇
12	〇	〇	〇	〇	〇
13	〇	〇	〇	〇	〇
14	〇	〇	〇	〇	〇
15	〇	〇	〇	〇	〇
16	〇	〇	〇	〇	〇
17	〇	〇	〇	〇	〇
18	〇	〇	〇	〇	〇
19	〇	〇	〇	〇	〇
20	〇	〇	〇	〇	〇
21	〇	〇	〇	〇	〇
22	〇	〇	〇	〇	〇
23	〇	〇	〇	〇	〇
24	〇	〇	〇	〇	〇
25	〇	〇	〇	〇	〇
26	〇	〇	〇	〇	〇
27	〇	〇	〇	〇	〇
28	〇	〇	〇	〇	〇
29	〇	〇	〇	〇	〇
30	〇	〇	〇	〇	〇
31	〇	〇	〇	〇	〇
32	〇	〇	〇	〇	〇

Correct Answers For The Foregoing Questions

(Check your answers with these that we provide. You should find considerable correspondence between them. If not, you'd better go back and find out why. On the next page we have provided concise clarifications of basic points behind the key answers. Please go over them carefully because they may be quite useful in helping you pick up extra points on the exam.)

1.B	6.C	11.B	16.A	21.A	26.D
2.C	7.A	12.B	17.A	22.A	27.B
3.A	8.C	13.C	18.D	23.C	28.B
4.B	9.D	14.A	19.A	24.B	29.A
5.B	10.D	15.D	20.A	25.C	30.A

EXPLANATORY ANSWERS CLARIFYING CARDINAL POINTS

The core of the Question and Answer Method . . . getting help when and where you need it. Even if you were able to write correct key answers for the preceding questions, the following explanations illuminate fundamental facts, ideas, and principles which just might crop up in the form of questions on future tests.

Bold-face references in the following answers direct you to paragraphs in the Arco Grammar Text, where fuller explanations are provided.

ANSWER 1.

B I have always had a sincere **interest in** and admiration for the important work of the teacher. REASON: The preposition **in (interest in)** is required to introduce the object of the preposition (**work**). **(53a)**

ANSWER 2.

C I spent the summer swimming, boating, fishing, and **doing** anything else I could find to do at the lake. REASON: The gerund **doing** is required for parallelism with the other gerunds (**swimming, boating, fishing**). **(56a)**

ANSWER 3.

A Everyone **concurs in** the judge's decision. REASON: We **concur in** a matter; we **concur with** a person. **(50)**

ANSWER 4.

B He says that he has no recollection **of**, or interest in, his father. REASON: The preposition **of** is necessary to complete the prepositional phrase (**of his father**). **(53)**

ANSWER 5.

B Two qualities of a true gentleman are **respect for** and trust in his fellow men. REASON: The preposition **for** is necessary in order to complete the prepositional phrase (**for fellow men**). **(53)**

ANSWER 6.

C Although I received an invitation, I don't know **whether** I can go. REASON: A choice is expressed by **whether** — not by **if**. **(58i)**

ANSWER 7.

A **Whether or not** the State Legislature shall pass laws permitting off-track betting is not for us to predict. REASON: The correct expression is **whether or not**. **(58j)**

ANSWER 8.

C Give them several hours **more; they** will have the package ready for you. REASON: The original statement, consisting of two sentences, is run-on without the semi-colon break. **(56e, 62)**

ANSWER 9.

D In fact, Schultz also reportedly offered the officer a house in Westchester **provided that** the officer would not take him in as a racketeer. REASON: The link between the two clauses is **provided that**. **(57b)**

ANSWER 10.

D My closest friend is studying **to** be a French teacher. REASON: **for a French teacher** is awkward and unidiomatic. **(49a)**

ANSWER 11.

B   In 1966, February 22 fell on a **Tuesday; consequently,** workers could not have a long weekend vacation. REASON: We have a run-on sentence in the original. The semicolon is needed to split the independent clauses.   **(56e, 63)**

ANSWER 12.

B   I bought this set **from** the dealer. REASON: One doesn't buy something **off of**.   **(49a)**

ANSWER 13.

C   Helen had a **habit of** postponing her homework. REASON: the idiom is **habit of**.   **(49a)**

ANSWER 14.

A   Commissioner Simpson's speech **consisted of** many remarks that were offensive. REASON: In detailing the contents of something, we say **consisted of**.   **(50)**

ANSWER 15.

D   His mother forbade him **to play** football until his marks improved REASON: The infinitive (**to play**) follows the verb **to forbid**.   **(49a)**

ANSWER 16.

A   He has an interest **in** and an aptitude for his work. REASON: The preposition (**in**) is necessary for the understood prepositional phrase (**in his work**).   **(53)**

ANSWER 17.

A   This is the report for which we were looking and with which he took action. REASON: The original sentence lacks parallel structure.   **(56a)**

ANSWER 18.

D   The play, for all its much-heralded novelty, was not **nearly so** challenging as we had expected it to be. REASON: **nearly**, an adverb, is used to modify the adjective (**challenging**). Also, in a negative comparison, the expression is **not. . .so. . .as**.   **(56c)**

ANSWER 19.

A   Each applicant was required to give his name, age and **residence**. REASON: Consistency of construction is required. Just as **name** and **age** are direct object nouns, the third in the series should be a direct object noun (**residence**).   **(56a)**

ANSWER 20.

A   Jack liked all sports: tennis, basketball, football, etc. REASON: **and** is omitted since it is redundant.   **(58b)**

ANSWER 21.

A   Her gown was of heavy green brocade, which was most becoming to her. REASON: **and** is redundant.   **(58c)**

ANSWER 22.

A   Much to his surprise, his classmates **agreed to** the proposal to cancel the picnic. REASON: **agreed at the proposal** is incorrect.   **(50)**

ANSWER 23.

C   It is evident that they like nothing but dancing, racing around in hot-rod cars, and, hour after hour, **listening** to the records of the Beatles. REASON: Parallel construction requires the use of the gerund **listening**.   **(56a)**

ANSWER 24.

B   My friend planned a trip to several countries, but it cost more than he could afford. REASON: Clarity requires the elimination of **which** in this sentence.   **(58c)**

ANSWER 25.

C   We are looking for a candidate with a knowledge of accounting who is willing to accept assignment in Washington. REASON: Omit **and** — it is unnecessary. **(58c)**

ANSWER 26.

D   He is **as good as**, if not better than, any other jumper in the country. REASON: The subordinate conjunction **as** must be included. **(56a)**

ANSWER 27.

B   Neither John **nor** I would join such an organization. REASON: The negative correlative conjunction is **neither-nor**. **(56c)**

ANSWER 28.

B   The teacher angrily insisted that a child **as** mischievous **as** William should be punished. REASON: The correlative **as...as** is used affirmatively. **(56c)**

ANSWER 29.

A   Participation in active sports produces both release from tension and physical well-being. REASON: The correlative conjunctions (**both-and**) are needed. The parallel construction clarifies meaning. **(56c)**

ANSWER 30.

A   The machine is not easy to fool, **nor** is it entirely foolproof. REASON: We have here what amounts to a "neither...nor" construction. **(56c)**

TEST XVI. MODIFIERS AND CONNECTIVES

TIME: 19 Minutes

*DIRECTIONS: Each question in this test begins with a sentence containing a word or expression in **boldface** type. Then follow four grammatical descriptions of the **boldface** type. They are lettered (A) (B) (C) (D). Choose the correct grammatical description, and mark your answer sheet with the letter of the correct answer.*

Explanations of the key points behind these questions appear with the answers at the end of this test. The explanatory answers provide the kind of background that will enable you to answer test questions with facility and confidence.

The mountains loomed in the distance, **peak after peak**.

(A) an adverbial phrase
(B) an adjective phrase
(C) a nominative absolute
(D) incorrect in usage

I bring fresh showers **for the thirsting flowers**.

(A) adverbial phrase
(B) complete predicate
(C) noun clause
(D) independent clause

"Hasten slowly" is an **Italian** proverb.

(A) common noun
(B) proper adjective
(C) relative pronoun
(D) coordinate conjunction

Struggling to earn a living and to complete his education, he became so ill that he had to be hospitalized.

(A) nominative absolute
(B) participial phrase
(C) gerundial phrase
(D) adjective clause

The time has come **when we must begin to think about Christmas shopping**.

(A) adverbial clause
(B) adjective clause
(C) noun clause in apposition with time
(D) noun clause used as an objective complement

How we are going to make both ends **meet** is beyond me.

(A) verb of main clause
(B) verb of subordinate clause
(C) infinitive
(D) adjective

I heard the telephone **ringing** as I opened the door.

(A) gerund
(B) verb
(C) participle
(D) adverb

In the phrase, "**The** more, the merrier," the syntax of the word **the** is

(A) an adverb
(B) an expletive
(C) an article
(D) a preposition

S1857

We heard the people **scream** when the car skidded.

(A) direct object
(B) indirect object
(C) infinitive
(D) predicate verb

There is a tide **in the affairs** of men.

(A) adverbial clause
(B) participial phrase
(C) noun clause
(D) prepositional phrase

My mind being made up, I sent in my resignation.

(A) predicate nominative
(B) nominative of direct address
(C) nominative absolute
(D) subject in a causal clause

To be conscious that you are ignorant is a great step to knowledge.

(A) intransitive verb
(B) infinitive
(C) participle
(D) article

The speaker bade the audience **listen** to him.

(A) verb
(B) infinitive
(C) gerund
(D) participle

Please don't go **without** me.

(A) simple preposition
(B) phrasal preposition
(C) idiomatic preposition
(D) compound preposition

Take me to the place **where** you left your book.

(A) subordinating conjunction
(B) a coordinating conjunction
(C) a relative adverb
(D) an adverb of place

Fools who came to scoff remained **to pray**.

(A) nominative of direct address　　(C) participial phrase
(B) compound noun　　(D) adverbial infinitive

John Grove's attempt **to break** away from his family ended in failure.

(A) modifies **John Grove**　　(C) modifies **attempt**
(B) subject of the verb　　(D) verb in dependent clause

Standing high above the crowd, the officer was able to control the traffic.

(A) a nominative absolute　　(C) a participle
(B) a gerund　　(D) an adverb

He has a job to do and the spirit **to do it well**.

(A) infinitive phrase with spirit as its subject
(B) object of the verb **has**
(C) objective complement
(D) infinitive phrase modifying **spirit**

There was once a city **on the outskirts** of which lay a pestilential morass.

(A) modifies **city**　　(C) modifies **lay**
(B) modifies **which**　　(D) modifies **morass**

The wine tastes **sour**, if you are not accustomed to its flavor.

(A) adverb　　(C) predicate adjective
(B) objective complement　　(D) adjective modifying **flavor**

He had a hard, time-consuming task **to complete** before he could stop for lunch.

(A) an infinitive used as adjective
(B) an infinitive used as objective complement
(C) an infinitive used as adverb
(D) an infinitive used as direct object

There's not a man alive **but** has known sorrow.

(A) conjunction joining two coordinate clauses
(B) preposition with clause as its object
(C) pronoun, subject of verb
(D) adverb in subordinate clause

Her work completed, she left the office for the day.

(A) object of **with** understood
(B) subject of **completed**
(C) nominative absolute
(D) modifier of **she**

His fumbling attempts **to prove his point** seemed pathetic.

(A) prepositional phrase
(B) noun phrase
(C) adjective phrase
(D) subject of **seemed**

CONSOLIDATE YOUR KEY ANSWERS HERE

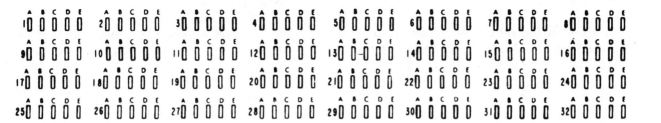

Correct Answers For The Foregoing Questions

(Check your answers with these that we provide. You should find considerable correspondence between them. If not, you'd better go back and find out why. On the next page we have provided concise clarifications of basic points behind the key answers. Please go over them carefully because they may be quite useful in helping you pick up extra points on the exam.)

1.C	4.B	7.C	10.D	13.B	16.D	19.D	22.A
2.A	5.B	8.A	11.C	14.D	17.C	20.C	23.C
3.B	6.C	9.C	12.B	15.C	18.C	21.C	24.C
							25.C

TEST XVI. MODIFIERS AND CONNECTIVES

EXPLANATORY ANSWERS CLARIFYING CARDINAL POINTS

The core of the Question and Answer Method . . . getting help when and where you need it. Even if you were able to write correct key answers for the preceding questions, the following explanations illuminate fundamental facts, ideas, and principles which just might crop up in the form of questions on future tests.

Bold-face *references in the following answers direct you to paragraphs in the Arco Grammar Text, where fuller explanations are provided.*

ANSWER 1.

C   REASON: The first noun **peak** forms with the other underlined words, a virtual adverbial clause (**as peak appeared after peak**). Since **peak after peak** is, in its present form, not related grammatically to the rest of the sentence, it constitutes a nominative absolute.   **(12f)**

ANSWER 2.

A   REASON: **For the thirsting flowers** is an adverbial phrase of purpose modifying the verb **bring**.   **(45)**

ANSWER 3.

B   REASON: **Italian** is an adjective modifying the noun **proverb**. A proper adjective is always capitalized (just as a proper noun is).   **(38)**

ANSWER 4.

B   REASON: **Struggling** is a present participle modifying the subject (**he**) of the main clause. The entire phrase (**struggling . . . education**) is a participial phrase since it begins with a participle.   **(44d)**

ANSWER 5.

B   REASON: The clause **when we . . . shopping** is a clause used adjectivally modifying the noun **time**.   **(46a)**

ANSWER 6.

C   REASON: **(to) Meet** is an infinitive used as an objective complement, completing the meaning of the direct object **ends**.   **(13g, 44a)**

ANSWER 7.

C   REASON: **Ringing** is a present participle modifying the noun **telephone**.   **(44c)**

ANSWER 8.

A   REASON: In this case, **The** is an adverb of degree modifying the adverb **more**.   **(39)**

ANSWER 9.

C   REASON: **Scream (to scream)** is an infinitive which completes the meaning of, and further describes, the direct object **people**. **Scream**, then, is an objective complement.   **(13g, 44a)**

ANSWER 10.

D   REASON: **In the affairs** is a prepositional phrase because it starts with a preposition. Functionally, the phrase is adverbial, expressing place and modifying the verb **is**.   **(5b)**

ANSWER 11.

C   REASON: Since **my mind being made up** has no grammatical connection with the rest of the sentence—although there is a thought connection—the expression is a nominative absolute.   **(44g)**

ANSWER 12.

B   REASON: **To be** is an infinitive. The infinitive phrase **To be conscious** plus the clause **that you are ignorant**, comprise the subject of the verb **is**.   **(44a)**

ANSWER 13.

B   REASON: **Listen** (really, **to listen**) is an infinitive used as an objective complement completing the meaning of the direct object **audience**.   **(13g, 44a)**

ANSWER 14.

D   REASON: Compound prepositions are one-word prepositions made up of two words. Other compound prepositions are **around, inside, upon**.   **(48b)**

ANSWER 15.

C   REASON: **Where** is an adverb modifying the verb **left**. The antecedent of **where** is **place**.   **(46a)**

ANSWER 16.

D   REASON: **To pray** is an infinitive used as an adverb of purpose to modify the verb **remained**.   **(44a)**

ANSWER 17.

C   REASON: **To break** is an infinitive used as an adjective to modify the noun **attempt**.   **(44a)**

ANSWER 18.

C   REASON: **Standing** is a participle modifying the subject **officer**.   **(44c)**

ANSWER 19.

D   REASON: **To do it well** is an infinitive phrase used as an adjective to modify the noun **spirit**.   **(44a, b)**

ANSWER 20.

C   REASON: **On the outskirts** is an adverbial phrase describing where the **morass lay**.   **(45)**

ANSWER 21.

C   REASON: **Sour** is an adjective. Since it somes after a copulative verb (**tastes**) and refers back to the subject (**wine**), **sour** is a predicate adjective.   **(40d)**

ANSWER 22.

A   REASON: **To complete** is used as an adjective modifying the noun **task**.   **(44a)**

ANSWER 23.

C   REASON: **But**, here, is a relative pronoun after a negative (**not**). In this sentence, **but** means **who not**.   **(46d)**

ANSWER 24.

C   REASON: Since **Her work completed** is, in its present form, not related grammatically to the rest of the sentence, it is a nominative absolute.   **(12f, 44g)**

ANSWER 25.

C   REASON: **To prove his point** is an adjective phrase modifying the noun **attempts**.   **(45)**

TEST XVII.MODIFIERS AND CONNECTIVES

TIME: 18 Minutes

*DIRECTIONS: Most questions in this test begin with a sentence containing a word or expression in **boldface** type. Then follow four grammatical descriptions of the **boldface** type. They are lettered (A) (B) (C) (D). Choose the correct grammatical description, and mark your answer sheet with the letter of the correct answer.*

Explanations of the key points behind these questions appear with the answers at the end of this test. The explanatory answers provide the kind of background that will enable you to answer test questions with facility and confidence.

The more he had to wait, **the** angrier he became.

(A) adverb
(B) article
(C) pronoun
(D) predicate adjective

The stone image of the God stood **tall** on the hill.

(A) adjective   (C) predicate nominative
(B) adverb   (D) object of the verb

Either your father **or** your mother must visit the school.

(A) coordinate conjunctions
(B) conjunctive adverbs
(C) subordinate conjunctions
(D) correlative conjunctions

The women looked so **attractive** in their Easter bonnets.

(A) direct object
(B) retained object
(C) predicate noun
(D) predicate adjective

Will you let us **see** your collection of stamps?

(A) objective complement
(B) part of compound verb
(C) infinitive
(D) verb in elliptical subordinate clause

Generally speaking, scientific investigations today are planned on a larger scale than formerly.

(A) nominative absolute
(B) adjective phrase
(C) expletive
(D) independent participle

Although he has only a learner's permit, we let him **drive** to the camp.

(A) infinitive
(B) participle
(C) gerund
(D) predicate verb

A little learning is a dangerous thing.

(A) indefinite article   (C) demonstrative adjective
(B) personal pronoun   (D) direct object

We have not seen him **since** the breaking up of the picnic we attended.

(A) preposition
(B) conjunctive adverb
(C) relative pronoun
(D) subordinate conjunction

10

The corn grew tall and **plentiful**

(A) modifies **grew**   (C) predicate adjective
(B) predicate adverb   (D) part of prepositional phrase

They judged him guilty, the evidence to the contrary **notwithstanding**.

(A) present participle
(B) adverb
(C) adjective
(D) preposition

Tennyson **as well as** Browning must be considered among the great Victorian poets.

(A) adjective modifying **Browning**
(B) preposition
(C) adverbial phrase
(D) correlative conjunction

I gave you a front seat **in order that** you might hear better.

(A) subordinate conjunction
(B) compound preposition
(C) relative adverb
(D) adverbial phrase

There was no one in the school **but** wished success to the brave child with such a handicap.

(A) conjunction connecting coordinate clauses
(B) conjunctive adverb
(C) preposition
(D) relative pronoun

We never did know **where** we were going.

(A) relative adverb
(B) direct object
(C) coordinating conjunction
(D) conjunctive adverb

He has agreed to go, **provided** proper accommodations can be obtained.

(A) predicate verb
(B) past participle
(C) preposition
(D) subordinate conjunction

He has put forth a great effort; **therefore**, I must praise him.

(A) subordinate conjunction
(B) coordinate conjunction
(C) conjunctive adverb
(D) absolute construction

Whoever excelled in any art or science was sure to be regarded by him **as** a rival.

(A) relative pronoun
(B) correlative conjunction
(C) preposition
(D) coordinating conjunction

He knew the answer; **moreover**, he was prepared to act.

(A) subordinate conjunction
(B) preposition
(C) conjunctive adverb
(D) interjection

Provided you follow this diet carefully, you can expect to lose weight gradually.

(A) past participle
(B) preposition
(C) conjunction
(D) verb

We shall gladly consider your plan **provided** you present it in outline at our next meeting.

(A) past participle
(B) conjunction
(C) preposition
(D) verb

The speaker was unsatisfactory in many respects: **for instance**, he swallowed his words and wandered from the topic.

(A) an adverb modifying **swallowed**
(B) a conjunction
(C) an independent element
(D) a prepositional phrase

Which sentence is incorrect?

(A) We don't know whether it's going to rain.
(B) The child likes candy, cakes, fruit and etc.
(C) Since the report was due, she worked late.
(D) But why must you cry?

(24)

Which sentence is incorrect?

(A) She was accompanied by her aunt.
(B) The pupil acceded to the teacher's request.
(C) The suspect was acquitted from the charge.
(D) Can one identify a bird by a tweet?

TEST XVI. MODIFIERS AND CONNECTIVES

CONSOLIDATE YOUR KEY ANSWERS HERE

[answer grid: rows numbered 1–24, columns A B C D E]

KEY ANSWERS FOR THE FOREGOING QUESTIONS

Check our key answers with your own. You'll probably find very few errors. In any case, check your understanding of all questions by studying the following explanatory answers. They illuminate the subject matter. Here you will find concise clarifications of basic points behind the key answers.

1.A	5.C	9.A	13.A	17.C	21.B
2.A	6.D	10.C	14.D	18.C	22.B
3.D	7.A	11.D	15.A	19.C	23.B
4.D	8.A	12.B	16.D	20.C	24.C

EXPLANATORY ANSWERS CLARIFYING CARDINAL POINTS

The core of the Question and Answer Method ... getting help when and where you need it. Even if you were able to write correct key answers for the preceding questions, the following explanations illuminate fundamental facts, ideas, and principles which just might crop up in the form of questions on future tests.

ANSWER 1.

A REASON: **The** is an adverb of degree, modifying the adjective **angrier**. **(39)**

ANSWER 2.

A REASON: The verb **stood** is copulative in this sentence, taking the predicate adjective **tall**. **(40d)**

ANSWER 3.

D REASON: Correlative conjunctions work in pairs to show that words and ideas are parallel. **(56c)**

ANSWER 4.

D REASON: **Attractive** is a predicate adjective after the copulative verb **looked** and refers to the subject **women**. **(40d)**

ANSWER 5.

C REASON: **See** (really **to see**) is an infinitive, the subject of which is **us** (the subject of an infinitive is in the objective case). **(44a)**

ANSWER 6.

D REASON: **Generally speaking** is a participial phrase that modifies the entire sentence without specific reference. **(44f)**

ANSWER   7.

   A   REASON: **To** is understood before **drive**; **to drive** is an infinitive. **We let him drive** may be replaced by **we allowed him to drive**. In the latter construction, **to drive** is obviously an infinitive. Incidentally, **to to drive**. In the latter construction, **to drive** is obviously an infinitive.   **(44a)**

ANSWER   8.

   A   REASON: **A** and **an** are indefinite articles; **the** is the definite article.   **(38a)**

ANSWER   9.

   A   REASON: **Since** is a preposition introducing the gerund (verbal noun) **breaking** in the prepositional phrase **since the breaking up.**   **(44e)**

ANSWER   10.

   C   REASON: **Plentiful** is a predicate adjective after the copulative verb **grew**. The predicate adjective refers to the subject **corn.**   **(40d)**

ANSWER   11.

   D   REASON: **Notwithstanding** is a preposition introducing the noun **evidence**. In other words, the sense is: **notwithstanding the evidence to the contrary.**   **(45)**

ANSWER   12.

   B   REASON: **As well as** is a phrasal preposition, the object of which is Browning.   **(48c)**

ANSWER   13.

   A   REASON: **In order that** is a subordinate conjunction connecting the main clause (**I gave . . . seat**) and the subordinate clause (**you might hear better**).   **(57b)**

ANSWER   14.

   D   REASON: **But** here is a relative pronoun after a negative (**no one**). In this sentence **but** means **who did not.**   **(57c)**

ANSWER   15.

   A   REASON: The relative adverb **where** introduces an adjective clause (**where we were going**) which modifies the understood noun **place.**   **(57d)**

ANSWER   16.

   D   REASON: **Provided** here means the same as the subordinate conjunction **if**. Note that **provided** and **providing** are synonymous.   **(57b)**

ANSWER   17.

   C   REASON: The conjunctive adverb **therefore** connects two independent clauses: **He has . . . effort** and **I . . . him**. The latter clause, though grammatically independent, is logically dependent on the first clause.   **(56d)**

ANSWER   18.

   C   REASON: **As** may be a substitute for the preposition **like**, **rival** being the object of the preposition. Though the choice is not given for this question, a subordinate conjunction could also be a correct designation for **as** in this sentence — that is, . . . **regarded by him as a rival is regarded by him.**   **(13c, 57b)**

ANSWER   19.

   C   REASON: **Moreover** is a conjunctive adverb since it functions as a device for logical transition between two independent clauses (**He . . . answer** and **he . . . to act.**)   **(56d)**

ANSWER   20.

   C   REASON: **Provided** could be replaced by the subordinate conjunction **if**.   **(57b)**

ANSWER   21.

   B   REASON: **Provided** is a subordinate conjunction meaning the same as **if**. It connects the main clause (**we shall . . . plan**) with the subordinate clause (**you present . . .**).   **(57b)**

ANSWER   22.

   B   REASON: **For instance** is a conjunctive adverb connecting two independent clauses.   **(56d)**

ANSWER   23.

   B   REASON: **Etc.** means **and so forth**. We certainly don't want to say **fruit and and so forth.**   **(58b)**

ANSWER   24.

   C   REASON: One is acquitted **of** a charge.   **(50)**

VIII. PUNCTUATION

59 Use the period:

. . . to mark the end of a sentence that is not a question or an exclamation.

> An agreement was reached on that case last week.

. . . after a request — to distinguish it from a direct question.

> Will you please send us three copies of the January 17 memo.
> Will you let us know whether you can attend the conference.

. . . after words or phrases that stand as sentences. (This is not an endorsement of fragmentary sentences; but if sentence fragments must be used, they are followed by periods.)

> True.
> What time will you be back? By noon.

. . . after abbreviations and initials.

> My neighbor, R. D. Pale, M.D., is employed by the Central Medical Association.

. . . to show that material has been omitted from a quotation. Omissions are usually shown by three periods, in addition to any other punctuation needed at that point in the material.

> The report stated, "Preliminary investigations . . . disclose no reason for discontinuing the procedure at this time."
> The report stated, "Preliminary investigations by the committee members disclose no reason for discontinuing the procedure. . . ."

60 Use the question mark:

. . . after a sentence that asks a *direct question.* (Not after a request, even though it is phrased as a question.)

> Have you heard from Mr. Rollins this morning?
> You know the letter I mean, don't you?
>
> But: He asked where Mr. Rollins was. (Indirect question.)

. . . to indicate doubt about the correctness of a statement.

> The company was established in 1960(?) and was incorporated in 1961.
> About a year after the company was established (1960?), it was incorporated.

61 Use the exclamation point:

. . . after an exclamatory sentence or remark, to show strong feeling. (The exclamation point should be used sparingly — rarely in expository writing.)

> That's the longest report I've seen yet!
> Whew! What a day!

62 Use the comma:

. . . to separate long main clauses joined by a coordinate conjunction.

> The two warring nations have been in negotiation for several weeks, but peace still seems to be a long way off.
> The case has been closed since last April, yet no official report has been filed.

62 Use the comma (continued):

NOTE: The comma may be used to separate main clauses only when the main clauses have been linked by a connective. A violation of this use of the comma is called the *comma splice* or the *run-on sentence*.

Not: Agreement has been reached by both sides, there will be no strike.

But: Agreement has been reached by both sides. There will be no strike.

or: . . . sides, so there will be no strike.

. . . to set off a nonrestrictive adjective modifier.

Mr. Jameson, *whom you met last week*, will help you.
The "X" Company, *established in 1873*, is the city's oldest business firm.
Exhausted from a long day of meetings, he stuffed some papers into his briefcase and left for the airport.
Elated, he called his staff in to tell them the news.

. . . to set off a nonrestrictive adverbial modifier at the end of a sentence, especially if it is long or needs special emphasis.

I will call you at 4 o'clock, *after the messenger brings the mail.*

I have not seen him since Tuesday, *when he spoke at the luncheon.*

We must finish this report by Friday, *even if we have to work on it at night.*

. . . to set off a nonrestrictive appositive.

My brother, *James*, has been visiting me.

James, *my youngest brother*, has been visiting me.

Office equipment, *such as typewriters and adding machines*, must be oiled regularly.

Restrictive and Nonrestrictive Modifiers

Modifiers and appositives are classed as *restrictive* or as nonrestrictive.

A *restrictive modifier* or appositive cannot be omitted without changing the meaning of the sentence. It restricts or limits the word preceding it, and by answering the question, "Which one?" also serves an identifying function. Because restrictive modifiers are essential parts of the sentence, they are *not set off by commas.*

A *nonrestrictive modifier* or appositive, on the other hand, is not essential to the meaning of the sentence. It may add interesting or helpful information, but it is not necessary as a restrictive modifier is. To show that they contain ideas of secondary importance, nonrestrictive modifiers are *set off by commas.*

. . . to set off an introductory adverbial modifier. (If the modifier is short and if no confusion will result, it is not set off.)

When you get back to the office, look up that information and call me.

If your figures are correct, we will have enough money left to buy that new equipment.

Because she was familiar with the files in the division, she was able to assemble the data on time.

. . . to set off an introductory prepositional phrase that demands special emphasis.

In spite of his head cold, he put in a full day at the office.

In the light of his objections, we may reconsider the proposed change.

. . . to set off an introductory transitional expression that is not closely related to the meaning of the sentence.

On the other hand, his statement may be based on nothing more than opinion.

In the first place, we do not have the funds to undertake the project right now.

. . . to set off an interrupting transitional expression.

We may, *of course*, postpone the meeting indefinitely.
He will, *therefore*, be forced to submit a written statement.
We must be sure, *however*, that he understands the serious nature of the charges.

. . . to set off an interrupting expression identifying speaker or source.

A little change of pace, *we decided*, was just what we needed.
The report, *as you may remember*, was not approved immediately.
That, *I feel*, may be the root of our problem.
"Your organization," *he said*, "has done an outstanding job."

. . . to set off addresses, dates, titles.

He moved to Omaha, *Nebraska*, shortly after he graduated.
You letter of July 6, *1969*, explains the problem clearly.
The reports are due in the office of the Director, *Personnel Division*, by noon Friday.

. . . to set off a nominative absolute phrase.

The meal having been paid for, he felt he must eat it.
The report having been submitted, he prepared an errata sheet.

. . . to set off words in direct address.

Sir, your letters are ready for signature.
Your letters are ready for signature, *Mr. Brown*.
May I interrupt, *Mr. Chairman*, to ask that the question be repeated.

. . . to separate coordinate items in a series

He asked that paper, pencils, and ashtrays be placed in the conference room.
He said it had been an exciting, exhausting day.

. . . in a direct quotation (see Section 67).

Mary remarked, "That's a pretty dress."
"I hope to do it soon," she said.
"When I have the time to do it," the teacher explained, "we'll review the lesson."

. . . in order to effect clearness.

After smoking, his mother went to the beauty parlor.
To Jim, Smith seemed very unfair.

. . . in letter closings.

Sincerely, . . . Very truly, . . . Cordially, . . .
. . . after the salutation in a friendly letter.
Dear Gary,

NOTE: Avoid the use of unnecessary commas. Be sure that, when you do use a comma, you have a good reason for using it. If you have any doubt about using a comma, don't use it.

63 Use the semicolon:

. . . to separate logically connected main clauses not joined by a coordinate conjunction.

We submitted the project plans to the Director this morning; they were approved by noon.
The Director publicly commended us for our work; he is particularly pleased about the new accounts system.
We have completed the summary; that is, we have completed the first draft.

. . . to separate main clauses joined by a conjunctive adverb.

The boss publicly commended us for our report; however, he later asked us to rewrite the conclusion.
The new system is scheduled to begin next Monday; we will, therefore, need the manuals by Friday.

. . . to separate main clauses joined by a coordinate conjunction when the clauses contain commas (if the semicolon is needed for clarity).

You will, of course, want to notify him; and, unless he is out of town, he will surely attend. (Comma after *and* is optional.)
He has given his tentative approval; but, naturally, he will wait until after the trial run to make a final decision.

... to separate coordinate items in a series when the items contain internal commas.

> Attending were representatives from Omaha, Nebraska; Los Angeles, California; Salem, Oregon; and San Francisco, California.
>
> Meeting to discuss the new plan were: Wilson, just in from New York; Addison, here only for the day; and James, only recently back from his place in the country.

64 Use the colon:

... between main clauses when the second clause completes or explains the first.

> There are two courses open to us: We can demand that the issue be reopened, or we can abide by the decision until the group meets again in the fall.

... after an expression that formally introduces a list, an explanation, or a quotation.

> Our new secretary will need to possess three qualities: endurance, patience, and humor.
>
> Our supply list includes the following items: one ream of bond paper, one box of pencils, and three typewriter ribbons.
>
> The topic of the conference is: An Appraisal of the Jacobs System.
>
> In his talk the Director said: "This division has, in the past few months, made great strides in reducing the backlog of cases."

... after the salutation in a business letter.

> Gentlemen:
> Dear Mr. Johnson:

NOTE: Do not use a colon after the salutation in a friendly letter; use a comma (see Section 62).

65 Use the dash:

... between main clauses when the second clause explains or summarizes the first.

> The decision was obvious—we would have to recall all tests until we could recheck them.
>
> He has done two things of which he is enormously proud—he has led the division to increased production, and he has helped increase the prestige of the division throughout the organization.

... to set off a nonrestrictive modifier or parenthetical element that contains internal commas.

> The Williams Building—built, it is believed, in 1900—was torn down three years ago.

... to emphasize a nonrestrictive modifier or parenthetical element that is normally set off by commas.

> He was—fortunately—able to deliver the pictures by the deadline.
>
> I plan to ask Wade—who is the person who surely ought to know—how this plan was first devised.

... to set off a nonrestrictive appositive for special emphasis.

> Only one member—the chairman—can break a tie vote.
>
> There is just one thing wrong with the filing system—you can't find anything!

66 Use parentheses:

... to enclose a nonrestrictive modifier or parenthetic element that is only loosely connected with the thought of the sentence.

> The book (published in 1969) has been most helpful to me.
>
> His discussion of those principles (pages 44-49) is one of the best I've seen.
>
> Mr. X (who probably knows more about production than anyone else in the company is being transferred to our Atlanta office.

NOTE: If other punctuation is needed at the place in the sentence where the parentheses occur, it follows the closing parenthesis. But if the punctuation pertains to the parenthetic matter it is placed within the parentheses.

> If you plan to attend the meeting (to be held at the Statler Hotel), please notify us by June 1.
>
> The director has approved our report (Publication No. 333); it will be released later this week.
>
> His promotion is barred by the Whitten Amendment. (See C.S. Reg. 2.501 (j).)
>
> His promotion is barred by the Whitten Amendment (C.S. Reg. 2.501 (j)).

67 Use quotation marks as follows:

...Beginning Quote

"Please return my keys," she said.
"Where are the children?" asked the grandmother.

...End Quote

The old man mumbled, "Times have certainly changed."
He yelled, "Give me my money!"

NOTE: The first word of a direct quotation is always capitalized. (*Times*, *Give*)

...Broken Quote

"This is quite a bargain," she said, "when you consider all that they do for you."
"I want to get off here," the passenger called out. "Please stop the bus."

NOTE 1: When a direct quotation is broken, the first word of the second half of the sentence is *not* capitalized. (*when*)

NOTE 2: When the second half of a broken quotation begins with a *new sentence*, the first word of the new sentence is capitalized. (*Please*)

Use single quotation marks to enclose a quotation within a quotation.

Addison remarked, "The phrase 'initiate any appropriate action' seems to leave a lot to the imagination."

When a quotation is given in indirect form, no quotation marks are used. An indirect quotation is usually introduced by *that*.

Direct quotation: He said, "I mailed my tax return yesterday."
Indirect quotation: He said that he mailed his tax return yesterday.

Quotation Marks With Other Marks of Punctuation

The comma and period are placed inside the quotation marks, whether or not they are a part of the quoted material.

"I wonder," he said, "if we will ever finish it."

The semicolon and colon are placed outside the quotation marks unless they are a part of the quoted matter.

"We have come far, but we have farther to go"; that is the note on which he began his speech.
I have only one thing to say about the "X Report": it will be a long time before we hear the last of it.

The question mark and exclamation mark are placed inside the quotation marks if they are a part of the quotation; outside if they are not.

He asked, "Do you plan to attend the meeting?"
Could we describe the project as "essentially completed"?

Use *only one* terminal punctuation mark at end of sentences. *Examples*: (1) Who was it who said, "Know thyself"? (2) He frowned when she asked, "Why?" (3) Which student asked, "Why?"

When enclosing a title with quotation marks, place the comma and the period inside the quotation marks.

The student enjoyed reading "Catcher in the Rye."
We recommend this book, "Good English With Ease," to all of you.

68 Use the apostrophe:

...to indicate omission.

We're (for *We are*) leaving shortly.
It's (for *It is*) six *o'clock* (for *of the clock*).

...to form the plural of letters and numbers.

Battalion is spelled with two *t*'s.
His license plate has three *6*'s.

For use of the apostrophe to show possession, see Sections 14a-h.

69 Use the hyphen:

... for the numbers from twenty-one through ninety-nine.

> There are no longer *forty-nine* stars in the flag.

... for a fraction used as a modifier.

> The bottle is *one-fourth* full.
> But: They received *three fourths* of the vote.
> (*three fourths* is used as a noun.)

... for a compound adjective when it precedes the noun modified.

> Picasso is a *well-known* painter.
> But: Picasso is *well known*. (The modifier is after the noun.)

... for certain compound nouns.

> *son-in-law, father-in-law, great-grandparents*
> But: *stepmother, half sister, grandfather*

70 Capitalization Rules

1. The first word of a sentence:

> *With* cooperation, a depression can be avoided.

2. All proper names:

> America, Santa Fe Chief, General Motors, Abraham Lincoln.

3. Days of the week and months:

> The check was mailed on *Thursday*.

NOTE: The seasons are not capitalized
Example: In Florida, *winter* is mild.

4. The word **dear** when it is the first word in the salutation of a letter:

> *Dear* Mr. Jones:
> but
> My *dear* Mr. Jones:

5. The first word of the complimentary close of a letter:

> *Truly* yours,
> but
> Very truly yours,

6. The first, and the important words in a title:

> The *Art* of *Salesmanship*

7. A word used as part of a proper name:

> William *Street* (but-That *street* is narrow.) Morningside *Terrace* (but: We have a *terrace* apartment.)

8. Titles, when they refer to a particular official or family member:

> The report was read by *Secretary* Marshall. (but: Miss Shaw, our *secretary*, is ill.)
> Let's visit *Uncle* Harry.
> (but: I have three *uncles*.)

9. Points of a compass, when they refer to particular regions of a country:

> We're going *South* next week. (but: New York is *south of Albany*.)

> Write: the Far West, the Pacific Coast, the Middle East, etc.

10. The first word of a direct quotation:

> It was Alexander Pope who wrote, "A little learning is a dangerous thing."

Now, push forward! Test yourself and practice for your test with the carefully constructed quizzes that follow. Each one presents the kind of question you may expect on your test. And each question is at just the level of difficulty that may be expected. Don't try to take all the tests at one time. Rather, schedule yourself so that you take a few at each session, and spend approximately the same time on them at each session. Score yourself honestly, and date each test. You should be able to detect improvement in your performance on successive sessions.

TEST XVIII. PUNCTUATION

TIME: 19 Minutes

DIRECTIONS: In each of the following groups of sentences, select the one sentence that is grammatically INCORRECT. Mark the answer sheet with the letter of that incorrect sentence.

Explanations of the key points behind these questions appear with the answers at the end of this test. The explanatory answers provide the kind of background that will enable you to answer test questions with facility and confidence.

1
(A) Although she appeared to be well, she lay in bed all day yesterday.
(B) The embezzler, whom you sentenced last week, has escaped.
(C) My uncle hasn't had much formal education, and yet he is an authority on Greek literature.
(D) The Chicago White Sox cannot possibly lose the pennant this year.

2
(A) The policeman told us that there had been another robbery at the house next door to us.
(B) "How do you like my dress?" Mary asked me, "it was a gift from my aunt."
(C) Is he wearing that blue overcoat again?
(D) The residents of the area rejected the proposed school budget.

3
(A) The General Organization must be a well-run school program, otherwise, its purpose is nullified.
(B) However, you may look at it, the problem is a serious one.
(C) The charge, if supported by fact, is enough to send all of them to prison.
(D) To be guilty of an overt act is a crime against the state.

4
(A) A slip of the tongue may cause intense embarrassment.
(B) The garret was cluttered with old furniture, discarded toys, moth-eaten clothing, etc.
(C) Interpret the lines as you will, their relevancy to the author's theme is questionable.
(D) Snow's thesis is that the world of science and the world of the humanities are irreconcilable.

5
(A) "It can be seen from our house, said Jack."
(B) Books, stationery, office furniture—all are sold in the new store.
(C) Such a harrowing experience can easily unnerve a sensitive child.
(D) Several chapters of the book were accidentally sent to the wrong department.

6
(A) If we meet the deadline, we shall have paid our debt to their satisfaction.
(B) The secretary's only reply was, "no comment."
(C) Please come to school on Wednesday, for we must talk about your son's grades.
(D) It occurred to the four courageous boys that they could divide the reward among them.

7
(A) "Why," she asked, "must I be responsible for training new employees to work the switchboard"?
(B) You must not doubt your ability to learn to prepare payroll reports.
(C) Learning to operate duplicating machines is an important part of a secretary's duties.
(D) I realize the values of promptness and accuracy in the office.

8
(A) A whole truckload of old clothes has been collected for the community drive.
(B) Frank ran all the way, he was certain he'd be late.
(C) If I were you, I should tell the entire truth.
(D) His incoherence and the guttural quality of his speech made it difficult for the audience to understand him.

9

(A) I read Golding's "Lord of the Flies".
(B) The orator at the civil rights rally thrilled the audience when he said, "I quote Robert Burn's line, 'A man's a man for a' that'"
(C) The phrase "producer to consumer" is commonly used by market analysts.
(D) The lawyer shouted, "Is not this evidence illegal?"

10

(A) "John told me," said James, "That he was not going with us."
(B) During the course, I read not only four plays but also three historical novels.
(C) The assortment of candies, nuts, and fruits is excellent.
(D) Worn out by the days of exposure and storm, the sailor clung pitifully to the puny raft.

11

(A) The judge listened carefully to the testimony of all the witnesses.
(B) The parisian influence is apparent in all of her dresses.
(C) What enthusiasm, energy, and skill the youngsters showed!
(D) His roommate was a typical mixture of hypocrisy and conceit.

12

(A) "This composition is well written, said the teacher, but I doubt that it represents your best work."
(B) To realize how greatly our environement has changed, one has only to review the past.
(C) If you compare Bill and Joe, you will conclude that the former is brighter.
(D) The author of the prize novel was feted.

13

(A) We're sure she'll respond if your careful about the suggestions she's given each day.
(B) I have always been of the opinion that that kind of examination is of little value.
(C) The papers will not blow away if you lay the paper weight on them.
(D) He had scarcely finished his lines when the audience began to applaud wildly.

14

(A) The feasibility of mass inoculations has made all governments aware of the necessity of maintaining a public health service.
(B) There are students who have not passed all their courses.
(C) What you decide to do about military service is your own business.
(D) We were intrigued by Professor Martin's interpretation of "On First Looking into Chapman's Homer".

15

(A) Although we are working under adverse conditions, let us strive to attain our objectives.
(B) If you ask me, being first in this contest required little intelligence, anybody could have done it.
(C) Stores try to discourage stealing by making customers feel that they are under close surveillance.
(D) You should know whether or not William the Conqueror lived during the Middle Ages.

16

(A) Martin says "that his cat's eyes shine in the dark."
(B) The murmur of voices could now be heard.
(C) There is a stationery store on each side of the street.
(D) Ichabod sat down carefully on the three-legged stool.

17

(A) The incidence of vitamin deficiency correlates positively with the level of family income.
(B) The "population explosion" is a threat to our survival, however, relatively little has been done to combat it.
(C) As for automation, its social implications have affected policy decisions in the highest echelons of government.
(D) Shakespeare's skill as a playwright stemmed from his experience in the theatre.

18

(A) "Doesn't this book interest you," asked the librarian?
(B) There are three 5's and two 4's in 54,545.
(C) This article will be sold to whoever makes the highest bid.
(D) Mortimer is one of those children who are always looking for attention.

19

(A) Joe's account of his lateness is incredible. I will not give him a second chance.
(B) Her willingness to take a typing course was due to her desire to submit a neat term paper.
(C) They scheduled their lunch hours in such a way that the switchboard could be covered constantly.
(D) She replenished her supply of clips, staples, bond paper, and pencils.

20

(A) I find music and poetry complementary, not competitive.
(B) "Don't be a perfectionist," they tell us, "it's impractical."
(C) I don't like his lackadaisical attitude.
(D) "I'm willing to concede the point," he said.

(A) The announcer said that variable cloudiness would be a feature of the weather on Sunday.
(B) Before starting to hunt John cleaned his rifle.
(C) All classes in Italian that meet at 3:30 today will be canceled.
(D) Had I known your address, I should have asked you to come with us.

(A) Much as I like to attend the theater, I feel strong disgust if the dialogue is blasphemous.
(B) The pupil who first discovers an acceptable solution to this problem will be invited to explain it to the club.
(C) Regardless of all that has been written on the Civil War, authors still find the struggle between the north and the south a fertile source of inspiration.
(D) Whether nineteenth century classics should be taught today has become a matter of controversy.

23

(A) That the Russian dramatist Chekhov should have died of tuberculosis at the comparatively early age of forty-four seems, to all lovers of literature and drama, a great pity.
(B) Thornton Wilder's play, Our Town, is being continually revived.

(C) At the theater last week I saw no fewer than four assemblymen, two senators and several well-known judges.
(D) Whoever you think is best able to lead us, we promise to follow loyally.

(A) There was a time when the Far North was unknown territory. Now American soldiers manning radar stations there wave to Boeing jet planes zooming by overhead.
(B) Exodus, the psalms, and Deuteronomy are all books of the Old Testament.
(C) Linda identified her china dishes by marking their bottoms with india ink.
(D) Harry S. Truman served as a captain.

(A) Mr. Prendergast, as a disinterested mediator, remained at the meeting all night in an effort to settle the strike.
(B) "For goodness' sake, children," cried the mother, "lower you voices"!
(C) An unpracticed liar, Mary explained her absence from school with an incredible tale of derring-do in which she played the role of heroine.
(D) I must repeat that these are the facts of the case.

CONSOLIDATE YOUR KEY ANSWERS HERE

Correct Answers For The Foregoing Questions

(Check your answers with these that we provide. You should find considerable correspondence between them. If not, you'd better go back and find out why. On the next page we have provided concise clarifications of basic points behind the key answers. Please go over them carefully because they may be quite useful in helping you pick up extra points on the exam.)

1. B	5. A	9. A	13. A	17. B	21. B	25. B
2. B	6. B	10. A	14. D	18. A	22. C	
3. A	7. A	11. B	15. B	19. A	23. B	
4. C	8. B	12. A	16. A	20. B	24. B	

TEST XVIII   PUNCTUATION

EXPLANATORY ANSWERS CLARIFYING CARDINAL POINTS

The core of the Question and Answer Method ... getting help when and where you need it. Even if you were able to write correct key answers for the preceding questions, the following explanations illuminate fundamental facts, ideas, and principles which just might crop up in the form of questions on future tests.

Bold-face references in the following answers direct you to paragraphs in the Arco Grammar Text, where fuller explanations are provided.

ANSWER 1.

B   The embezzler whom you sentenced last week has escaped. REASON: The restrictive clause (**whom ... week**) takes no commas.   **(62)**

ANSWER 2.

B   "How do you like my dress?" Mary asked me. "**It** was a gift from my aunt." REASON: The second half of the broken quotation begins with a new sentence. Therefore, **It** must begin with a capital.   **(67)**

ANSWER 3.

A   The General Organization must be a well-run school program; otherwise, its purpose is nullified. REASON: The semicolon is necessary before **otherwise**. With the comma instead of the semicolon, we have a run-on sentence.   **(62, 63)**

ANSWER 4.

C   Interpret the lines as you **will—their** relevancy to the author's theme is questionable. REASON: The original sentence is run-on. We must split the two independent clauses with a dash or a period—not with a comma.   **(62, 65)**

ANSWER 5.

A   "It can be seen from our house," said Jack. REASON: The quotation mark was misplaced.   **(67)**

ANSWER 6.

B   The secretary's only reply was, "**No** comment." REASON: The capital letter is used to begin the quotation.   **(67)**

ANSWER 7.

A   "Why," she asked, "must I be responsible for training new employees to work the switchboard?" REASON: The question mark belongs inside of the second quote.   **(67)**

ANSWER 8.

B   Frank ran all the **way; he** was certain he'd be late. REASON: The original sentence has a run-on construction.   **(63)**

ANSWER 9.

A   I read Golding's "Lord of the Flies." REASON: The period is placed inside the quotation marks—not outside.   **(67)**

ANSWER 10.

A   "John told me," said James, "**that** he was not going with us." REASON: The second part of the broken quotation begins with a small letter (**that**).   **(67)**

ANSWER 11.

B   The **Parisian** influence is apparent in all of her dress. REASON: This adjective (derived from the name of a city) begins with a capital.   **(38, 70)**

ANSWER 12.

A "This composition is well written," said the teacher, "**but** I doubt that it represents your best work." REASON: The quotation marks must be placed after the first part and before the second part of the broken quotation. **(67)**

ANSWER 13.

A We're sure she'll respond if **you're** careful about the suggestions she's given each day. REASON: The sentence requires **you are (you're)**. **(68)**

ANSWER 14.

D We were intrigued by Professor Martin's interpretation of "On First Looking into Chapman's Homer." REASON: When a quoted title ends a sentence, the period comes inside of the quotation mark. Incidentally, the verb **to intrigue** is now accepted to mean **to fascinate**. **(67)**

ANSWER 15.

B If you ask me, being first in this contest required little intelligence, since anybody could have done it. REASON: The subordinate conjunction (**since**) is necessary. Without it, we would have a run-on sentence. **(62)**

ANSWER 16.

A Martin says that his cat's eyes shine in the dark. REASON: The quotation marks are omitted in indirect discourse. **(67)**

ANSWER 17.

B The "population explosion" is a threat to our **survival; however**, relatively little has been done to combat it. REASON: The semicolon is required before the conjunctive adverb **however**. **(63)**

ANSWER 18.

A "Doesn't this book interest you?" asked the librarian. REASON: The question mark should be enclosed within the direct quotation. **(67)**

ANSWER 19.

A Joe's account of his lateness is incredible. I will not give him a second chance. REASON: The period must be used to break up the two main clauses. The original sentence is a run-on sentence. **(59, 62)**

ANSWER 20.

B "Don't be a perfectionist," they tell us. "**It's** impractical." REASON: The period after **us** ends the first sentence in the broken quotation. **It's** (with a capital) begins the second sentence of the broken quotation. **(67)**

ANSWER 21.

B Before starting to **hunt**, **John** cleaned his rifle. REASON: The comma is used as a pause, for clarity. **(62)**

ANSWER 22.

C Regardless of all that has been written on the Civil War, authors still find the struggle between the **North** and the **South** a fertile source of inspiration. REASON: Capital letters are needed to refer to particular regions. **(70)**

ANSWER 23.

B Thornton Wilder's play, "Our Town," is being continually revived. REASON: The name of a play is enclosed by quotation marks or is italicized (in print). **(67)**

ANSWER 24.

B Exodus, **Psalms**, and Deuteronomy are all books of the Old Testament. REASON: **Psalms**, a book of the Old Testament, must have an initial capital. Also, we do not use the definite article (**the**) preceding it. **(70)**

ANSWER 25.

B "For goodness' sake, children," cried the mother, "lower your voices!" REASON: The exclamation mark is placed inside the quotation marks since it is part of the quotation. **(67)**

TEST XIX. PUNCTUATION

TIME: 20 Minutes

DIRECTIONS: In each of the following groups of sentences, select the one sentence that is grammatically INCORRECT. Mark the answer sheet with the letter of that incorrect sentence.

Explanations of the key points behind these questions appear with the answers at the end of this test. The explanatory answers provide the kind of background that will enable you to answer test questions with facility and confidence.

1

(A) Harry's perseverance was praised by those who had observed his efforts to learn the part.
(B) Is the present system detrimental to the interests of both the producer and the consumer?
(C) Why should we give him our books, when he had extras he refused to share them with us?
(D) Although he tried hard to pass all of his tests, he failed one of them.

2

(A) I don't understand why people like Paul and me should be required to fill out this questionnaire.
(B) The Declaration of Independence opens with these words: "When in the course of human events...."
(C) The stranger wore a long, buttonless, tattered cloak.
(D) "It is unlikely," said the lecturer in response to my question; "that man will ever reach the outer planets."

3

(A) To learn about the Middle Ages you would do well to read *Life On A Medieval Barony.*
(B) There were Mary and Ellen in front of the school door.
(D) "Frank's dog is still in the yard," my father said, "perhaps he had better stay there until we have finished our dinner."
(D) The English Channel has been swum by both men and women.

4

(A) The teacher asked, "Who is the author of 'The Purloined Letter'?"
(B) Courage, self-denial, a high sense of duty—these are the attributes of a great statesman.
(C) Our supply of drinking water which we assume is inexhaustible, becomes a precious commodity in times of drought.
(D) No government can guarantee economic security, however much it may desire to do so.

5

(A) The sight of the marching soldiers with their colorful uniforms, will remain with us forever.
(B) Did he plan the lesson, prepare the test, and mark the papers all by himself?
(C) Do not put into parentheses or brackets any of your own writing that you wish omitted.
(D) A crate of oranges is being sent to the winner of the essay contest.

6

(A) A picture of Martin Van Buren who was not one of our better-known presidents hangs on the rear wall of my room.
(B) My brother likes to go to New Hampshire with Uncle Bob to enjoy the winter sports.
(C) His work does not indicate the kind of perseverance needed.
(D) The speaker's habit of disparaging the achievements of great men was resented.

7

(A) A visit to the children's ward of St. Giles' hospital proved to be a heart-rending experience.
(B) Let's you and me take the matter into our own hands.
(C) Being the only man in the group, he found that the demands upon his gentlemanliness exhausted him.
(D) The detective, when he was looking for a suspect, never dreamed of its being me.

8

(A) Our English teacher used Poe's "The Bells" to illustrate the principle of onomatopoeia.
(B) "Were the delegates all seated when the speaker arrived," Hawkins asked?
(C) Why are we boys blamed for what those girls did?
(D) We may attribute the noticeable decline in the number of misspelled words to our emphasizing correct pronunciation.

9

(A) You have probably heard of the innovation in the regular morning broadcast.
(B) The pupils are required to stand, to salute, and to sing the fourth stanza of "America."
(C) None of the rocks which form the solid crust of our planet is more than two billion years old.
(D) "I have finished my assignment," said the pupil. "May I go home now"?

10

(A) He asked whether they had read, "Ulysses."
(B) In her first attempt to make fudge, she concocted a nauseous mess that had to be thrown away.
(C) The insignia on his uniform indicate that he has served overseas.
(D) The program was broadcast by stations all over the world.

11

(A) When Daniel Boone was captured by the Indians, the entire settlement was in danger.
(B) The wolverine, a powerful member of the weasel family is commonly found in the forests of Canada and Alaska.
(C) They played the game like professionals.
(D) Anyone with the necessary equipment can manufacture his own outdoor furniture.

12

(A) A serious student of any art would be surprised to find himself referred to as a dilettante.
(B) The conclusion of most American novels, at least in previous generations, was the typical happy ending.
(C) "The work will soon be finished," said John, "If everyone does his share."
(D) People who are too credulous are likely to be deceived by unscrupulous individuals.

13

(A) Jones seems slow on the track, but you will find few boys quicker than he on the basketball court.
(B) Many themes considered sacrilegious in the nineteenth century are treated casually on today's stage.
(C) Few members besides you think that the club should have a meeting every month.
(D) One of the great heroes of World War I was general John Pershing.

14

(A) Robert purchased five dollars' worth of candy for the party.
(B) Such activities certainly do not warrant official recognition.
(C) His brother, the captain of the squad scored many points.
(D) Caesar's refusal to heed the soothsayer's prophecy resulted in the success of the conspiracy against him.

15

(A) He cannot claim that his refusal to remit the proper sum was due to his not being informed of the requirement, for he was.
(B) When you are entertaining a potful of coffee is a good thing to have on hand.
(C) Letters of censure and of commendation may be signed only by the Commissioners.
(D) Although certain questions remain unanswered, the program is important and must go forward.

16

(A) You should understand, sir, that no draft that is not countersigned by the cashier of the company is valid.
(B) The teacher shouted at the class, "Stop bothering me with your foolish questions. Just leave me alone".
(C) All our fraternity brothers are truly fond of one another.
(D) No great naturalist of note has yet written so excellent an account.

17

(A) The agent asked, "Did you say, 'Never again?'"
(B) Kindly let me know whether you can visit us on the 17th.
(C) "I cannot accept that!" he exploded. "Please show me something else."
(D) Ed, will you please lend me your grass shears for an hour or so?

18

(A) Whether the book is John's or yours, I should like to borrow it for the duration of this unit.
(B) Neither Bonnie nor Clyde was chosen for the class play.
(C) The beautiful view from the hilltop, is the attraction that brings thousands of visitors here every year.
(D) Many look upon George Washington as the unparalleled hero of our country.

19

(A) The intensive study of Latin and English made the young man aware of their interrelationship.
(B) Chess, he believes, is the ideal thinker's pastime.
(C) We were told to read Charles Lamb's essays and Edgar Allan Poe's short stories.
(D) The seasoned campaigner heard the warning, he chose to ignore it.

20

(A) A home run that constant threat to the peace of mind of pitchers, was hit in the ninth inning.
(B) No form of prejudice having exhibited itself, the State Anti-Discrimination Commission decided to look elsewhere.
(C) When they arrived, they found no one but the children in the house.
(D) The traveller had an attack of appendicitis and was operated on immediately.

21

(A) The monograph was rather poorly received because of its pedantic style.
(B) As the work could not be finished that night, Mr. Small decided to go to bed.
(C) He would like to gamble, still, he fears that he can ill afford to lose.
(D) Defeated though he was, the chieftain carried himself proudly.

22

(A) He was wholly committed to a course of action many thought dangerous.
(B) She did the work very well, however, she showed no interest in anything beyond her assignment.
(C) Such fallacious reasoning can easily be detected by an experienced debater.
(D) I hope to have good news for you tomorrow.

23

(A) The sequel of their marriage was a divorce.
(B) We bought our car secondhand.
(C) His whereabouts is unknown.
(D) Jones offered to use his own car; providing the company would pay for gasoline, oil, and repairs.

24

(A) She needed the secretarial job to supplement her income.
(B) He felt bad when he heard the news.
(C) "They will soon be here," John replied, "Please wait for them."
(D) It was hard to believe that conscientious pupils could misspell so many words in their quizzes.

25

(A) Throughout the day, we waited in the vicinity of the attorney's residence.
(B) My sister was overjoyed to receive the citation.
(C) After all his adventures, he seemed unable to settle down to a steady job.
(D) We asked uncle Tim to take us to the circus.

26

(A) The weakened garrison did little to act as a deterrent force.
(B) Roberts, a man whom we trusted with the most difficult task of all proved loyal to his country.
(C) The consensus of those present favored the suggestion.
(D) Apples, pears, plums, and apricots were quickly sold to the eager children.

27

(A) "As I remember it, his words were, Please give me another chance," said Jim.
(B) The results of the poll had little or no effect on the actions of the legislature.
(C) We all asked him to be careful not to spoil the official reception.
(D) These platitudinous observations did little to embellish his speech.

CONSOLIDATE YOUR KEY ANSWERS HERE

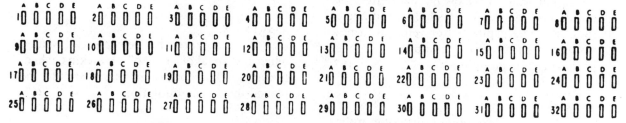

Correct Answers For The Foregoing Questions

(Check your answers with these that we provide. You should find considerable correspondence between them. If not, you'd better go back and find out why. On the next page we have provided concise clarifications of basic points behind the key answers.)

1. C	5. A	9. D	13. D	17. A	21. C	25. D
2. D	6. A	10. A	14. C	18. C	22. B	26. B
3. C	7. A	11. B	15. B	19. D	23. D	27. A
4. C	8. B	12. C	16. B	20. A	24. C	

TEST XIX. PUNCTUATION

EXPLANATORY ANSWERS CLARIFYING CARDINAL POINTS

The core of the Question and Answer Method ... getting help when and where you need it. Even if you were able to write correct key answers for the preceding questions, the following explanations illuminate fundamental facts, ideas, and principles which just might crop up in the form of questions on future tests.

Bold-face references in the following answers direct you to paragraphs in the Arco Grammar Text, where fuller explanations are provided.

ANSWER 1.

C Why should we give him our books? When he had extras, he refused to share them with us. REASON: The original sentence is run-on since it contains two independent clauses with no coordinate conjunction. **(62)**

ANSWER 2.

D "It is unlikely," said the lecturer in response to my **question**, "**that** man will ever reach the outer planets." REASON: The use of a semicolon is incorrect here. **(63, 67)**

ANSWER 3.

C "Frank's dog is still in the yard," my father said. "**Perhaps** he had better stay there until we have finished our dinner." REASON: The capital letter refers to a new sentence. There are two complete sentences in this broken quotation. **(67)**

ANSWER 4.

C Our supply of drinking **water, which** we assume is inexhaustible, becomes a precious commodity in times of drought. REASON: The nonrestrictive adjective clause is enclosed by commas. **(62)**

ANSWER 5.

A The sight of the marching soldiers with their colorful uniforms will remain with us forever. REASON: The comma is not to be used here—it breaks up the thought. **(62)**

ANSWER 6.

A A picture of Martin Van Buren, who was not one of our better-known presidents, hangs on the rear wall of my room. REASON: A nonrestrictive clause should be set off by commas. A nonrestrictive clause is not an organic part of the whole sentence. Such a clause may be omitted without destroying the essential meaning of the sentence. **(62)**

ANSWER 7.

A A visit to the children's ward of St. Giles' **Hospital** proved to be a heart-rending experience. REASON: A word (**Hospital**) used as part of a proper name should be capitalized. **(10a, 70)**

ANSWER 8.

B "Were the delegates all seated when the speaker arrived?" Hawkins asked. REASON: The question mark should be placed inside the quotation. **(67)**

ANSWER 9.

D "I have finished my assignment," said the pupil. "May I go home now?" REASON: The question mark, being part of the quotation, is placed inside the quotation marks. **(67)**

ANSWER 10.

A He asked whether they had read "Ulysses." REASON: There is no reason for the comma after **read**. **(62)**

ANSWER 11.

B The wolverine, a powerful member of the weasel **family, is** commonly found in the forests of Canada and Alaska. REASON: A comma is needed to enclose the appositive (**a powerful . . . family**). **(62)**

ANSWER 12.

C "The work will soon be finished," said John, "**if** everyone does his share." REASON: The first word of the second part of a broken quotation begins with a small letter. **(67)**

ANSWER 13.

D One of the great heroes of World War I was **General** John Pershing. REASON: **General** is capitalized since it is part of the proper noun **Pershing**. **(70)**

ANSWER 14.

C His brother, the captain of the **squad**, scored many points. REASON: The comma sets off the appositive. **(62)**

ANSWER 15.

B When you are **entertaining, a** potful of coffee is a good thing to have on hand. REASON: The comma is necessary to avoid confusion. **(62)**

ANSWER 16.

B The teacher shouted at the class, "Stop bothering me with your foolish question. Just leave me **alone**." REASON: The period should be enclosed within the original quotation. **(67)**

ANSWER 17.

A The agent asked, "Did you say, 'Never again'?" REASON: The question mark is placed between the single and double quotes because the **never again** quote is not the question. The question is the entire **"Did you say, 'Never again'?"** **(67)**

ANSWER 18.

C The beautiful view from the **hilltop is** the attraction that brings thousands of visitors here every year. REASON: The comma is not to be used here—it breaks up the thought. **(62)**

ANSWER 19.

D The seasoned campaigner heard the warning, **but** he chose to ignore it. REASON: The coordinate conjunction (**but**) should be used to avoid the run-on sentence. **(62)**

ANSWER 20.

A A home **run, that** constant threat to the peace of mind of pitchers, was hit in the ninth inning. REASON: The appositive (**that constant threat to the peace of mind of pitchers**) must be set off by commas. **(62)**

ANSWER 21.

C He would like to **gamble; still,** he fears that he can ill afford to lose. REASON: The semicolon is required to separate main clauses joined by a conjunctive adverb (**still**). The original sentence is run on. **(62, 63)**

ANSWER 22.

B She did the work very **well; however,** she showed no interest in anything beyond her assignment. REASON: The semicolon is necessary before the conjunctive adverb **however**, if we are to avoid a run-on sentence. **(62, 63)**

ANSWER 23.

D Jones offered to use his own **car providing** the company would pay for gasoline, oil, and repairs. REASON: No punctuation mark belongs after **car**. **(62, 63)**

ANSWER 24.

C "They will soon be here," John **replied**. "Please wait for them." REASON: The period is necessary after **replied** since it marks the end of the first sentence in the broken quotation. **(67)**

ANSWER 25.

D We asked **Uncle Tim** to take us to the circus. REASON: **Uncle** is capitalized because it is part of the family name. **(70)**

ANSWER 26.

B Roberts, a man whom we trusted with the most difficult task of all, proved loyal to his country. REASON: The appositive (**a man . . . of all**) must be set off by commas. **(62c)**

ANSWER 27.

A "As I remember it, his words were, 'Please give me another chance'," said Jim. REASON: A quotation within a quotation is enclosed by a pair of single quotation marks. **(67)**

2

PART TWO

Correct English Usage.

A Glossary Correcting Common Errors.
Two Test-Type Quizzes.
66 Questions With Explanatory Answers.

Knowledge of grammar and English usage is fundamental to almost every exam. Firstly it's required in order to understand and answer the questions correctly. Secondly, many exams ask direct questions involving correct English usage and grammar. This book was written to help you on any exam you might have to take. The grammar is as simple as we could make it, while still solving the problems generally posed by a wide variety of tests. Every significant rule of grammar is concisely explained in eighty indexed pages, reasonably arranged in seven chapters. Each chapter is followed by examination-type questions that explain, clarify, and illustrate the rules in that chapter. Each multiple-choice question is answered both by key letter and by a fuller explanation. These explanations contain frequent references back to the numbered rules of grammar involved. Learning correct English usage should be a pleasure because you will have so many concrete illustrations of the rules which, in the past, were abstract and dry.

CORRECT ENGLISH USAGE

Here is where educated, literate people have the greatest difficulty in making themselves readily understood. They know enough words and their grammar seldom slips. But too often they put words together into sentences that are just too hard to understand. The suggestions discussed here are based on a study of the things that can make your writing much more effective.

FIRST of all, it is important for you to know the essential difference between two special categories in the study of Correct Usage —

COLLOQUIAL ENGLISH and SLANG.

COLLOQUIAL (or INFORMAL) ENGLISH — This is English customarily used in conversation and informal types of writing (notes, diaries, friendly letters, etc.). It is ACCEPTABLE.

SLANG — This is used by people who are poor in vocabulary and/or lazy. It is generally UNACCEPTABLE.

WORDS THAT WON'T WORRY YOU AGAIN

abbreviate—means *to shorten by omitting.*
abridge—means *to shorten by condensing.*
> New York is *abbreviated* to N. Y., Tennesee to *Tenn.*
> In order to save time in the reading, the report was *abridged.*

ability—means a *developed, actual* power.
capacity—means an *undeveloped, potential* power.
> He now has fair writing *ability*, but additional courses in college will develop his *capacity* beyond the average level.

above—Avoid *above* except in business forms where it may be used in reference to a preceding part of the text. In normal writing use *foregoing* or *preceding*, instead of *above.*
> *Unacceptable*: The *above* books are available in the library.
> *Acceptable*: The *above* prices are subject to change without notice.

accede—means *to agree with.*
concede—means *to yield*, but not necessarily in agreement.

exceed—means *to be more than.*
> We shall *accede* to your request for more evidence.
> To avoid delay, we shall *concede* that more evidence is necessary.
> Federal expenditures now *exceed* federal income.

accept—means *to take when offered.*
except—means *excluding.* (preposition)
except—means *to leave out.* (verb)
> The draft board will *accept* all seniors as volunteers before graduation.
> All eighteen-year-olds *except* seniors will be called.
> The draft board will *except* all seniors until after graduation.

access—means *availability.*
excess—means *too much.*
> The lawyer was given *access* to the grand jury records.
> The expenditures this month are far in *excess* of income.

accidently—No such word. The word is *accidentally* (adverb). Pronounce it ak-si-DENT-ally.

in accord with—means *in agreement with a person*.

I am *in accord with* you about this.

in accordance with—means *in agreement with a thing*.

The police officer acted *in accordance with* the law.

acoustics—when used in the *singular* means *the science* of sound.

Acoustics is a subdivision of physics.

acoustics—when used in the *plural* denotes the *qualities* of sound.

The *acoustics* of Carnegie Hall are incomparable.

Note: *Athletics* is an *activity* (or *are activities*) that will aid in weight-reducing.

Politics is a method (or *are methods*) of getting favors.

Physics is a science. (*singular* as a *branch of science*).

Physics are used to relieve sickness. (*plural* as a *medicine*)

Economics is taught in most high schools. (*singular only*)

acquiesce in—means *to accept with or without objection*. Do NOT use *acquiesce* WITH or *acquiesce* TO.

Although there is some doubt about your plan, I shall *acquiesce in* its adoption.

ad—this abbreviation for *advertisement* is colloquial; it is not to be used in formal speech or writing.

Other colloquial words of this type, with the formal word in parentheses, are *exam* (examination) *auto* (automobile); *phone* (telephone); *gym* (gymnasium).

adapt—means *to adjust or change*.

adopt—means *to take as one's own*.

adept—means *skillful*.

Children can *adapt* to changing conditions very easily.

The war orphan was *adopted* by the general and his wife.

Proper instruction makes children *adept* in various games.

NOTE: adapt *to*, adopt *by*, adept *in* or *at*.

adapted to—implies *original or natural suitability*.

The gills of the fish are *adapted to* underwater breathing.

adapted for—implies *created suitability*.

Atomic energy is constantly being *adapted for* new uses.

adapted from—implies *changed to be made suitable*.

Many of Richard Wagner's opera librettos were *adapted from* old Norse sagas.

addicted to—means *accustomed to by strong habit*.

subject to—means *exposed to* or *liable to*.

People *addicted to* drugs or alcohol need constant medical care.

The coast of Wales is *subject to* extremely heavy fogs.

addition—means *the act or process of adding*.

edition—means *a printing of a publication*.

In *addition* to a dictionary, he always used a thesaurus.

The first *edition* of Shakespeare's plays appeared in 1623. —

admit—means *to give entrance to* or *to grant as true*.

admit of—means *to allow* or *permit*.

This ticket *admits* one person to the game.

I *admit* the possibility of error in this experiment.

The scope of the experiment will *admit of* not more than four research assistants.

admit—means *to grant the existence of error*, without original intent.

confess—means *to grant the existence of error*, with original intent.

I *admit* that I was mistaken in my calculations.

I *confess* that I am guilty of tax evasion.

admittance—means *permission to enter*.

admission—means *permission to enter, with certain privileges*.

No *admittance* to the laboratory was permitted.

Friendly aliens may secure *admission* to this country.

advantage—means *a superior position.*

benefit—means *a favor conferred* or *earned* (as a profit).

He had an *advantage* in experience over his opponent.

The rules were changed for his *benefit.*

Note: To *take* advantage *of,* to *have* an advantage *over.*

adverse—means *unfavorable.* (pronounced AD-verse)

averse—means *disliking.* (pronounced a-VERSE)

He took the *adverse* decision in poor taste.

Many students are *averse* to criticism by their classmates.

advise—best means *to give advice. Advise* is losing favor as a synonym for *notify.*

Acceptable: The teacher will *advise* the student in habits of study.

Unacceptable: We are *advising* you of a delivery under separate cover. (SAY *notifying*)

affect—means *to influence.* (a verb)

effect—means *an influence.* (a noun)

effect—means *to bring about.* (a verb)

Your education must *affect* your future.

The *effect* of the last war is still being felt.

A diploma *effected* a tremendous change in his attitude.

Note: *affect* also has a meaning of *pretend.*

She had an *affected* manner.

affection—means *feeling.*

affectation—means *pose.*

Alumni develop a strong *affection* for their former school.

The *affectation* of a Harvard accent is no guarantee of success.

affinity—means an *attraction to a person or thing.*

infinity—means an *unlimited time, space* or *quantity.*

She has an *affinity* for men who own Cadillac cars.

That the universe has *infinity* is questionable.

after—is unnecessary with the *past* participle.

SAY: *After* checking the timetable, I left for the station.

DON'T say: *After having checked* (omit *after*) the timetable, I left for the station.

aggravate—means *to make worse.*

exasperate—means *to irritate* or *annoy.*

His cold was *aggravated* by faulty medication.

His inability to make a quick recovery *exasperated* him exceedingly.

agree—means *to be in general accord.*

concur—means *to be in specific agreement.*

The judges *agreed* with the plaintiff who was seeking relief under the law.

Nevertheless, the five judges *concurred* in the verdict for the defendant.

Note: For agree *with,* agree *to,* agree *on* see "Guide to Grammar" (Prepositions).

ain't—is an *unacceptable* contraction for *am not, are not,* or *is not.*

aisle—is *a passageway* between seats.

isle—is *a small island.* (both words rhyme with *pile*)

alibi—is an explanation on the basis of being *in another place.*

excuse—is an *explanation* on *any basis.*

His *alibi* offered at the trial was that he was twenty miles away from the scene of the crime at the time indicated.

His *excuse* for failing on the test was that he was sick.

alimentary—refers to the process of *nutrition.*

elementary—means *primary.*

The *alimentary* canal includes the stomach and the intestines.

Elementary education is the foundation of all human development.

all ready—means *everybody* or *everything ready.*

already—means *previously.*

They were *all ready* to write when the teacher arrived.

They had *already* begun writing when the teacher arrived.

alright—is *unacceptable*.
all right is *acceptable*.

all-round—means *versatile* or *general*.
all around—means *all over a given area*.
Rafer Johnson, decathlon champion, is an *all-round* athlete.
The police were lined up for miles *all around*.

all together—means *everybody* or *everything together*.
altogether—means *completely*.
The boys and girls sang *all together*.
This was *altogether* strange for a person of his type.

all ways—means *in every possible way*.
always—means *at all times*.
He was in *all ways* acceptable to the voters.
His reputation had *always* been spotless.

allege—means *to state without proof*, (same as *assert* or *maintain*)
claim—means *to state ownership by proof*, NOT *to assert* or *maintain*.
He *alleges* that Plato was Aristotle's teacher.
The informant *claimed* the reward for having helped catch the thief.

allow—does NOT mean *to suppose*. It DOES mean *to give permission*.
Acceptable: The teacher *allows* adequate time for study in class.
Unacceptable: I *allow* I haven't ever seen anything like this.

allude—means *to make a reference to*.
elude—means *to escape from*.
Only incidentally does Coleridge *allude* to Shakespeare's puns.
It is almost impossible for one to *elude* tax collectors.

allusion—means *a reference*.
illusion—means *a deception of the eye or mind*.
The student made *allusions* to his teacher's habits.

Illusions of the mind, unlike those of the eye, cannot be corrected with glasses.

alongside of—means *side by side with*.
Bill stood *alongside of* Henry.
alongside—means *parallel to the side*.
Park the car *alongside* the curb.

alot—is *unacceptable*. It should always be written as two words: *a lot*.
allot—means *to apportion*.
We bought *a lot* of land on which to build a small house.
Before the attack, we shall *allot* the ammunition to the troops.
Note: *A lot* should never be used in formal English to signify *very much*, or *a large quantity*.
Unacceptable: I like spinach *a lot*. (SAY *very much*)

altar—means *a platform*.
alter—means *to change*.
The bride and groom approached the *altar*.
The tailor *altered* the old-fashioned suit.

alternate—(the noun) means *a substitute* or *second choice*.
alternative—means *a statement* or *offer of two things, both equally preferable, but only one of which may be accepted*.
He served as an *alternate* to the delegate selected.
Since there was no *alternative*, I had to accept the position.

alumnus—means *a male graduate*.
alumna—means *a female graduate*.
With the granting of the diploma, he became an *alumnus* of the school.
Note: The masculine plural form of *alumnus* is *alumni* (*ni* rhymes with *high*)
She is an *alumna* of Hunter College.
Note: The feminine plural form is *alumnae* (*ae* rhymes with *key*)

amend—means *to correct*.
emend—means *to correct a literary work; to edit*.
Our Constitution, as *amended* by the Bill of Rights, was finally ratified.

Before publication, several chapters of the book had to be *emended.*

among—is used with *more than two persons or things.*

Note: *Amongst* should be avoided.

between—is used with *two persons or things.*

The inheritance was equally divided *among* the four children.

The business, however, was divided *between* the oldest and the youngest one.

amount—applies to quantities *that cannot be counted one by one.*

number—applies to quantities *that can be counted one by one.*

A large *amount* of grain was delivered to the storehouse.

A large *number* of bags of grain was delivered.

and—should NOT be used before *etc.*

etc.—is the Latin expression *et cetera* meaning *and other things, and so forth.* Since the *et* means *and,* a combination of the two would have to be translated "and and so forth."

Acceptable: Oranges, peaches, cherries, *etc.* are healthful.

Unacceptable: Pickles, pizza, frankfurters, *and etc.* should be eaten sparingly.

angel—is *a heavenly creature.*

angle—is *a point at which two sides meet,* also *a corner.*

Lucifer was the most famous of the fallen *angels.*

A line perpendicular to another line forms a right *angle.*

angry at—means *annoyed by a thing.*

angry with—means *annoyed by a person.*

We were *angry at* the gross carelessness of the attendant.

We were *angry with* the careless attendant.

annual—means *yearly.*

biannual—means *twice a year.* (*semiannual* means the same).

biennial—means *once in two years* or *every two years.*

another such—is *acceptable.*

such another—is *unacceptable.*

Another such error may lead to legal prosecution.

After his illness, he seemed *quite another* person *from* what he had been. (NOT *such another*)

ante—is a prefix meaning *before.*

anti—is a prefix meaning *against.*

The *ante*chamber is the room just before the main room.

An *anti*-fascist is one who is opposed to fascists.

anxious—means *worried.*

eager—means *keenly desirous.*

We were *anxious* about our first airplane flight.

We are *eager* to fly again.

any—should not be used for *at all.*

SAY I haven't rested *at all* (NOT *any*) during this Easter vacation.

Note: When a comparison is indicated, say *any other*—NOT *any.*

Acceptable: He likes France better than *any other* country.

anywheres—is *unacceptable.*

anywhere—is *acceptable.*

SAY we can't find it *anywhere.*

Also SAY $\begin{cases} nowhere \text{ (NOT nowheres)} \\ somewhere \text{ (NOT somewheres)} \end{cases}$

appraise—means *to set a value.*

apprise—means *to inform.*

The jeweler *appraised* the diamond at a very high value.

We were *apprised* of their arrival by the honking of the car horn.

apprehend—means *to catch the meaning of something.*

comprehend—means *to understand a thing completely.*

It is fairly simple to *apprehend* the stupidity of war.

It is far more difficult to *comprehend* the Euclidean postulates.

Note: *Apprehend* may also mean *to take into custody.*

The sheriff succeeded in *apprehending* the rustler.

apt—suggests *habitual behavior.*
likely—suggests *probable behavior.*
liable—suggests an exposure to something *harmful.*

Boys are *apt* to be rather lazy in the morning.
A cat, if annoyed, is *likely* to scratch.
Cheating on a test may make one *liable* to expulsion from school.

aren't I—is colloquial. Its use is to be discouraged.
SAY *Am I not* entitled to an explanation? (preferred to *Aren't I* . . .)

argue—means *to prove something by logical methods.*
quarrel—means *to dispute without reason or logic.*

The opposing lawyers *argued* before the judge.
The lawyers became emotional and *quarreled.*

around—meaning *about* or *near* is a poor colloquialism.

It's *about* ten o'clock. (NOT *around*)
We'll be *near* the house. (NOT *around*)

artisan—means *mechanic* or *craftsman.*
artist—means *one who practises the fine arts.*

Many *artisans* participated in the building of the Sistine Chapel.
The basic design, however, was prepared by the *artist* Michelangelo.

as—(used as a conjunction) is followed by a verb.
like—(used as a preposition) is NOT followed by a verb.

Do *as* I do, not *as* I say.
Try not to behave *like* a child.
Unacceptable: He acts *like* I do.

as far as—expresses *distance.*
so far as—indicates *a limitation.*

We hiked *as far as* the next guest house.
So far as we know, the barn was adequate for a night's stay.

as good as—should be used *for comparisons only.*
This motel is *as good as* the next one.
Note: *As good as* does NOT mean *practically.*
Unacceptable: They *as good as* promised us a place in the hall.
Acceptable: They *practically* promised us a place in the hall.

as if—is correctly used in the expression, "He talked *as if* his jaw hurt him."
Unacceptable: "He talked *like* his jaw hurt him."

as much—is *unacceptable* for *so* or *this.*
He thought *so.*
They admitted *this* freely.
NOT He thought *as much*, or They admitted *as much* freely.

as per—is poor usage for *according to* or *in accordance with.*
The secretary typed the letter *in accordance with* the manager's directions. (NOT *as per*)

as regards to—is *unacceptable*. So is *in regards to.*
SAY, *in regard* to or *as regards.*
The teacher would say nothing *in regard to* the student's marks.

ascared—no such word. It is *unacceptable* for *scared.*
The child was *scared* of ghosts. (NOT *ascared*).

as to whether—is *unacceptable. Whether* includes the unnecessary words *as to.*
Acceptable: I don't know *whether* it is going to rain.

ascent—is *the act of rising.*
assent—means *approval.*

The *ascent* to the top of the mountain was perilous.
Congress gave its *assent* to the President's emergency directive.

assay—means *to try* or *experiment.*
essay—means *to make an intellectual effort.*

We shall *assay* the ascent to the mountain tomorrow.

Why not *essay* a description of the mountain in composition?

astonish—means *to strike with sudden wonder.*

surprise—means *to catch unaware.*

The extreme violence of the hurricane *astonished* everybody.

A heat wave in April would *surprise* us.

at—should be avoided where it does not contribute to the meaning.

SAY Where shall I meet you? (DON'T add the word *at*)

at about—should not be used for *about.*

The group will arrive *about* noon.

attend to—means to *take care of.*

tend to—means to *be inclined to.*

One of the clerk's will *attend to* mail in my absence.

Lazy people *tend* to gain weight.

audience—means *a group of listeners.*

spectators—refers to *a group of watchers.*

Leonard Bernstein conducted a concert for the school *audience.*

The slow baseball game bored the *spectators.*

Note: A group that both watches and listens is called an *audience.*

aught—is *the figure* O (zero); it also means *nothing* (same as *naught.*)

ought—expresses *obligation.*

Add a *naught.*

You *ought* to do it.

Note: The expression *had ought* is unacceptable.

average—means *conforming to norms* or *standards.*

ordinary—means *usual, customary,* or *without distinction.*

A book of about 300 pages is of *average* length.

The contents of the book were rather *ordinary.*

avocation—means *a temporary interest* or *employment.*

vocation—means *one's regular employment.*

Fishing and swimming are two of my favorite *avocations.*

I am by *vocation* a civil engineer.

award—means *the result of a decision of many; a decision.*

reward—means *pay for good* or *evil done.*

The judge gave him an *award* of $100.00 in damages in the case.

Satisfactory marks are the *reward* for intensive study.

awful—means *inspiring fear or respect.* It is an *unacceptable* synonym for *bad, ugly, shocking, very.*

The *awful* shadow of the bomber's wings threw terror into their hearts.

Unacceptable: I received an *awful* mark in history.

ay, aye—both mean *always* or *ever,* when rhyming with *may.* Both mean *yes,* when rhyming with *my.*

I shall love you *forever and aye.*

Those in favor of the bill, please say "*Aye.*"

back—should NOT be used with such words as *refer* and *return* since the prefix *re* means *back.*

Unacceptable: Refer *back* to the text, if you have difficulty recalling the facts.

backward } Both are *acceptable* and may be
backwards } used interchangeably as an adverb.

We tried to run *backward.* (or *backwards*)

Backward as an adjective means *slow in learning.* (DON'T say *backwards* in this case)

A *backward* pupil should be given every encouragement.

balance—meaning *remainder* is *acceptable* only in commercial usage.

Use *remainder* or *rest* otherwise.

Even after the withdrawal, his bank *balance* was considerable.

Three of the students voted for John; the *rest* voted for Jim.

bazaar—is a *market place* or a *charity sale.*

bizarre—means *odd* or *strange.*

> We are going to the *bazaar* to buy things.
> He dresses in a *bizarre* manner.

being that—is *unacceptable* for *since* or *because.*

> SAY, *Since* (or *Because*) you have come a long way, why not remain here for the night?

berth—is *a resting place.*

birth—means *the beginning of life.*

> The new liner was given a wide *berth* in the harbor.
> He was a fortunate man from *birth.*

beside—means *close to.*

besides—refers *to something that has been added.*

> He lived *beside* the stream.
> He found wild flowers and weeds *besides.*

better—means *recovering.*

well—means *completely recovered.*

> He is *better* now than he was a week ago.
> In a few more weeks, he will be *well.*

better part of—implies *quality.*

greater part of—implies *quantity.*

> The *better part of* his performance came in the first act of the play.
> Fortunately for the audience, the first act took *the greater part of the time.*

biannual—means *twice a year.*

biennial—means *every two years.*

> Most schools have *biannual* promotion, in January and June.
> The *biennial* election of Congressmen is held in the even-numbered years.

blame on—is *unacceptable* for *blame* or *blame for.*

> *Blame* the person who is responsible for the error.
> Don't *blame* me for it.
> *Unacceptable*: Why do you put the *blame on* me?

born—means *brought into existence.*

borne—means *carried.*

> All men are *born* free.

We have *borne* our burdens with patience.

both—means *two considered together.*

each—means *one of two* or *more.*

> *Both* of the applicants qualified for the position.
> *Each* applicant was given a generous reference.
>
> Note: Avoid using such expressions as the following:
>
> *Both* girls had a new typewriter. (Use *each girl* instead).
> *Both* girls tried to outdo the other. (Use *each girl* instead).
> They are *both* alike. (Omit *both*).

bouillon—(pronounced boo-YON) is a *soup.*

bullion—(pronounced BULL-yun) means *gold* or *silver* in the form of bars.

> This restaurant serves tasty *bouillon.*
> A mint makes coins out of *bullion.*

breath—means *an intake of air.*

breathe—means *to draw air in and give it out.*

breadth—means *width.*

> Before you dive in, take a very deep *breath.*
> It is difficult to *breathe* under water.
> In a square, the *breadth* should be equal to the length.

bridal—means *of a wedding.*

bridle—means *to hold back.*

> The *bridal* party was late in arriving at the church.
> You must learn to *bridle* your short temper as you grow older.

bring—means *to carry toward the person who is speaking.*

take—means *to carry away from the speaker.*

> *Bring* the books here.
> *Take* your raincoat with you when you go out.

broach—means to *mention for the first time.*

brooch—(pronounced BROACH) means an *ornament* for clothing.

> At the meeting, one of the speakers *broached* the question of salary increases.

The model was wearing an expensive *brooch*.

broke—is the past tense of *break*.

broke—is *unacceptable* for *without money*.
He *broke* his arm.
"Go for broke" is a slang expression widely used in gambling circles.

bunch—refers to *things*.

group—refers to *persons* or *things*.
This looks like a delicious *bunch* of bananas.
What a well-behaved *group* of children!
Note: The colloquial use of bunch applied to *persons* is to be discouraged.
A bunch of the boys were whooping it up. (*number* is preferable)

burgle
burglarize } are humorous ways of expressing the idea of committing burglary.
SAY, Thieves *broke* into (NOT *burglarized*) the store.

burst—is *acceptable* for *broke*.

bust—is *unacceptable* for *broke* (or broken).
Acceptable: The balloon *burst*.
Unacceptable: My pen is *busted*.
Acceptable: That is a *bust* of Wagner.

business—is sometimes incorrectly used for work.
Unacceptable: I went to *business* very late today. (SAY, work).
Acceptable: He owns a thriving *business*.

but—should NOT be used after the expression *cannot help*.
Acceptable: One *cannot help noticing* the errors he makes in English.
Unacceptable: One *cannot help but* notice...

byword—is *a pet expression*.

password—is *a secret word uttered to gain passage*.
In ancient Greece, truth and beauty were *bywords*.
The sentry asked the scout for the *password*.

calculate—means *to determine mathematically*.
It does NOT mean *to think*.

Some Chinese still know how to *calculate on* an abacus.
Unacceptable: I *calculate* it's going to rain.

calendar—is *a system of time*.

calender—is *a smoothing and glazing machine*.

colander—is *a kind of sieve*.
In this part of the world, most people prefer the twelve-month *calendar*.
In ceramic work, the potting wheel and the *calender* are indispensable.
Garden-picked vegetables should be washed in a *colander* before cooking.

Calvary—is *the name of the place of the Crucifixion*.

cavalry—is *a military unit on horseback*.
Calvary and Gethsemane are place-names in the Bible.
Most of our modern *cavalry* is now motorized.

can—means *physically able*.

may—implies *permission*.
I *can* lift this chair over my head.
You *may* leave after you finish your work.

cannon—is *a gun* for heavy firing.

canon—is *a rule* or *law* of the church.
Don't remain near the *cannon* when it is being fired.
Churchgoers are expected to observe the *canons*.

cannot help—must be followed by an *ing* form.
We cannot help *feeling* (NOT *feel*) distressed about this.
Note: cannot help *but* is unacceptable.

can't hardly—is a *double negative*. It is unacceptable.
SAY, The child *can hardly* walk in those shoes.

capital—is *the city*.

capitol—is *the building*
Paris is the *capital* of France.
The Capitol in Washington is occupied by the Congress. (The Washington *Capitol* is capitalized).
Note: *capital* also means wealth.

catalog—is a *systematic* list. (also **catalogue**)

category—is a *class* of things.

> The item is precisely described in the sales *catalog*.
>
> A trowel is included in the *category* of farm tools.

cease—means *to end*.

seize—means *to take hold of*.

> Will you please *cease* making those sounds?
>
> *Seize* him by the collar as he comes around the corner.

celery—is *a vegetable*.

salary—means *payment*. (generally a fixed amount, as opposed to wages)

> *Celery* grows in stalks.
>
> Your starting *salary* may appear low, but bonuses will make up for it.

censor—means *to examine for the purpose of judging moral aspects*.

censure—means *to find fault with*.

> The government *censors* films in some countries.
>
> She *censured* her husband for coming home late.

cent—means *a coin*.

scent—means *an odor*.

sent—is the past tense of *send*.

> The one-*cent* postal card is a thing of the past.
>
> The *scent* of roses is pleasing.
>
> We were *sent* to the rear of the balcony

center around—is *unacceptable*. Use *center in* or *center on*.

> The maximum power was *centered in* the nuclear reactor.
>
> All attention was *centered on* the launching pad.

certainly—(and *surely*) is an *adverb*.

sure—is an *adjective*.

> He was *certainly* learning fast.
>
> *Unacceptable*: He *sure* was learning fast.

cession—means *a yielding*.

session—means *a meeting*.

> The *cession* of a piece of territory could have avoided the war.
>
> The legislative *session* lasted three months.

character. Do NOT use for a strange or eccentric person.

> *Unacceptable*: He's as unpredictable as they come—what a *character*! (SAY eccentric person).

childish—means *silly, immature*.

childlike—means *innocent, unspoiled*.

> Pouting appears *childish* in an adult.
>
> His *childlike* appreciation of art gave him great pleasure.

choice—means *a selection*.

choose—means *to select*.

chose—means *have selected*.

> My *choice* for a career is teaching.
>
> We may *choose* our own leader.
>
> I finally *chose* teaching for a career.

cite—means *to quote*.

sight—means *seeing*.

site—means *a place for a building*.

> He was fond of *citing* from the Scriptures.
>
> The *sight* of the wreck was appalling.
>
> The Board of Education is seeking a *site* for the new school.

climatic—refers *to climate*.

climactic—refers to *climax*.

> New York City has many *climatic* changes.
>
> The *climactic* parts of novels are often the most interesting.

climate—is the average weather *over a period of many years*.

weather—is the *hour by hour or day by day* condition of the atmosphere.

> He likes the *climate* of California better than that of Illinois.
>
> The *weather* is sometimes hard to predict.

coarse—means *vulgar* or *harsh.*

course—means a *path* or a *study.*

He was shunned because of his *coarse* behavior.

The ship took its usual *course.*

Which *course* in English are you taking?

come to be—should NOT be replaced with the expression *become to be,* since *become* means *come to be.*

True freedom will *come to be* when all tyrants have been overthrown.

comic—means *intentionally funny.*

comical—means *unintentionally funny.*

A clown is a *comic* figure.

The peculiar hat she wore gave her a *comical* appearance.

comma—is *a mark of punctuation.*

coma—means *a period of prolonged unconsciousness.* (rhymes with *aroma*)

A *comma* can never separate two complete sentences.

The accident put him into a *coma* lasting three days.

common—means *shared equally by two or more.*

mutual—means *interchanged.*

The town hall is the *common* pride of every citizen.

We can do business to our *mutual* profit and satisfaction.

compare to—means *to liken to something which has a different form.*

compare with—means *to compare persons or things with each other when they are of the same kind.*

contrast with—means *to show the difference between two things.*

A minister is sometimes *compared to* a shepherd.

Shakespeare's plays are often *compared with* those of Marlowe.

The writer *contrasted* the sensitivity of the dancer *with* the grossness of the pugilist.

complement—means *a completing part.*

compliment—is *an expression of admiration.*

His wit was a *complement* to her beauty.

He received many *compliments* on his valedictory speech.

complected—is *unacceptable* for *complexioned.*

SAY, Most South Sea Islanders are *dark-complexioned.*

comprehensible—means *understandable.*

comprehensive—means *including a great deal.*

Under the circumstances, your doubts were *comprehensible.*

Toynbee's *comprehensive* study of history covers many centuries.

comprise—means *to include.*

compose—means *to form the substance of.*

Toynbee's study of history *comprises* seven volumes.

Some modern symphonies are *composed* of as little as one movement.

concur in—must be followed by *an action.*

concur with—must be followed by *a person.*

I shall *concur in* the decision reached by the majority.

I cannot *concur with* the chairman, however much I respect his opinion.

Note: See **agree – concur.**

conducive to—means *leading to.*

conducive for—is *unacceptable.*

Your proposals for compromise are *conducive to* a setttlement of our disagreement.

conform to—means *to adapt one's self to.*

conform with—means *to be in harmony with.*

Youngsters are inclined to *conform to* a group pattern.

They feel it dangerous not to *conform with* the rules of the group.

conscience—means *sense of right.*

conscientious—means *faithful.*

conscious—means *aware of one's self.*

Man's *conscience* prevents him from becoming completely selfish.

We all depend on him because he is *conscientious.*

The injured man was completely *conscious.*

considerable—is properly used *only as an adjective*, NOT as a noun.
> *Acceptable*: The fraternal organization invested a *considerable amount* in government bonds.
> *Unacceptable*: He lost *considerable* in the stock market.

consistently—means *in harmony.*
constantly—means *regularly, steadily.*
> If you choose to give advice, act *consistently* with that advice.
> Doctors *constantly* warn against overexertion after forty-five.

consul—means *a government representative.*
council—means *an assembly which meets for deliberation.*
counsel—means *advice.*
> Americans abroad should keep in touch with their *consuls.*
> The City *Council* enacts local laws and regulations.
> The defendant heeded the *counsel* of his friends.

contact—meaning *to communicate with a person* should be left for business usage only.
> *Acceptable*: The owner *contacted* his salesmen.
> *Unacceptable*: *Contact* me if you want to play bridge some evening. (say *telephone* me)

contagious—means *catching.*
contiguous—means *adjacent or touching.*
> Measles is a *contagious* disease.
> The United States and Canada are *contiguous* countries.

contemptible—means *worthy of contempt.*
contemptuous—means *feeling contempt.*
> His spying activities were *contemptible.*
> It was plain to all that he was *contemptuous* of his co-workers.

continual—means *happening again and again at short intervals.*
continuous—means *without interruption.*
> The teacher gave the class *continual* warnings.

Noah experienced *continuous* rain for forty days.

convenient to—should be followed by a *person.*
convenient for—should be followed by a *purpose.*
> Will these plans be *convenient to* you? You must agree that they are *convenient for* the occasion.

copy—is *an imitation of an original work.* (not necessarily an exact imitation)
facsimile—is *an exact imitation of an original work.*
> The counterfeiters made a crude *copy* of the hundred-dollar bill.
> The official government engraver, however, prepared a *facsimile* of the bill.

core—means *the heart of something.*
corps—(pronounced like *core*) means an *organized military body.*
corpse—means *a dead body.*
> The *core* of the apple was rotten.
> The *corps* consisted of three full-sized armies.
> The *corpse* was quietly slipped overboard after a brief service.

co-respondent—is a *joint defendant* in a divorce case.
correspondent—is *one who communicates.*
> The *co-respondent* declared that he loved the other man's wife.
> Max Frankel is a special *correspondent* for the New York Times.

corporeal—means *bodily as the opposite of spiritual.*
corporal—means *bodily as it pertains to a person.*
> Many believe that our *corporeal* existence changes to a spiritual one after death.
> *Corporal* punishment is not recommended in modern schools.

costumes—are *garments belonging to another period.*
customs—are *habitual practices.*
> The company played "Macbeth" in Elizabethan *costumes.*

Every country has its own distinctive *customs*.

could of—is *unacceptable*. (*should of* is also *unacceptable*)

could have—is *acceptable*. (*should have* is acceptable)

Acceptable: You *could have* done better with more care.

Unacceptable: I *could of* won.

AVOID ALSO: *must of, would of*.

couple—refers *to two things that are joined*.

pair—refers *to two things that are related, but not necessarily joined*.

Four *couples* remained on the dance floor.

The left shoe in this *pair* is a size seven; the right is a size nine.

Note: *couple* refers to *two*. Do not use couple for more than two or for an undetermined number.

The *couple* has just become engaged.

Phone me in a *few* (NOT *couple of*) days.

credible—means *believable*.

creditable—means *worthy of receiving praise*.

credulous—means *believing too easily*.

The pupil gave a *credible* explanation for his lateness.

Considering all the handicaps, he gave a *creditable* performance.

Politicians prefer to address *credulous* people.

cute—is an abbreviated form of the word *acute*.

It may mean *attractive* in colloquial usage. AVOID IT.

data—has *plural* meaning.

The *data* for the report are (NOT *is*) ready.

Note 1: The singular (*datum*) is seldom used.

Note 2: *errata, strata, phenomena* are plural forms of *erratum, stratum, phenomenon*.

deal—is *acceptable* when it means a quantity.

When it means a business transaction it is *unacceptable*.

Acceptable: I have a great *deal* of confidence in you.

Unacceptable: Let's make a *deal* and I'll buy your car.

decease—means *death*.

disease—means *illness*.

The court announced the *decease* of the crown prince.

Leukemia is a deadly *disease*.

decent—means *suitable*.

descent—means *going down*.

dissent—means *disagreement*.

The *decent* thing to do is to admit your fault.

The *descent* into the cave was treacherous.

Two of the nine justices filed a *dissenting* opinion.

decided—means *unmistakable* when used of persons or things.

decisive—means *conclusive*, and is used of things only.

He was a *decided* supporter of the left-wing candidate.

The atom-bomb explosion over Hiroshima was the *decisive* act of World War II.

deduction—means *reasoning from the general (laws or principles) to the particular (facts)*.

induction—means *reasoning from the particular (facts) to the general (laws or principles)*.

All men are mortal. Since John is a man, he is mortal. (*deduction*)

There are 10,000 oranges in this truckload. I have examined 100 from various parts of the load and find them all of the same quality. I conclude that the 10,000 oranges are of this quality. (*induction*)

deference—means *respect*.

difference—means *unlikeness*.

In *deference* to his memory, we did not play yesterday.

The *difference* between the two boys is unmistakable.

definite—means *clear, with set limits.*

definitive—means *final, decisive.*

> We would prefer a *definite* answer to our *definite* question.
>
> The dictionary is the *definitive* authority for word meanings.

delusion—means *a wrong idea* which will probably influence action.

illusion—means *a wrong idea* that will probably *not* influence action.

> People were under the *delusion* that the earth was flat.
>
> It is just an *illusion* that the earth is flat.

deprecate—means *to disapprove.*

depreciate—means *to lower the value.*

> His classmates *deprecated* his discourtesy.
>
> The service station *depreciated* the value of our house.

desirable—means *that which is desired.*

desirous—means *desiring or wanting.*

> It was a most *desirable* position.
>
> He was *desirous* of obtaining it. (Note the preposition *of*)

despise—means *to look down upon.*

detest—means *to hate.*

> Some wealthy persons *despise* the poor.
>
> I *detest* cold weather. (NOT *despise*)

despite—means *notwithstanding, nevertheless.*

in spite of—is a synonym.

> *Despite* the weather, he went on the hike. (*Note*: no preposition)
>
> *In spite of* the weather, he went on the hike.

desert—(pronounced DEZZ-ert) means *an arid area.*

desert—(pronounced di-ZERT) means *to abandon;* also *a reward or punishment.*

dessert—(pronounced di-ZERT) means *the final course of a meal.*

> The Sahara is the world's most famous *desert.*
>
> A husband must not *desert* his wife.

Execution was a just *desert* for his crime.

We had plum pudding for *dessert.*

device—means *a way to do something.* (a noun)

devise—means *to find the way.* (a verb)

> A hook is a good fishing *device.*
>
> Some fishermen prefer to *devise* other ways for catching fish.
>
> Note: *Advice* (noun), *advise* (verb); *prophecy* (noun), *prophesy* (verb).

differ from—is used when there is a difference *in appearance.*

differ with—is used when there is a difference *in opinion.*

> A coat *differs from* a cape.
>
> You have the right to *differ with* me on public affairs.

different from—is *acceptable.*

different than—is *unacceptable.*

> *Acceptable*: Jack is *different from* his brother.
>
> *Unacceptable*: Florida climate is *different than* New York climate.

discover—means to find something already in existence.

invent—means to create something that never existed before.

> Pasteur *discovered* the germ theory of disease.
>
> Whitney *invented* the cotton gin.

discomfit—means to *upset.* (a verb)

discomfort—means *lack of ease.* (a noun)

> The general's plan was designed to *discomfit* the enemy.
>
> This collar causes *discomfort.*

discreet—means *cautious.*

discrete—means *separate.*

> The employee was *discreet* in her comments about her employer.
>
> Since these two questions are *discrete*, you must provide two separate answers.

disinterested—means *impartial.*

uninterested—means *not interested.*

> The judge must always be a *disinterested* party in a trial.

As an *uninterested* observer, he was inclined to yawn at times.

dissociate } Both mean to *separate one's self.*
disassociate } Although both are *acceptable, use dissociate.*

After graduation, he *dissociated* himself from his former friends.

dissuade from—means *to urge against.* (Note the preposition *from*)

Acceptable: We tried to *dissuade* him *from* his rash scheme.

Unacceptable: He *dissuaded* me *against* going on a trip.

divers—means *several.* (pronounced DIE-vurz)

diverse—means *different.* (pronounced di-VERSE)

The store had *divers* foodstuffs for sale. Many of the items were completely *diverse* from staple foods.

doubt that—is *acceptable.*

doubt whether—is *unacceptable.*

Acceptable: I *doubt that* you will pass this term.

Unacceptable: We *doubt whether* you will succeed.

doubtless—is *acceptable.*

doubtlessly—is *unacceptable.*

Acceptable: You *doubtless* know your work; why, then, don't you pass?

Unacceptable: He *doubtlessly* thinks that you can do the job well.

drouth—(rhymes with MOUTH) and **drought** (rhymes with OUT) are two forms of the same word; the second is preferred.

The lengthy *drought* caused severe damage to the crops.

dual—means *relating to two.*

duel—means *a contest between two persons.*

Dr. Jekyl had a *dual* personality.

Alexander Hamilton was fatally injured in a *duel* with Aaron Burr.

due to—is *unacceptable* at the beginning of a sentence. Use *because of, on account of,* or some similar expression instead.

Unacceptable: *Due to* the rain, the game was postponed.

Acceptable: *Because of* the rain, the game was postponed.

Acceptable: The postponement was *due to* the rain.

each other—refers to *two persons.*

one another—refers to *more than two persons.*

The two girls have known *each other* for many years.

Several of the girls have known *one another* for many years.

eats—is *unacceptable* as a synonym for *food.*

We enjoyed the *food* (NOT *eats*) at the party.

economic—refers to *the subject of economics.*

economical—means *thrifty.*

An *economic* discussion was held at the United Nations.

A housewife should be *economical.*

either ... or—is used when referring to choices.

neither ... nor—is the *negative* form.

Either you *or* I will win the election.

Neither Bill *nor* Henry is expected to have a chance.

elegy—is a *mournful* or *melancholy* poem.

eulogy—is a speech in praise of a deceased person.

Gray's "*Elegy* Written in a Country Churchyard" is one of the greatest poems ever written.

The minister delivered the *eulogy.*

eligible—means *fit to be chosen.*

illegible—means *impossible to read* or *hard to read.*

Not all thirty-five year-old persons are *eligible* to be President.

His childish handwriting was *illegible.*

eliminate—means *to get rid of.*

illuminate—means *to supply with light.*

Let us try to *eliminate* the unnecessary steps.

Several lamps were needed to *illuminate* the corridor.

else—is superfluous in such expressions as the following:

Unacceptable: We want *no one else* but you.

Acceptable: We want *no one* but you.

Note: The possessive form of *else* is *else's*.

emerge—means *to rise out of.*

immerge—means *to sink into.* (also **immerse**)

The swimmer *emerged* from the pool.

The laundress *immerged* the dress in the tub of water.

emigrate—means *to leave one's country for another.*

immigrate—means *to enter another country.*

The Norwegians *emigrated* to America in mid-1860.

Many of the Norwegian *immigrants* settled in the Middle West.

enclosed herewith—is *unacceptable.*

enclosed—is *acceptable.*

Acceptable: You will find *enclosed* one copy of our brochure.

Unacceptable: *Enclosure herewith* is the book you ordered.

endorse—means *to write on the back of.*

Acceptable: He *endorsed* the check.

Unacceptable: He *endorsed* the check *on the back.*

enormity—means *viciousness.*

enormousness—means *vastness.*

The *enormity* of his crime was appalling.

The *enormousness* of the Sahara exceeds that of any other desert.

enthused—should be avoided.

enthusiastic—is preferred.

Acceptable: We were *enthusiastic* over the performance.

Unacceptable: I am truly *enthused* about my coming vacation.

equally as good—is *unacceptable.*

just as good—is *acceptable.*

Acceptable: This book is *just as good* as that.

Unacceptable: Your marks are *equally as good* as mine.

eruption—means *a breaking out.*

irruption—means *a breaking in.*

The *eruption* of Mt. Vesuvius caused extensive damage.

The *irruption* of the river devastated the coastal town.

everyone—is written as one word when it is a *pronoun.*

every one—(two words) is used when each individual is stressed.

Everyone present voted for the proposal.

Every one of the voters accepted the proposal.

Note: *Everybody* is written as one word.

every bit—is *incorrectly* used for *just as.*

Acceptable: You are *just as* clever as she is.

Unacceptable: He is *every bit* as lazy as his father.

every so often—is *unacceptable.*

ever so often—is *acceptable.*

We go to the ball game *ever so often.* (NOT *every* so often)

everywheres—is *unacceptable.*

everywhere—is *acceptable.*

We searched *everywhere* for the missing book.

Note: *Everyplace* (one word) is likewise *unacceptable.*

every which way—meaning *in all directions* is *unacceptable.*

every way—is *acceptable.*

He tried to solve the problem in *every* (OMIT *which*) *way.*

exceed—means *going beyond the limit.*

excel—refers *to superior quality.*

You have *exceeded* the time allotted to you.

All-round athletes are expected to *excel* in many sports.

except—is *acceptable.*

excepting—is *unacceptable.*

Acceptable: All *except* Joe are going.

Unacceptable: All cities, *excepting* Washington, are in a state.

Note: Don't use *except* for *unless*.
Unacceptable: He won't consent *except* you give him the money. (SAY *unless*)

exceptional—means *extraordinary*.
exceptionable—means *objectionable*.
Exceptional children learn to read before the age of five.
The behavior of exceptional children is sometimes *exceptionable*.

excessively—means *beyond acceptable limits*.
exceedingly—means *to a very great degree*.
In view of our recent feud, he was *excessively* friendly.
The weather in July was *exceedingly* hot.

expand—means *to spread out*.
expend—means *to use up*.
As the staff increases, we shall have to *expand* our office space.
Don't *expend* all your energy on one project.

expect—means *to look forward to*.
suspect—means *to imagine to be bad*.
We *expect* that the girls will come home before New Year's Day.
They *suspect* that we have a plan to attack them.

factitious—means *unnatural* or *artificial*.
fictitious—means *imaginary*.
His *factitious* enthusiasm did not deceive us.
Jim Hawkins is a *fictitious* character.

faint—means *to lose consciousness*.
feint—means *to make a pretended attack*.
The lack of fresh air caused her to *faint*.
First he *feinted* his opponent out of position; then he lobbed the ball over the net.

fair—means *light in color, reasonable, pretty*.
fare—means *a set price*.
Your attitude is not a *fair* one.
Children may ride the bus for half-*fare*.

farther—is used to describe *concrete distance*.
further—is used to describe *abstract ideas*.
Chicago is *farther* from New York than Cincinnati is.

I'll explain my point of view *further*.

faze—meaning *to worry* or *disturb* may be used colloquially.
Don't let his angry look *faze* you.
phase—means *an aspect*.
A crescent is a *phase* of the moon.

feel bad—means *to feel ill*.
feel badly—means *to have a poor sense of touch*.
I *feel bad* about the accident I saw.
The numbness in his limbs caused him to *feel badly*.

feel good—means *to be happy*.
feel well—means to be in *good health*.
I *feel* very *good* about by recent promotion.
Spring weather always made him *feel well*.

fellow—means *man* or *person* in the *colloquial* sense only.

fever—refers to an *undue rise of temperature*.
temperature—refers to the *degree of heat* which may be normal.
We had better call the doctor—he has a *fever*.
The *temperature* is 80 degrees.

fewer—refers to *persons or things that can be counted*.
less—refers to *something considered as a mass*.
We have *fewer* customers this week than last week.
I have *less* money in my pocket than you have.

finalize—is a new word meaning *conclude* or *complete*. The word has not yet received complete acceptance.
SAY, Labor and management *completed* arrangements for a settlement. (NOT *finalized*)

financial—refers to *money matters in a general sense*.
fiscal—refers to the *public treasury*.
Scholars are usually not *financial* successes.
The government's *fiscal year* begins July 1 and ends June 30.

fix—*means to fasten in place.* There are certain senses in which *fix* should *NOT* be used.
Acceptable: He *fixed* the leg to the table.
Unacceptable: The mechanic *fixed* the Buick. (SAY *repaired*)
Unacceptable: How did I ever get into this *fix*? (SAY *predicament*)

flout—means *to insult.*
flaunt—means *to make a display of.*
He *flouted* the authority of the principal.
Hester Prynne *flaunted* her scarlet "A."

flowed—is the past participle of *flow.*
flown—is the past participle of *fly.*
The flood waters had *flowed* over the levee before nightfall.
He had *flown* for 500 hours before he crashed.

folk—means *people in the sense of a group.* It is no longer used alone, but in combination with other words.
folks—is *unacceptable* for *friends, relatives, etc.*
Unacceptable: I'm going to see my *folks* on Sunday.
Acceptable: Anthropologists study *folk*ways, *folk*lore, and *folk*songs.

forbear—means *to refrain from doing something.* (accent on second syllable)
forebear—means *ancestor.* (accent on first syllable)
Forbear seeking vengeance.
Most of our *forebears* came from England.

formally—means *in a formal way.*
formerly—means *at an earlier time.*
The letter of reference was *formally* written.
He was *formerly* a delegate to the convention.

former—means *the first of two.*
latter—means *the second of two.*
The *former* half of the book was in prose.
The *latter* half of the book was in poetry.

fort—means *a fortified place.*
forte—(rhymes with *fort*) means *a strong point.*
A small garrison was able to hold the fort.

Conducting Wagner's music was Toscanini's forte.
Note: forte (pronounced FOR-tay) is a musical term meaning *loudly.*

forth—means *forward.*
fourth—*comes after third.*
They went *forth* like warriors of old.
The *Fourth* of July is our Independence Day.
Note: spelling of *forty* (40) and *fourteen* (14).

freeze—means *to turn into ice.*
frieze—is *a decorated band in or on a building.*
As the temperature dropped, the water began to *freeze.*
The *friezes* on the Parthenon are wonders of art.

funny—means *humorous* or *laughable.*
That clown is truly *funny.*
Note: *Funny* meaning *odd* or *strange* is a colloquial use that should be avoided.
SAY I have *queer* feeling in my stomach. (NOT *funny*)

genial—means *cheerful.*
congenial—means *agreeing in spirit.*
Genial landlords are rare today.
A successful party depends on *congenial* guests.

genius—means *extraordinary natural ability,* or *one so gifted.*
genus—means *class* or *kind.*
Mozart showed his *genius* for music at a very early age.
The rose-of-Sharon flower probably does not belong to the *genus* of roses.
Note: A particular member of a genus is called *a species.*

get—is a verb which strictly means *to obtain.*
Please *get* my bag.
There are many slang forms of GET that should be avoided:
AVOID: Do you *get* me? (SAY, Do you *understand* me?)
You can't *get* away with it. (SAY,

You won't *avoid* punishment if you do it.)

Get wise to yourself. (Say, *Use* common sense.)

We didn't *get* to go. (SAY, We didn't *manage* to go.)

get-up—meaning *dress* or *costume* should be *avoided.*

gibe } (pronounced alike) - both
jibe } mean *to scoff.*

We are inclined to *gibe* at awkward speakers.

Jibe also means *to agree.*

The two stories are now beginning to *jibe.*

got—means *obtained.*

He *got* the tickets yesterday.

AVOID: You've *got* to do it. SAY, You *have* to do it.)

We *have got* no sympathy for them. (SAY, We *have* no sympathy for them.)

They have *got* a great deal of property. (SAY, They *have* a great deal of property.)

gourmand—is *one who eats large quantities of food.* (rhymes with POOR-mund)

gourmet—is *one who eats fastidiously; a connoisseur.* (rhymes with POOR-may)

His uncontrollable appetite soon turned him into a *gourmand.*

The *gourmet* chooses the right wine for the right dish.

graduated—is followed by the prep. *from.*

He *graduated* (or *was graduated*) from high school in 1961.

Unacceptable: He *graduated* college.

Note: A *graduated* test tube is one that has markings on it to indicate volume or capacity.

guess—is *unacceptable* for *think* or *suppose.*

SAY, I *think* I'll go downtown. (NOT I *guess*)

habit—means *an individual tendency to repeat a thing.*

custom—means *group habit.*

He had a *habit* of breaking glasses before each ball game.

The *custom* of the country was to betroth girls at the age of ten.

had ought—is *unacceptable.*

SAY, You *ought* not to eat fish if you are allergic to it.

hanged—is used in reference to a *person.*

hung—is used in reference to *a thing.*

The prisoner was *hanged* at dawn.

The picture was *hung* above the fireplace.

happen—means *to take place.*

transpire—means *to come to general knowledge.*

The meeting *happened* last year.

The decisions reached at that meeting did not *transpire* until recently.

healthy—means *having health.*

healthful—means *giving health.*

The man is *healthy.*

Fruit is *healthful.*

heap—means a *pile.*

heaps—is *unacceptable* in the sense of *very much.*

Unacceptable: Thanks *heaps* for the gift.

Note: LOTS is also *unacceptable* for very much.

help—meaning employees is *unacceptable.*

Unacceptable: Some of the *help* are sick. (SAY, *employees*)

him }
his } Use these pronouns correctly:

We saw *him working* from sunup to sunset. (The *object* of saw is *him.*)

We saw *his working* as a means of solving a financial problem.

(The object of saw is *his working*).

Note: The same rule applies to *me — my, you — your, them — their.*

holy—means *sacred.*

holey—means *with holes.*

wholly—means *completely or altogether.*

Easter Week is a *holy* time in many lands.

Old stockings tend to become *holey* after a while.

We are *wholly* in agreement with your decision.

however—means *nevertheless*.

how ever—means *in what possible way*.

We are certain, *however*, that you will like this class.

We are certain that, *how ever* you decide to study, you will succeed.

human—is *unacceptable* in the sense of *human being*.

Love is one of the basic needs of all *human beings*. (not *humans*)

Love is a basic *human* (as adj. only) need.

hypercritical—refers to a person *who finds fault easily*.

hypocritical—refers to a person *who pretends*.

Don't be so *hypercritical* about the meals at such low prices.

It is better to be sincere than to be *hypocritical*.

identical with—means *agreeing exactly in every respect*.

similar to—means *having a general likeness* or *resemblance*.

By coincidence, his plan was *identical with* mine.

He had used methods *similar to* mine.

idle—means *unemployed* or *unoccupied*.

idol—means *image* or *object of worship*.

Idle men, like *idle* machines, are inclined to lose their sharpness.

Some dictators prefer to be looked upon as *idols* by the masses.

if—introduces a *condition*.

whether—introduces *a choice*.

I shall go to Europe *if* I win the prize.

He asked me *whether* I intended to go to Europe. (not *if*)

if it was—implies that *something might have been true in the past*.

if it were—implies *doubt*, or indicates *something that is contrary* to fact.

If your book was there last night, it is there now.

If it were summer now, we would all go swimming.

immunity—implies *resistance to a disease*.

impunity—means *freedom from punishment*.

The Salk vaccine helps develop an *immunity* to poliomyelitis.

Because he was an only child, he frequently misbehaved with *impunity*.

imply—means *to suggest* or *hint at*. (The speaker *implies*)

infer—means *to deduce* or *conclude*. (The listener *infers*)

Are you *implying* that I have disobeyed orders?

From your carefree attitude, what else are we to *infer*?

in—usually refers to *a state of being*. (no motion)

into—is used for *motion from one place to another*.

The records are *in* that drawer.

I put the records *into* that drawer.

Note: "We were walking in the room" is correct even though there is motion. The motion is *not* from one place to another.

in back of—means *behind*.

in the back of—(or *at the back of*) means *in the rear of*.

The shovel is in *back of* (that is, *behind*) the barn.

John is sitting *in the back* of the theatre.

inclement—(pronounced in-CLEM-ent) refers to *severe weather*, such as a heavy rainfall or storm. It does NOT mean threatening.

Because of the *inclement* weather, we were soaked to the skin.

indict—(pronounced *indite*) means *to charge with a crime*.

indite—means *to write*.

The grand jury *indicted* him for embezzlement.

Modern authors prefer the expression *to write*, rather than *indite*; the latter is now a stuffy sort of expression.

infect—means *to contaminate with germs.*

infest—means *to be present in large numbers* (in a *bad sense*)

The quick application of a germicide can prevent *infection.*

The abandoned barn was *infested* with field mice.

ingenious—means *skillful, imaginative.*

ingenuous—means *naive, frank, candid.*

The *ingenious* boy created his own rocket.

One must be *ingenuous* to accept the Communist definition of freedom.

inside
inside of } When referring to time, use WITHIN

She is arriving *within* two hours. (NOT *inside* or *inside of*)

invite—is *unacceptable* for *invitation.*

SAY, We received an *invitation* to the party.

irregardless—is *unacceptable.*

regardless—is *acceptable.*

Unacceptable: Irregardless of the weather, I am going to the game.

Acceptable: Regardless of his ability, he is not likely to win.

irresponsible—means *having no sense of responsibility.*

not responsible for—means *not accountable for something.*

Irresponsible people are frequently late for appointments.

Since you came late, we are *not responsible* for your having missed the first act.

its—means *belonging to it.*

it's—means *it is.*

The house lost *its* roof.

It's an exposed house, now.

join together—is incorrect for *connect.* Omit *together.*

Acceptable: I want to *join* these pieces of wood.

Unacceptable: All of us should *join together* to fight intolerance.

judicial—means *pertaining to courts* or *to the law.*

judicious—means *wise.*

The problem required the *judicial* consideration of an expert.

We were certainly in no position to make a *judicious* decision.

jump at—means *to accept eagerly.*

jump to—means *to spring to.*

We would be foolish not to *jump at* such an opportunity.

At the sound of the bell, they all *jumped to* attention.

just terrible—is barely *acceptable.*

SAY, The sight of the accident was *simply* (or *quite*) *terrible.*

kid—meaning *child* is colloquial. Don't use it formally.

My cousin is a clever *kid.* (*acceptable* in the informal use)

Note: *kid* meaning *to make fun of* is *unacceptable.*

SAY, You must be *making fun of me.* (NOT *kidding*)

kind of
sort of } are *unacceptable* for *rather.*

SAY, We are *rather* disappointed in you.

kinfolks—is *unacceptable* for *kinfolk,* or *kinsfolk.*

SAY, We now know that the Irish and the Welsh are distant *kinfolk.*

last—refers to *the final member in a series.*

latest—refers to *the most recent in time.*

latter—refers to *the second of two.*

This is the *last* bulletin. There won't be any other bulletins.

This is the *latest* bulletin. There will be other bulletins.

Of the two most recent bulletins, the *latter* is more encouraging.

later on—is *unacceptable* for *later.*

SAY, *Later,* we shall give your request fuller attention.

lay—means *to place.* (**transitive** verb)
lie—means *to recline.* (**intransitive** verb) } see Grammar Section (verbs)

Note the forms of **each verb:**

TENSE	LAY (PLACE)	LIE (RECLINE)
PRESENT	The chicken *is laying* an egg.	The child *is lying* down.
PAST	The chicken *laid* an egg.	The child *lay* down.
PRES. PERF.	The chicken *has laid* an egg.	The child *has lain* down.

learn—means *to acquire knowledge.*
teach—means *to give knowledge.*
> We can *learn* many things just by observing carefully.
> In technical matters it is better to get someone to *teach* you.

least—means *the smallest.*
less—means *the smaller of two.*
> This was the *least* desirable of all the locations we have seen.
> We may finally have to accept the *less* desirable of the two locations we last saw.

leave—means *to go away from.* (A verb is NOT used with *leave*)
let—means *to permit.* (A verb is used with *let*)
> *Leave* this house at once.
> *Let* me remain in peace in my own house.
> (*remain* is the verb used with *let*)

legible—means *able to be read.*
readable—means *able to be read with pleasure.*
> Your themes have become increasingly more *legible.*
> In fact, I now find most of them extremely *readable.*

lengthened—means *made longer.*
lengthy—means *annoyingly long.*
> The essay, now *lengthened,* is more readable.
> However, try to avoid writing *lengthy* explanations of obvious facts.

levy—(rhymes with *heavy*) means *to impose a tax.*
levee—(pronounced like *levy*) means *an embankment.*
> It is the duty of Congress to *levy* taxes.
> The Mississippi River is held in with massive *levees.*

libel—is *a written and published statement injurious to a person's character.*

slander—is *a spoken statement of the same sort.*
> The unfavorable references to me in your book are *libelous.*
> When you say these vicious things about me, you are committing *slander.*

lief—(rhymes with *thief*) means *gladly.*
> He had as *lief* give me the tools as sell them to me.
> He would *liefer* (*more gladly*) give me the tools as sell them to me.

lightening—is the present participle of to *lighten.*
lightning—means *the flashes of light accompanied by thunder.*
> Leaving the extra food behind resulted in *lightening* the pack.
> Summer thunderstorms produce startling *lightning* bolts.

line—meaning occupation is *unacceptable.*
> He is in the engineering *profession.*
> *Unacceptable:* What *line* are you in? (SAY, *occupation*)

lineament—means *outline* or *contour.*
liniment—is *a medicated liquid.*
> His face had the *lineaments* of a Greek Adonis.
> After the football game, we all applied *liniment* to our legs.

loan—is a *noun.*
lend—is a *verb.*
> The bank was willing to grant him a *loan* of $500.00.
> The bank was willing to *lend* him $500.00.

locate—means *to discover the position of.*
> We *located* my uncle's whereabouts.
> AVOID these uses of LOCATE:
> > The school is *located* on the north side of the street. (omit *located*)
> > Have you *located* the book? (SAY, *found*)

Note: *locate* meaning *to settle* is colloquial.

Example: We have *located* in Texas. This use is *unacceptable* in formal English.

lonely—means *longing for companionship.*
solitary—means *isolated.*

Some people are forced to live *lonely* lives.

Sometimes *solitary* surroundings are conducive to deep thought.

lots—(or *a lot, a whole lot*) meaning *a great deal, much,* is *unacceptable.*

Unacceptable: He has *lots* of friends. (SAY, *many*)

Unacceptable: I have a *lot* of trouble. (SAY, *a great deal of*)

luxuriant—means *abundant growth.*
luxurious—implies *wealth.*

One expects to see *luxuriant* plants in the tropics.

The *luxurious* surroundings indicated both wealth and good taste.

majority—means *more than half of the total number.*
plurality—means an *excess* of votes received by the leading candidate over *those* received by the next candidate.

Example: A received 251 votes.

B received 127 votes.

C received 123 votes.

A received a *majority*, or 1 vote more than half of the total.

A received a *plurality* of 124 votes over B.

many—refers to *a number.*
much—refers to *a quantity in bulk.*

How *many* inches of rain fell last night? I don't know; but I would say *much* rain fell last night.

material—means *of or pertaining to matter.*
materiel—(accent the last syllable, EL) is French, and means *material equipment,* the opposite of *personnel* (*manpower*).

His *material* assets included an automobile and two suits of clothing.

The small army was rich in *materiel,* poor in personnel.

may—is used in the *present tense.*
might—is used in the *past tense.*

We are hoping that he *may* come today.

He *might* have done it if you had encouraged him.

it's I—is always *acceptable.*
it's me—is *acceptable* only in colloquial speech or writing.

It's him
This is her   always
It was them   *unacceptable*

It's he
This is she   always
It was they   *acceptable*

my—must be used in such expressions as, Why do you object to *my going* (NOT *me going*)?

SEE HIM — HIS.

measles—is plural in form, singular in meaning.

SAY, *Measles* is now a minor childhood disease.

Note also, *mumps, shingles, chills, etc.* is . . .

medieval—means *of or pertaining to the Middle Ages* (1000-1400 A.D.).
middle-aged—refers to persons *in the middle period of life.*

Serfs and feudal baronies were part of *medieval* times.

According to the Bible, the *middle-aged* man has thirty-five more years of life to look forward to.

memorandum—is *a reminder.* The plural is *memoranda.*

Send me a short *memorandum* of his meeting with you.

The *memoranda* will help me reconstruct the story of the meeting.

Note: *addendum - addenda; bacterium - bacteria; datum-data; dictum - dicta; erratum-errata; medium - media; stratum - strata.*

Messrs.—(rhymes with *guessers*) used instead of "Misters" ("Misters" is *unacceptable*.)

The meeting was attended by *Messrs.* Smith, Jones, Brown, and Swift.

metal—is *the common chemical element.*
mettle—means *spirit.*

Lead is one of the more familiar *metals.*
One had to admire his *mettle* in the face of a crisis.

mighty—means *powerful* or *bulky.* Do NOT use it to mean *very.*

Samson was a *mighty* warrior.
The Philistines were all *very* (NOT *mighty*) unhappy to meet him.

minutiae—(pronounced min-YEW-she-ee) is the plural of *minutia,* and means *minor details.*

A meticulous person spends much time on *minutiae.*

miss out on—is *unacceptable* for *miss.*

SAY, We almost *missed* (not *missed out on*) seeing the game because of the traffic tieup.

Mmes.—is the abbreviation for Mesdames. (pronounced med-DAM)

It introduces a series of names of married women.
The party was attended by the *Mmes.* Jones, Smith, Wilson, and Miss Brown.
Note: The plural of Miss is *Misses.*

moment—is a *brief, indefinite space of time.*
minute—means *the sixtieth part of an hour.*

The lightning flared for a *moment.*
The thunder followed one *minute* afterwards—or so it seemed.
Unacceptable: I'll be there in a *minute* (SAY *moment* if you mean *briefly.*)

moneys—is *the plural of money.*

We shall vote on the disposition of the various *moneys* in the treasury.
Note: *alley - alleys; monkey - monkeys; valley - valleys.*

moral—means *good or ethical;* also, *an ethical lesson to be drawn.*

morale—(pronounced more-AL) means *spirit.*

The *moral* of the story is that it pays to be honest.
The *morale* of the troops rose after the general's inspiring speech.

more than—is correct. Do not add *rather* to this construction.

SAY, I depend *more* on you *than* (NOT *rather than*) on him.
BUT, I depend on you *rather than* on him.

most—is an adjective in the *superlative degree.*
almost—is an adverb, meaning *nearly.*

He is the *most* courteous boy in the class.
It's *almost* time to go to school.

myself—is *unacceptable* for *I* or *me.*

SAY, My son and *I* will play.
He is a better player than *I.*
They gave my son and *me* some berries.
Note: *Myself* may be used if the subject of the verb is I.
Since I know *myself* better, let me try it my way.

nauseous—means *causing sickness.* (NAWSH-us)
nauseated—means *being sick.* (NAW-she-ate-id)

The odor is *nauseous.*
I feel *nauseated.* (NOT *nauseous*)

naval—refers *to ships.*
nautical—refers *to navigation and seamen.*

John Paul Jones was a famous *naval* commander.
A *nautical* mile is a little longer than a land mile.

near—is an adjective meaning *close.*
nearly—is an adverb meaning *almost.*

Before 1933, only *near* beer was available.
Unacceptable: It is *near* a week since you called. (SAY *nearly*)

needless to say—Avoid this expression—it doesn't mean anything.

Unacceptable: Needless to say, I refused to go. (omit *needless to say*)

neither—means *not either of two*, and should NOT be used for *none* or *not one*.

Neither of his two books was very popular.

Of the many plays he has written, *not one* (or *none*) was very popular.

never—means *at no time*. Do NOT use it for *not*.

SAY, Shakespeare was *never* in Italy.

Shakespeare was *not* very fond of France.

nevertheless—means *notwithstanding*.

none the less—means *not any the less*, and is always followed by an adjective.

I have often warned you; *nevertheless*, you have persisted in doing the wrong thing.

I am *none the less* willing to give you a second chance.

nice—means *precise* or *exact*.

Your argument makes a *nice*, logical distinction.

Some use *nice* for anything and everything that is *pleasing*.

*Try to be more exact in your descriptive word.

AVOID: This is *nice* weather. (SAY *sunny*, or whatever you really mean)

He is such a *nice* person. (SAY *kind*, or whatever you really mean.)

*Other trite "blanket" expressions to avoid are: *fine, elegant, grand, lovely, splendid, terrific, swell, wonderful*—also, *rotten, lousy, miserable, terrible, awful*.

Note: NICELY is *unacceptable* for *well*. Considering the seriousness of his illness, he is now doing *well*. (NOT *nicely*)

no-account—(and *no-good* and *no-use*) is *unacceptable* for *worthless*.

of no account—meaning *useless* is *acceptable*.

SAY, He is a *worthless* (NOT *no-account*) painter.

He will always be a painter *of no account*.

no better—(or **no worse**) is *acceptable* in colloquial use.

He is *no better* than this record.

Note: *No different* is *unacceptable*.

SAY, Your proposal is *not different* from mine.

noplace—as a solid word, is *unacceptable* for *no place* or *nowhere*.

Acceptable: You now have *nowhere* to go.

nohow—is *unacceptable* for *regardless*.

Unacceptable: I can't do this *nohow*.

no sooner . . . than—(NOT *no sooner . . . when*) is the *acceptable* expression.

SAY, *No sooner* did the rain start *than* (not *when*) the game was called off.

nowhere near—is *unacceptable* for *not nearly*.

SAY, The work was *not nearly* finished by nightfall.

nowheres—is *unacceptable*.

nowhere—is *acceptable*.

The child was *nowhere* (NOT *nowheres*) to be found.

nominate—means *to propose as a candidate*.

denominate—means *to describe*.

Nixon was *nominated* for President in 1960.

He was *denominated* a "favorite son" from the State of California.

notable—means *remarkable*.

notorious—means *of bad reputation*.

December 7, 1941, was a *notable* day.

At that time, the *notorious* Tojo commanded the Japanese forces.

nothing more or less—is *unacceptable* for *nothing more nor less*.

SAY, Correct English is *nothing more nor less* than a matter of careful practice.

number—is singular *when the total is intended*.

The *number* (of pages in the book) is 500.

number—is plural *when the individual units are referred* to.

A *number* of pages (in the book) were printed in italic type.

obligate—implies *a moral or legal responsibility*.

oblige—means *to do a favor to*, or *to accommodate*.

The principal felt *obligated* to disqualify himself in the dispute between the pupils.

Please *oblige* me by refraining from discussing this matter with anyone else.

observance—means the *act of complying.*

observation—means the *act of noting.*

In *observance* of the new regulation, we shall omit further tests.

His scientific *observations* became the basis for a new rocket theory.

occupancy—refers to *the mere act of occupying,* usually legally.

occupation—means *the forceful act of occupying.*

According to the lease, the tenant still had *occupancy* of the apartment for another month.

The *occupation* of the enemy worried the townspeople.

oculist—is an M.D. who *treats diseases of the eye.*

optometrist—is a person who *measures the eye* to prescribe glasses.

optician—is a person who *makes the glasses.*

Note: An *oculist* is also called an *ophthalmologist* (ahf-thal- (like pal)- MOLL-ogist)

Note: An *optometrist* may also be an *optician.*

of any—(and *of anyone*) is *unacceptable* for *of all.*

SAY, His was the highest mark *of all.* (NOT *of any* or *of anyone*)

off of—is *unacceptable.*

SAY, He took the book *off* the table.

oftentimes—is *unacceptable* for *often.*

SAY, He *often* went back to the scenes of his childhood.

O.K.—is *acceptable* for *all right* or *approved* in informal business and informal social usage.

AVOID the use of O.K. in formal situations.

Acceptable: This retyped letter is O.K.

on account of—is *unacceptable* for *because.*

SAY, We could not meet you *because* (NOT *on account of*) we did not receive your message in time.

one and the same—is repetitious. Omit *one and.*

Your plan and mine are *the same.*

one ... one—is the acceptable construction in such expressions as:

The more *one* listens to President Kennedy's speeches, the more *one* (NOT *he*) wonders how a young man can be so wise.

SAY, The more a *person* listens to President Kennedy's speeches, the more *he* wonders how a young man can be so wise.

oral—means *spoken.*

verbal—means *expressed in words,* either spoken or written.

In international intrigue, *oral* messages are less risky than written ones.

Shorthand must usually be transcribed into *verbal* form.

ordinance—means *regulation.*

ordnance—refers to *guns, cannon, and the like.*

The local *ordinance* restricted driving speeds to thirty-five miles an hour.

Some rockets and guided missiles are now included in military *ordnance.*

ostensible—means *shown (usually for the purpose of deceiving others).*

ostentatious—means *showy.*

Although he was known to be ambitious, his *ostensible* motive was civic pride.

His *ostentatious* efforts in behalf of civic improvement impressed no one.

other ... than—is *acceptable; other ... but* (or *other ... except*) is *unacceptable.*

SAY, We have no *other* motive *than* friendship in asking you.

other—is an adjective and means *different.*

otherwise—is an adverb and means *in a different way.*

What you did was *other* (NOT *otherwise*) than what you had promised.

I cannot look *otherwise* (NOT *other*) than with delight at the improvement in your work.

SAY, All students, *except* (NOT *other than*) those exempted, should take the examination.

All students, *unless* **they have** been exempted (NOT *otherwise*), **will** take the examination.

out loud—is *unacceptable* for *aloud*.

SAY, he read *aloud* to his family every evening.

outdoor—(and *out-of-door*) is an adjective.

outdoors—is an adverb.

We spent most of the summer at an *outdoor* music camp.

Most of the time we played string quartets *outdoors*.

Note: *Out-of-doors* is *acceptable* in either case.

over—is *unacceptable* for *at*.

SAY, We shall be *at* (NOT *over*) your house tonight.

overly—is *unacceptable* for *over*.

SAY, We were *over-anxious* (not *overly anxious*) about the train's delay.

over with—is *unacceptable* for *completed*.

SAY, Thank goodness, that job is now *over!*

packed—means *full*.

pact—means *a treaty*.

The crate is *packed* with mixed fruits.

The peace *pact* between the former enemy nations was signed today.

part—means *a fraction of a whole*.

portion—means *an allotted* or *designated part*.

We had time to read just a *part* of the story.

Tomorrow, each of us will be responsible for reading a *portion* of the story.

part from—*a person*.

part with—*a thing*.

It was difficult for him to *part from* his classmates.

It will be difficult for him to *part with* his memories as well.

partial to—is *unacceptable* for *fond of*.

SAY, I am *fond of* (or *prefer*) bamboo fishing rods. (NOT *partial to*)

party—refers to a *group*, NOT an *individual*.

A *party* of men went on a scouting mission.

I told the woman (NOT *party*) that she was using the phone too long.

Note: *Party* may be used in a legal sense —The *party* of the second part . . .

passed—is the past tense of *to pass*.

past—means *just preceding*.

The week *passed* very slowly.

The *past* week was a very dull one.

patron—means *supporter*.

customer—is a *buyer*.

Mrs. Kennedy is a *patron* of early American art.

The rain kept the *customers* away.

pedal—means *a lever operated by foot*. (AVOID *foot* pedal)

peddle—means *to sell from door to door*.

It is impossible to ride a bicycle without moving the *pedals*.

The traveling salesman today seldom *peddles* from farm door to farm door.

people—comprise *a united* or *collective group of individuals*.

persons—are *individuals that are separate and unrelated*.

Only five *persons* remained in the theater after the first act.

The *people* of New York City have enthusiastically accepted "Shakespeare-in-the-Park" productions.

per—is Latin and is *chiefly commercial*.

per diem (by the day); *per minute*, etc.

AVOID *as per* your instruction, (SAY *according to*)

percent— (also **per cent**) expresses rate of interest.

percentage—means a part or proportion of the *whole*.

The interest rate of some banks is 4 *percent*.

The *percentage* of unmarried people in our community is small.

persecute—means *to make life miserable for someone*. (It's non-legal)

prosecute—means *to conduct a criminal investigation*. (It's legal)

Some racial groups insist upon *persecuting* other groups.

The District Attorney is *prosecuting* the racketeers.

personal—refers *to a person.*

personnel—means *an organized body of individuals.*

> The general took a *personal* interest in every one of his men.
>
> He believed that this was necessary in order to maintain the morale of the *personnel* in his division.

perspicacity—means *keenness in seeing* or *understanding.*

perspicuity—means *clearness to the understanding.*

> The teacher showed *perspicacity* in respect to the needs of his class.
>
> The class, in turn, appreciated the *perspicuity* of his explanations.

physic—means *a drug.*

physics—means *a branch of science.*

physique—means *body structure.*

> A doctor should determine the safe dose of a *physic.*
>
> Nuclear *physics* is the most advanced of the sciences.
>
> Athletes must take care of their *physiques.*

plain—means *simple,* or *a prairie.*

plane—means *a flat surface,* or *a tool.*

> The Great *Plains* are to be found in Western America.
>
> In *plane* geometry, we are concerned with two dimensions: *length* and *width.*

pled—is *unacceptable* as the past tense for *plead* (use *pleaded*).

> All the men who were arrested *pleaded* not guilty.

plenty—is a noun; it means *abundance.*

> America is land of *plenty.*
>
> SAY, There is *plenty of* (NOT *plenty*) room in the compact car for me.
>
> Note: *plenty* as an adverb is *unacceptable.*
>
> Note: *plenty* as an adj. is *unacceptable.*
>
> SAY, The compact car is *quite* (NOT *plenty*) large enough for me.

pole—means *a long stick.*

poll—means *vote.*

> We bought a new *pole* for the flag.

> The seniors took a *poll* to determine the graduate most likely to succeed.

poorly—meaning in poor health is *unacceptable.*

> Grandfather was feeling *in poor health* (NOT *poorly*) all last winter.

pour—is to send flowing *with direction and control.*

spill—is to send flowing *accidentally.*

> Please *pour* some cream into my cup of coffee.
>
> Careless people *spill* things.

posted—meaning informed is *unacceptable.*

> SAY, One can keep *well-informed* (NOT *well-posted*) by reading *The New York Times* daily.

practicable—means *useful, usable,* or *workable,* and is applied only to objects.

practical—means *realistic, having to do with action.* It applies to persons and things.

> There is as yet no *practicable* method for resisting atomic bomb attacks.
>
> *Practical* technicians, nevertheless, are attempting to translate the theories of the atomic scientists into some form of defense.

precede—means *to come before.*

proceed—means *to go ahead.* (*procedure* is the noun)

supersede—means *to replace.*

> What are the circumstances that *preceded* the attack?
>
> We can then *proceed* with our plan for resisting a second attack.
>
> It is then possible that Plan B will *supersede* Plan A.

predominately—is *unacceptable* for *predominantly,* meaning *powerfully* or *influentially.*

> SAY, The *predominantly* rich people in the area resisted all governmental attempts to create adequate power facilities.

prescribe—means *to lay down a course of action.*

proscribe—means *to outlaw* or *forbid.*

> The doctor *prescribed* plenty of rest and good food for the man.

Mark Antony *proscribed* many of Brutus' followers after Brutus' death.

principal—means *chief* or *main* (as an adjective); *a leader* (as a noun).

principle—means *a fundamental truth* or *belief*.

His *principal* supporters came from among the peasants.

The *principal* of the school asked for cooperation from the staff.

Humility was the guiding *principle* of Buddha's life.

Note: *Principal* may also mean *a sum placed at interest.*

Part of his monthly payment was applied as interest on the *principal*.

prodigy—means *a person endowed with extraordinary gifts or powers.*

protégé—means *someone under the protection of another.*

Mozart was a musical *prodigy* at the age of three.

For a time, Schumann was the *protege* of Johannes Brahms.

prophecy—(rhymes with *sea*) is the noun meaning *prediction*.

prophesy—(rhymes with *sigh*) is the verb meaning *to predict.*

The *prophecy* of the three witches eventually misled Macbeth.

The witches had *prophesied* that Macbeth would become king.

proposal—means *an offer*.

proposition—means a *statement*.

Lincoln's *proposal* for freeing the slaves through government purchase was unacceptable to the South.

The *proposition* that all men are created equal first appeared in the writings of the French Encyclopedists.

propose—means *to offer*.

purpose—means *to resolve* or *to intend.*

Let the teacher *propose* the subject for our debate.

The teacher *purposed* to announce the subject of the debate next week.

put across—meaning *to get something accepted* is *unacceptable*.

SAY, A good teacher may be defined as one who *succeeds in her purpose*. (NOT *puts it across*)

put in—meaning *to spend, make* or *devote* is *unacceptable*.

SAY, Every good student should *spend* (NOT *put in*) at least four hours a day in studying.

SAY, Be sure to *make* (NOT *put in*) an appearance at the council meeting.

rain—means *water from the clouds.*

reign—means *rule*.

rein—means *a strap for guiding a horse.*

The *rain* in Spain falls mainly on the plain.

A queen now *reigns* over England.

When the *reins* were pulled too tightly, the horse reared.

raise—means *to lift, erect.*

raze—(pronounced like *raise*) means *to tear down.*

The neighbors helped him *raise* a new barn.

The tornado *razed* his barn.

AVOID *raise* in connection with rearing *children*.

SAY, She *brought up* three lovely girls. (NOT *raised*)

rarely or ever—is *unacceptable*.

Say *rarely ever, rarely if ever, rarely or never.*

One *rarely if ever* (NOT *rarely or ever*) sees a trolley car today.

Students today *seldom if ever* (NOT *seldom or ever*) read Thackeray's novels.

real—meaning *very* or *extremely* is *unacceptable*.

SAY, He is a *very* (NOT *real*) handsome young man.

He is *really* handsome.

reason is because—is *unacceptable* for *the reason is that*.

SAY, *The reason* young people do not read Trollope today *is that* his sentences are too involved.

Note: Avoid *due to* after *reason is*.

SAY, *The reason* he refused *was that he was proud* (NOT *due to his pride*).

rebellion—means *open, armed, organized resistance to authority.*

revolt—means *similar resistance on a smaller scale.*

revolution—means *the overthrowing of one government and the setting up of another.*

Bootlegging has sometimes been referred to as a *rebellion* against high whiskey taxes.

An increase in the grain tax caused a peasant's *revolt* agains the landowners.

Castro's Cuban *revolution* is a matter of grave concern to Latin America.

reckon—meaning *suppose* or *think* is unacceptable.

SAY, I *think* it may rain this afternoon.

recollect—means *to bring back to memory.*

remember—means *to keep in memory.*

Now I can *recollect* your returning the money to me.

I *remember* the occasion well.

reconciled to—means *resigned to* or *adjusted to.*

reconciled with—means *to become friendly again with someone;* also, *to bring one set of facts into harmony with another one.*

I am now *reconciled to* this chronic ache in my back.

The boy was *reconciled with* his parents after he had promised not to try to run away from home again.

How does one *reconcile* the politician's shabby accomplishments *with* the same politician's noble promises?

regular—meaning *real* or *true* is unacceptable.

SAY, He was a *real* (NOT *regular*) tyrant.

respectably—means *in a manner deserving respect.*

respectfully—means *with respect and decency.*

respectively—means *as relating to each, in the order given.*

Young people should conduct themselves *respectably* in school as well as in church.

The students listened *respectfully* to the principal.

John and Bill are the sons *respectively* of Mr. Smith and Mr. Brown.

restive—means *fretting under restraint.*

restless—means *fidgety.*

As the principal continued talking, the students became *restive*.

Spring always makes me feel *restless*.

retaliate—means *to return evil for evil.*

reciprocate—means *to return in kind—usually a favor for a favor.*

The private *retaliated* by putting a snake into the sergeant's bed.

When she received the mink coat, she *reciprocated* by cooking a delicious meal for her husband.

reverend—means *worthy of reverence* or *respect.*

reverent—means *feeling* or *showing respect.*

Shakespeare, the *reverend* master of the drama, still inspires most readers.

Sometimes a too *reverent* attitude toward Shakespeare causes the reader to miss much of the fun in his plays.

Note: *The Reverend* (abbreviated *Rev.*) John W. Smith is pastor of our church.

Reverend—should be used with the full name or the initials of the person.

Acceptable: The Reverend James Wilson will address us. (NOT the *Reverend Wilson*)

Unacceptable: The Reverend will conduct the services.

right along—is *unacceptable* for *continuously.*

SAY, His contemporaries were *continuously* (NOT *right along*) in opposition to Shakespeare.

Note: *Right away* and *right off* are *unacceptable* for *at once.*

SAY, Other of Shakespeare's contemporaries, especially Ben Jonson, *immediately* (NOT *right off* or *right away*) recognized his genius.

rob—one *robs* a *person.*

steal—one *steals* a *thing.*

They *robbed* the blind man of his money.

He *stole* my wallet.

Note: "They *robbed* the First National Bank" is correct because they actually robbed the persons working in the bank.

rout—(rhymes with *stout*) means *a defeat*.

route—(rhymes with *boot*) means *a way of travel*.

The *rout* of the army was near.

The milkman has a steady *route*.

same as—is *unacceptable* for *in the same way* and *just as*.

SAY, The owner's son was treated *in the same way as* any other worker. (NOT *the same as*)

AVOID *same* as a pronoun, except in *legal* usage.

SAY, If the books are available, please send *them* (NOT *same*) by parcel post.

saw—is the past tense of *see*.

seen—is the past participle of *see*.

We *saw* a play yesterday. (NOT *seen*)

I have never *seen* a live play before. (NOT *saw*)

scan—means to *examine carefully*. It does *not* mean to examine *hastily* or *superficially*.

You must *scan* a book on nuclear physics in order to understand it thoroughly.

DON'T SAY When I am in a hurry, I *scan* the headlines. (SAY *glance at*)

seem—as used in the expression *I couldn't seem to* and *I don't seem to* is *unacceptable*.

SAY, *We can't find* (NOT *We can't seem to find*) the address.

self-confessed—is *unacceptable* for *confessed*. Omit *self*.

He was a *confessed* slayer.

sensible of—means *aware of*.

sensitive to—means *affected by*.

I am very *sensible of* my shortcomings in written English.

He is *sensitive to* criticism.

sensual—means *pleasure-loving*.

sensuous—means *influenced through the senses*, *esthetic*.

The *sensual* man cares little about the salvation of his soul.

A *sensuous* person usually appreciates art and music.

settle—meaning *to pay* is *unacceptable*.

We *paid* all our former bills. (NOT *settled*)

AVOID: We'll *settle* you, We'll *settle* your hash, etc.

sewage—means *waste matter in a sewer*.

sewerage—means *the system* of *sewers*.

The careful disposal of *sewage* is essential to proper public health.

For such disposal, an adequate amount of *sewerage* is necessary.

shall⎫
will⎭ SAY I *shall*, we *shall* (Otherwise, say *will*—you *will*, he *will*, she *will*, they *will*, it *will*)

Note: In informal speech, I *will* (would) may be used instead of I *shall*.

Note: In cases of determination, reverse the foregoing rule: I certainly *will* insist on full payment.

They *shall* not pass.

shape—meaning *state* or *condition* is *unacceptable*.

SAY, The refugees were in a serious *condition* (NOT *shape*) when they arrived here.

show—meaning *opportunity* or *chance* is *unacceptable*.

The sailors on the torpedoed vessel *didn't have a chance* (NOT *didn't have a show*) of surviving in the wild waters.

show up—meaning *to make an appearance* is *unacceptable*.

SAY, We were all disappointed in the star's failure to *appear* (NOT *to show up*).

Note: *Show up* meaning *to expose* is *unacceptable*.

SAY, It is my firm intention to *expose* (NOT *show up*) your hypocrisy.

sign up—meaning *to enlist* or *enroll* is *unacceptable*.

SAY, Many young men hurried *to enlist* (NOT *sign up*) after the President's talk.

simple reason—is *unacceptable* for *reason*. Omit the word *simple* in similar expressions: *simple truth*, *simple purpose*, etc.

Unacceptable: I refuse to do it for the *simple reason* that I don't like your attitude.

Acceptable: The *truth* (omit *simple*) is that I feel tired.

simply—meaning *absolutely* is *unacceptable*.
SAY, The performance was *absolutely* (NOT *simply*) thrilling.

sit—means *take a seat.* (intransitive verb)

set—means *place.*   (transitive verb)
Note the forms of each verb:

TENSE	SIT (TAKE A SEAT)
PRESENT	He *is sitting* on a chair.
PAST	He *sat* on the chair.
PRES. PERF.	He *has sat* on the chair.

TENSE	SET (PLACE)
PRESENT	He *is setting* the lamp on the table.
PAST	He *set* the lamp on the table.
PRES. PERF.	He *has set* the lamp on the table.

size up—meaning *to estimate* is *unacceptable.*
SAY, The detectives were able *to estimate* (NOT *size up*) the fugitive's remaining ammunition supply from his careless shooting.

so—should be avoided for *very, great,* etc.
SAY, She is *very* (NOT *so*) beautiful! *So* should not be used for *so that* to express purpose.
Unacceptable: He gave up his seat *so* (SAY *so that*) the old lady could sit down.

sociable—means *friendly.*

social—means *relating to people in general.*
Sociable individuals prefer to have plenty of people around them.
The President's *social* program included old age insurance, housing, education, etc.

sole—means *all alone.*

soul—means *man's spirit.*
He was the *sole* owner of the business.
Man's *soul* is unconquerable.

some—meaning *somewhat* is *unacceptable.*
SAY, She is *somewhat* (NOT *some*) better today.

Note: *Some* is *unacceptable* in such expressions as the following:
We had a *very* (NOT *some*) strong scare this morning.

some time—means *a portion of time.*

sometime—means *at an indefinite time in the future.*

sometimes—means *occasionally.*
I'll need *some time* to make a decision.
Let us meet *sometime* after twelve noon.
Sometimes it is better to hesitate before signing a contract.

somewheres—is *unacceptable.*

somewhere—is *acceptable.*

specie—means *money as coins.* (*Specie* is singular only).

species—means *a class of related things.* (*Species* is singular and plural).
He preferred to be paid in *specie*, rather than in bank notes.
The human *species* is relatively young. (singular)
Several animal *species* existed before man. (plural)

stand—meaning *to tolerate* is *unacceptable.*
SAY, I refuse *to tolerate* (NOT *to stand for*) your nonsense.

start in—is *unacceptable* for *start.*
We shall *start* (NOT *start in*) to read the story in a few minutes.

state—means *to declare formally.*

say—means *to speak generally.*
Our ambassador *stated* the terms for a cease-fire agreement.
We *said* (NOT *stated*) that we would not attend the meeting.

stationary—means *standing still.*

stationery—means *writing materials.*
In ancient times people thought the earth was *stationary.*
We bought writing paper at the *stationery* store.

statue—means *a piece of sculpture.*

stature—means *height.*

statute—is *a law.*

The *Statue* of Liberty stands in New York Harbor.

The athlete was a man of great *stature*.

Compulsory education was established by *statute*.

stay—means *to remain*.

stop—means *to cease*.

We *stayed* (NOT *stopped*) at the hotel for three days.

The power failure caused the clock *to stop*.

Note: *To stop off, to stop over*, and *to stay put* are *unacceptable*.

stayed—means *remained*.

stood—means *remained upright* or *erect*.

The army *stayed* in the trenches for five days.

The soldiers *stood* at attention for one hour.

straight—means *direct* or *not crooked*.

strait—means *narrow, restricted*.

The road led *straight* to the deserted farmhouse.

The violent patient was placed in a *strait*-jacket.

strangled to death—is *unacceptable* for *strangled*. Omit *to death*.

Unacceptable: The girl was found *strangled to death*.

Acceptable: The madman attempted *to strangle* his victim.

summons—is singular; *summonses* is the plural.

We received a *summons* to appear in court.

This was the first of three *summonses* we were to receive that week.

Note: *Summons* is also a verb.

We were *summonsed* to appear in court. (also *summoned*)

sure—for *surely* is *unacceptable*.

SAY, You *surely* (NOT *sure*) are not going to write that!

surround—means *to inclose on all sides*. Do NOT add *on all sides* to it.

The camp was *surrounded* by heavy woods.

suspicioned—is *unacceptable* for *suspected*.

SAY, We *suspected* (NOT *suspicioned*) that he was ready to betray us.

take in—is *unacceptable* in the sense of *deceive* or *attend*.

SAY, We were *deceived* (NOT *taken in*) by his oily manner.

We should like to *attend* (NOT *take in*) a few plays during our vacation.

take stock in—is *unacceptable* for *rely on*.

SAY, We rarely *rely on* (NOT *take stock in*) the advice of younger employees.

tasteful—means *having good taste*.

tasty—means *pleasing to the taste*.

The home of our host was decorated in a *tasteful* manner.

Our host also served us very *tasty* meals.

tenants—are *occupants*.

tenets—are *principles*.

Several *tenants* occupied that apartment during the first month.

His religious *tenets* led him to perform many good deeds.

tender—means *to offer officially* or *formally*.

give—means *to donate* or *surrender something willingly*.

The discredited official decided to *tender* his resignation.

He *gave* testimony readily before the grand jury.

testimony—means *information given orally only*.

evidence—means *information given orally or in writing*.

He gave *testimony* readily to the grand jury.

The defendant presented written *evidence* to prove he was not at the scene of the crime.

that there ⎫
this here ⎭ are *unacceptable*. Omit *there, here*.

SAY, *That* (NOT *that there*) person is taller than *this* (NOT *this here*) one.

their—means *belonging to them*.

there—means *in that place*.

they're—means *they are*.

We took *their* books home with us.

You will find your books over *there* on the desk.

They're not as young as we expected them to be.

theirselves—is *unacceptable* for *themselves.*
SAY, Most children of school age are able to care for *themselves* in many ways.

therefor—means *for that.*
therefore—means *because of that.*
One day's detention is the punishment *therefor.*
You will, *therefore*, have to remain in school after dismissal time.

these kind—is *unacceptable.*
this kind—is *acceptable.*
I am fond of *this kind* of apples.
Note: *These kinds* would be also acceptable.

through—meaning *finished* or *completed* is unacceptable.
SAY, We'll finish (NOT *be through with*) the work by five o'clock.

thusly—is *unacceptable* for *thus.*
SAY, Speak words *thus:* ...

to my knowledge—implies *certain knowledge.*
to the best of my knowledge—implies *limited knowledge.*
He is, *to my knowledge*, the brightest boy in the class.
As for his character, he has never, *to the best of my knowledge*, been in trouble with the law.

tortuous—means *twisting.*
torturing—means *causing pain.*
The wagon train followed a *tortuous* trail through the mountains.
The *torturing* memory of his defeat kept him awake all night.
Note: *Torturesome* is unacceptable.

track—means *a path* or *road.*
tract—means *a brief but serious piece of writing; a piece of land.*
The horses raced around the fair grounds *track.*
John Locke wrote a famous *tract* on education.

The heavily wooded *tract* was sold to a lumber company.

treat—means *to deal with.*
treat of—means *to give an explanation of.*
treat with—means *to negotiate with.*
I shall *treat* that subject in our next lesson.
The lesson itself will *treat* of Shakespeare's humor.
I shall *treat* with the delinquent students at some other time.

try to—is *acceptable.*
try and—is *unacceptable.*
Try to come (NOT *try and* come).
Note: *plan on going* is *unacceptable.*
plan to go is *acceptable.*

two—is the *numeral 2.*
to—means *in the direction of.*
too—means *more than* or *also.*
There are *two* sides to every story.
Three *twos* (or 2's) equal six.
We shall go *to* school.
We shall go, *too.*
The weather is *too* hot for school.

type man—(*type book, type game,* etc.) is unacceptable for *type of man, type of book, type of game,* etc.
SAY, He is a high *type of man* for this position.

ugly—meaning *unpleasant* or *dangerous* is unacceptable.
SAY, This is a very *dangerous* (NOT *ugly*) situation.

ulterior—means *hidden underneath.*
underlying—means *fundamental.*
His noble words were contradicted by his *ulterior* motives.
Shakespeare's *underlying* motive in *Hamlet* was to criticize the moral climate of his own times.

unbeknownst to—is *unacceptable* for *without the knowledge of.*
SAY, The young couple decided to get married *without the knowledge of* (NOT *unbeknownst to*) their parents.

unique—means *the only one of its kind*, and therefore does not take *very, most, extremely* before it.

SAY, The First Folio edition of Shakespeare's works is *unique* (NOT *very unique*)

Note: The same rule applies to *perfect*.

uninterested—means *bored*.

disinterested—means *fair, impartial*.

I am *uninterested* in this slow-moving game.

Let us ask a *disinterested* person to settle this argument.

United States should always have *The* before it.

SAY, *The United States* of America is not the largest land mass in the Western Hemisphere. (Note the singular verb *is*)

The United States of Brazil is also a federal republic.

unmoral—(and *amoral*) means *not involving morality*.

immoral—means *contrary to moral law*.

The principles of science are considered *unmoral*.

The question of beauty is an *amoral* one.

It is *immoral* to steal or to bear false witness.

upwards of—is *unacceptable* for *more than*.

SAY, There are *more than* (NOT *upwards of*) one million people unemployed today.

valuable—means *of great worth*.

valued—means *held in high regard*.

invaluable—means *priceless*.

This is a *valuable* manuscript.

The expert gave him highly *valued* advice.

A good name is an *invaluable* possession.

venal—means *capable of being bribed*.

venial—means *pardonable*.

The *venal* councilman yielded to corruption.

A white lie is a *venial* sin.

veracity—means *truthfulness*.

truth—is *a true statement, a fact*.

Because he had a reputation for *veracity*, we could not doubt his story.

We would have questioned the *truth* of his story otherwise.

via—means *by way of* and should be used in connection with travel or motion only.

SAY, We shipped the merchandise *via* motor express.

I received the information through (NOT *via*) his letter.

virtue—means *goodness*.

virtuosity—means *technical skill*.

We should expect a considerable degree of *virtue* in our public officials.

The young pianist played with amazing *virtuosity* at his debut.

virtually—means *in effect*.

actually—means *in fact*.

A tie in the final game was *virtually* a defeat for us.

We had *actually* won more games than they at that time.

waive—means *to give up*.

wave—means *a swell* or *roll of water*.

As a citizen, I refuse to *waive* my right of free speech.

The *waves* reached the top deck of the ship.

was ⎫
were ⎭ If something is contrary to fact (not a fact), use *were* in every instance.

I wish I *were* in Bermuda.

Unacceptable: If he *was* sensible, he wouldn't act like that.

(SAY If he *were* . . .)

way back—(and *way down yonder, way behind us,*) is *unacceptable*.

SAY, We knew him from *early times*. (NOT *way back*)

ways—is *unacceptable* for *way*.

SAY, We climbed a little *way*, (NOT *ways*) up the hill.

went and took—(*went and stole*, etc.) is *unacceptable*.

SAY, They *stole* (NOT *went and stole*) our tools.

what—is *unacceptable* for *that*.

SAY, Everything *that* (NOT *what*) you write displeases me.

when—(and *where*) should NOT be used to introduce a definition of a noun.

SAY, A tornado *is a* twisting, high wind on land (NOT *is when a twisting, high wind is on land*).

A pool *is a place for swimming.* (NOT *is where people swim*)

whereabouts—is *unacceptable* for *where*.

SAY, Where (NOT *whereabouts*) do you live?

Note: *Whereabouts* as a noun meaning a place is *acceptable*.
Do you know his *whereabouts*?

whether—should NOT be preceded by *of* or *as to*.

SAY, The President will consider the question *whether* (NOT *of whether*) it is better to ask for or demand higher taxes now.

He inquired *whether* (NOT *as to whether*) we were going or not.

which—is used *incorrectly* in the following expressions:

He asked me to stay, *which I did.* (CORRECT: He asked me to stay and I did.)

It has been a severe winter, *which* is unfortunate. (CORRECT: Unfortunately, it has been a severe winter.)

You did not write; besides *which* you have not telephoned. (CORRECT: Omit *which*)

while—is *unacceptable* for *and* or *though*.

SAY, The library is situated on the south side; (OMIT *while*) the laboratory is on the north side.

Though (NOT while) I disagree with you, I shall not interfere with your right to express your opinion.

Though (NOT while) I am in my office every day, you do not attempt to see me.

who
whom } The following is a method (without going into grammar rules) for determining when to use WHO or WHOM.

"Tell me (*Who, Whom*) you think should represent our company?"

STEP ONE Change the who—whom part of the sentence to its natural order.

"You think (*who, whom*) should represent our company?"

STEP TWO—Substitute HE for WHO, HIM for WHOM.

"You think (*he, him*) should represent our company?"

You would say *he* in this case.

THEREFORE—"Tell me WHO you think should represent the company?" is correct.

who is
who am } Note these constructions:

It is I who *am* the most experienced.
It is he who *is* . . .
It is he or I who *am* . . .
It is I or he who *is* . . .
It is he and I who *are* . . .

whose—means *of whom*.
who's—means *who is*.

Whose is this notebook?
Who's in the next office?

win—you *win* a game.
beat—you *beat* another player.

We *won* the contest.
He *beat* me in tennis. (NOT *won* me)

Note: Don't use *beat* for swindle.
SAY, The peddler *swindled* the customer out of five dollars. (NOT *beat*)

worst kind—(and *worst way*) is *unacceptable* for *very badly* or *extremely*.

SAY, The school is *greatly in need of more teachers.* (NOT *needs teachers the worst way.*)

would have—is *unacceptable* for *had*.

SAY, I wish you *had* (NOT *would have*) called earlier.

you all—is *unacceptable* for *you* (plural).

SAY, We welcome *you*, the delegates from Ethiopia.

You are all welcome, delegates of Ethiopia.

TEST XX. CORRECT USAGE

TIME: 25 Minutes

DIRECTIONS: In each of the following groups of sentences, select the one sentence that is grammatically INCORRECT. Mark the answer sheet with the letter of that incorrect sentence.

Explanations of the key points behind these questions appear with the answers at the end of this test. The explanatory answers provide the kind of background that will enable you to answer test questions with facility and confidence.

1

(A) The dairy business was incidental to the regular grocery business.
(B) Speak to whom you see first.
(C) Our vacation has come to an end, I am sorry to say.
(D) The reason he retired is because he was old.

2

(A) The amount of G.I. returns is steadily increasing.
(B) Much information on the subject is available.
(C) They collected many details about the matter.
(D) Many persons are guilty of traffic violations.

3

(A) The stone made a very angry bruise on his forearm.
(B) Put the book in this drawer.
(C) In all likelihood, we shall be unable to go to the fair.
(D) He would have liked to go to the theatre with us.

4

(A) He carried out the order with great dispatch but with little effect.
(B) The cook's overbearing manner overawed his employer.
(C) All of us shall partake of the benefits of exercise.
(D) Miss Smith made less errors than the other typists.

5

(A) Leave us face it – the jury cannot make a determination of the facts.
(B) His precision resulted in a nice discrimination between their relative merits.
(C) Green vegetables are healthful foods.
(D) We shall attempt to ascertain whether there has been any tampering with the lock.

6

(A) Last night I visited a friend who has just returned to America.
(B) Due to his long absence he was unable to keep up with his class.
(C) "I have nothing further to say," he stated.
(D) Our country is proud of its powerful industries.

7

(A) Located on a mountainside with a babbling brook beside the door, it was a dream palace.
(B) Blessed are they that have not seen and yet have believed.
(C) The customs in that part of the country are much different than I expected.
(D) Politics, even in towns of small population, has always attracted ambitious young lawyers.

8

(A) You ought to begin, oughtn't you?
(B) When she graduates college she will be twenty-one.
(C) The law prescribed when and to whom the tax should be paid.
(D) We would rather die than surrender.

9

(A) I believe that we are liable to have good weather tomorrow.
(B) From what I could see, I thought he acted like the others.
(C) Perpetual motion is an idea which is not unthinkable.
(D) Many of us taxpayers are displeased with the service.

10

(A) He was charged with having committed many larcenous acts.
(B) Material wealth is certainly not something to be dismissed cavalierly.
(C) He is one of those people who do everything promptly.
(D) I hope to be able to retaliate for the assistance you have given me.

11

(A) There was, in the first place, no indication that a crime had been committed.
(B) She is taller than any other member of the class.
(C) Politics is nothing more or less than making the right connections.
(D) Haven't you any film in stock at this time?

12

(A) The reason why I am writing to you is that I wish to avoid further misunderstanding.
(B) On account of there was adequate police protection the march was not disrupted.
(C) Regardless of your decision, I shall have to go.
(D) I have only twenty pupils in this class.

13

(A) He fidgeted, like most children do, while the grown-ups were discussing the problem.
(B) I won't go unless you go with me.
(C) Sitting beside the charred ruins of his cabin, the frontiersman told us the story of the attack.
(D) Certainly there can be no objection to the boys' working on a volunteer basis.

14

(A) By rotating the secretaries' tasks, we should be able to train the entire office staff in all duties.
(B) The clerk who had fainted told me that he felt alright, so I didn't make out an accident report.
(C) The flowers that the secretary had brought added a delightful touch of color to the office.
(D) We shall have to work fast to complete the task before the deadline.

15

(A) What you are doing is mighty important.
(B) The enormousness of the animal was enough to make her gasp.
(C) The judge brought in a decision which aroused antagonism in the community.
(D) I asked the monitor to take the papers to the principal.

16

(A) Have you noted the unusual phenomena to be seen in that portion of the heavens?
(B) The storm raged continually for twelve hours.
(C) The enormity of the crime was such that we could not comprehend it.
(D) The collection of monies from some clients was long overdue.

17

(A) The secretary prepared a notice which was put in the mail boxes of all employees, including yourself.
(B) Do not yield to the temptation to deal with a poorly dressed person in a way which is different from the way in which you treat others.
(C) You will find the envelope directly behind the file folder headed "Correspondence."
(D) May I ask you to double-check the totals?

18

(A) If my trip is a success, I should be back on Thursday.
(B) We will send a copy of the article to you if you wish it.
(C) They will have gone before the notice is sent to their office.
(D) Can I use this information in my speech?

19

(A) He likes these pencils; how ever, they must have soft lead.
(B) That Jackson will be elected is evident.
(C) He does not approve of my dictating the letter.
(D) Ray should make some progress in his work each day.

20

(A) The instant Mr. Armstrong began to dictate, the bell rang, interrupting his train of thought.
(B) This is one of those machines that are constantly breaking down.
(C) She asked me whether I would remain a few additional minutes to check her work.
(D) Good Americans should join together to destroy racial prejudice.

21

(A) Listening intently to the heated discussion at the conference, Laura forgot to take notes; consequently, the minutes were incomplete.
(B) If I were going to prepare the payroll report, I would begin as long in advance as possible.
(C) She asked the student to bring the book to the principal.
(D) The secretaries agreed among themselves that each would do a certain amount of the correspondence.

22

(A) From the tone of the letter, it was easy to imply that the writer was grateful.
(B) We devised other means of communication since telephone extensions were nonexistent.
(C) The preparation of circulars and attendance reports requires considerable care.
(D) "Please direct me to room 205," said the visitor. "I have an appointment with Mr. Galbraith."

(23)

(A) He will study the lesson providing he can find his book.
(B) It looks like they will come.
(C) The meeting of the committee was held in the Rose Room.
(D) He decided to open a branch store.

(24)

(A) For the sake of expediency, we divided the work between the four of us.
(B) She quickly learnt to use a comptometer.
(C) Miss Smith would rather take dictation than operate the switchboard.
(D) The dimensions of the envelope determine the quantity of matter that may be enclosed.

(25)

(A) The slayer of Dr. King tried in every which way to avoid the death penalty.
(B) Should she be chosen, give her this letter of congratulation.
(C) He had respect for whosoever was in power.
(D) If you are not careful, you will fall off the platform.

(26)

(A) There were twenty 80's, four 70's, and no failures in the test.
(B) Neither his writings nor his speech qualifies him as an expert.
(C) Of all who were at the party, he was the one whom we most loved.
(D) The reason Frank is going to Arizona is that he despises a damp climate.

(27)

(A) The secretary and treasurer of the company was questioned by the investigating committee.
(B) John has grown much taller than Jim in the past two years.
(C) Get in touch with me in a couple of days.
(D) The executive said that the published story was inaccurate.

(28)

(A) Through a ruse, the prisoners affected their escape from the concentration camp.
(B) Constant exposure to danger has affected his mind.
(C) Her affected airs served to alienate her from her friends.
(D) Her vivacity was an affectation.

(29)

(A) Because they had been trained for emergencies, the assault did not catch them by surprise.
(B) They divided the loot between the four of them in proportion to their efforts.
(C) The number of strikes is gradually diminishing.
(D) Between acts we went out to the lobby for a brief chat.

(30)

(A) Copper and gold are what I need.
(B) There are a piano and a phonograph in the room.
(C) You always look well in those sort of clothes.
(D) The audience was enthusiastic.

(31)

(A) He promised that he would be here.
(B) Shall we go to the park?
(C) They are alike in this particular.
(D) I all ready anticipate the good times we shall have on our trip.

(32)

(A) I said nothing.
(B) It's I.
(C) Lend me five dollars.
(D) She walks like I do.

(33)

(A) It must be here somewhere.
(B) The reason is that there is no gasoline.
(C) I shall try and attend one meeting.
(D) He walked up the hill.

CONSOLIDATE YOUR KEY ANSWERS HERE

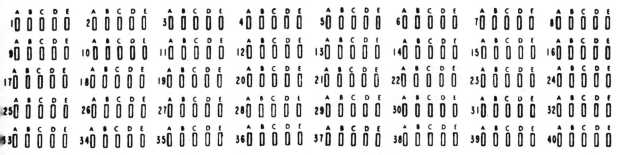

TEST XX. CORRECT USAGE

KEY ANSWERS FOR THE FOREGOING QUESTIONS

1.D	6.B	11.C	16.B	21.C	26.D	31.D
2.A	7.C	12.B	17.A	22.A	27.C	32.D
3.B	8.B	13.A	18.D	23.B	28.A	33.C
4.D	9.A	14.B	19.A	24.A	29.B	
5.A	10.D	15.A	20.D	25.A	30.C	

EXPLANATORY ANSWERS CLARIFYING CARDINAL POINTS

The core of the Question and Answer Method . . . getting help when and where you need it. Even if you were able to write correct key answers for the preceding questions, the following explanations illuminate fundamental facts, ideas, and principles which just might crop up in the form of questions on future tests.

Bold-face *references in the following answers direct you to paragraphs in the Arco Grammar Text, where fuller explanations are provided.*

ANSWER 1.

D   The reason he retired is **that** he was old. REASON: We say the **reason is that** — not the **reason is because**.   **(71)**

ANSWER 2.

A   The **number** of G.I. returns is steadily increasing. REASON: **amount** is used for bulk — **number** is used for countable items.   **(71)**

ANSWER 3.

B   Put the book **into** this drawer. REASON: Motion from one place to another is expressed by **into**.   **(71)**

ANSWER 4.

D   Miss Smith made **fewer** errors than the other typists. REASON: **fewer** refers to countable items — **less** refers to bulk items.   **(71)**

ANSWER 5.

A   Let us face it — the jury **cannot** make a determination of the facts. REASON: Since an infinitive **(to) face** follows, we must use **Let**. When there is no infinitive, we use **Leave (Leave us alone)**.   **(71)**

ANSWER 6.

B   **Because of** his long absence he was unable to keep up with his class. REASON: Never start a sentence with **Due to**.   **(71)**

ANSWER 7.

C   The customs in that part of the country are much **different from** what I expected. REASON: The correct expression is **different from** — not **different than**.   **(71)**

ANWER 8.

B When she **graduates from** college, she will be twenty-one. REASON: The correct expression for completing the schoolwork is **to graduate from**. Incidentally, this is better than the passive form, **to be graduated from**, though both usages are correct. **(71)**

ANSWER 9.

A I believe that we are **likely** to have good weather tomorrow. REASON: **liable** is used for undesirable happenings. **(71)**

ANSWER 10.

D I hope to be able to **reciprocate** for the assistance you have given me. REASON: **retaliate** means to strike back for some injury; **reciprocate** means to pay back for a kindness. **(71)**

ANSWER 11.

C Politics is **nothing more nor less** than making the right connections. REASON: **nothing more or less** is unacceptable. **(71)**

ANSWER 12.

B **Because** there was adequate police protection, the march was not disrupted. REASON: **on account of** cannot be used as a subordinate conjunction. **(71)**

ANSWER 13.

A He fidgeted, **as** most children do, while the grown-ups were discussing the problem. REASON: **like** is a preposition—it cannot act as a subordinate conjunction to introduce a clause. **As** does that job. **(71)**

ANSWER 14.

B The clerk who had fainted told me that he felt **all right**, so I didn't make out an accident report. REASON: **alright** is never correct. **(71)**

ANSWER 15.

A What you are doing is **very** important. REASON: Don't use **mighty** for **very**. **(71)**

ANSWER 16.

B The storm raged **continuously** for twelve hours. REASON: **continuously** means with no interruption. **(71)**

ANSWER 17.

A The secretary prepared a notice which was put **into** the mail boxes of all employees, including yourself. REASON: We **put into**—not **in**. **(71)**

ANSWER 18.

D **May** I use this information in my speech? REASON: **May** is used for permission—**Can** is used for a physical possibility. **(71)**

ANSWER 19.

A He likes these pencils; **however,** they must have soft lead. REASON: **however,** the conjunctive adverb, is a solid word. **(71)**

ANSWER 20.

D Good Americans should **join** to destroy racial prejudice. REASON: Omit **together** in this case. **(71)**

ANSWER 21.

C She asked the student to **take** the book to the principal. REASON: **take from** the speaker; **bring** to the speaker. **(71)**

ANSWER 22.

A From the tone of the letter, it was easy to infer that the writer was grateful. REASON: The listener infers - the speaker (or writer) implies - in this sentence, we are "listening" to the writer. **(71)**

ANSWER 23.

B   It looks **as if** they will come. REASON: **like** is a preposition — it cannot act as a subordinate conjunction to introduce a clause. **as if** serves that purpose. **(71)**

ANSWER 24.

A   For the sake of expediency, we divided the work **among** the four of us. REASON: **between** us is used for two — **among** for three or more. **(71)**

ANSWER 25.

A   The slayer of Dr. King tried in **every way** to avoid the death penalty. REASON: **every which way** is unacceptable. **(71)**

ANSWER 26.

D   The reason Frank is going to Arizona is that he **detests** a damp climate. REASON: **despise** means to look down upon. **(71)**

ANSWER 27.

C   Get in touch with me in a **few** days. REASON: **couple** is used for two things that are joined. **(71)**

ANSWER 28.

A   Through a ruse, the prisoners **effected** their escape from the concentration camp. REASON: **effected** means brought about — **affected** means influenced. **(71)**

ANSWER 29.

B   They divided the loot **among** the four of them in proportion to their efforts. REASON: **between** is used for two — **among**, for three or more. **(71)**

ANSWER 30.

C   You always look well in **that sort** of clothes. REASON: Since **sort** is a singular noun, its demonstrative adjective modifier (**that**) must be singular. See **these kind**. **(71)**

ANSWER 31.

D   I **already** anticipate the good times we shall have on our trip. REASON: **all ready** means that all persons (are) ready — **already** means previously. **(71)**

ANSWER 32.

D   She walks **as** I do. REASON: The conjunction **as** — not the preposition **like** — is required here. **(71)**

ANSWER 33.

C   I shall **try to** attend one meeting. REASON: Don't say **try and** — say **try to**. **(71)**

TEST XXI. CORRECT USAGE

TIME: 25 Minutes

DIRECTIONS: In each of the following groups of sentences, select the one sentence that is grammatically INCORRECT. Mark the answer sheet with the letter of that incorrect sentence.

Explanations of the key points behind these questions appear with the answers at the end of this test. The explanatory answers provide the kind of background that will enable you to answer test questions with facility and confidence.

1

(A) His speed was equal to that of a racehorse.
(B) His failure was due to weak eyes.
(C) His love for war is contemptuous.
(D) Of course, my opinion is worth less than a lawyer's.

2

(A) In spite of the fact that it had not been refrigerated for several hours, the milk was still sweet.
(B) No sooner had he finished his studies when he dashed out to play.
(C) "Will you ride to the game with me?" asked John.
(D) To see is to believe, but one must be sure that one sees clearly.

3

(A) There goes the last train with American soldiers.
(B) Such talk aggravates me.
(C) The scene opens quickly, and in walk John and Mary.
(D) I cough continually in the winter.

4

(A) Everyone was present but him for whom the meeting was called.
(B) The citizen was wholly within his rights.
(C) Not only did I eat too much, but I also drank to excess.
(D) Let's meet around six o'clock.

5

(A) He lost considerable in Wall Street.
(B) Last night, in a radio address, the President urged us to subscribe to the Red Cross.
(C) In the evening, light spring rain cooled the streets.
(D) "Un-American" is a word which has been used even by those whose sympathies may well be pro-Nazi.

6

(A) The professor finished the unit inside of a month.
(B) After stealing the bread, he ran like a thief.
(C) Swimming is more enjoyable than dancing.
(D) The scouts walked a mile further than they had intended.

7

(A) The meal was meant to be theirs.
(B) We all prefer those other kinds of candy.
(C) Has either of you a sharp pencil?
(D) That was a great bunch of people.

8

(A) Bob Kennedy was the choice of many.
(B) Bring all these books to the library.
(C) We are desirous of serving you.
(D) Anyone may attend.

9

(A) I beg leave to call upon you in case of an emergency.
(B) Do not deter me from carrying out the demands of my office.
(C) Please see me irregardless of the time of day.
(D) The attorney for the slayer insisted his client was innocent.

10

(A) It is the noise made by the crickets that you hear.
(B) She told us that she would be at home on Sunday.
(C) The Democratic Convention was about to drop Chicago as its site because of a telephone strike.
(D) Sandy is a very cute girl.

11

(A) In brief, jurors must exercise their very best judgment.
(B) If we can make a deal, I'll buy your paintings.
(C) The letter, having been corrected, was ready for his signature.
(D) Their disagreement soon developed into a bitter fight.

12

(A) I think that Report A is equally as good as Report B.
(B) Not only John but also his brothers have applied for admission to college.
(C) This book is more valauble than any other book in my library.
(D) My cousin said that he intended to go to camp with me.

13

(A) I prefer these kind of books to those.
(B) Did he say, "The test will be on Saturday"?
(C) When we reviewed the report, we felt that we oughtn't to incur any further expenses.
(D) It's time to give the baby its bath.

14

(A) Working hard at school during the day and in the post office during the night, he seemed to be utterly indefatigable.
(B) Do you think she is liable to win the fellowship?
(C) I found "Ode to a Skylark" in an anthology called "Singing Winds."
(D) Their stories being unintelligible, it's hard to say who's to blame for the disturbance.

15

(A) Many artisans participated in the building of the Sistine Chapel.
(B) The contrast between the two parties is patent.
(C) Although Richard graduated high school with honors, he failed three subjects as a college freshman.
(D) Neither the teacher nor the students have found the reference.

16

(A) I can read almost anything, but these childlike books disgust me.
(B) Neither of the candidates was able to secure a plurality of the votes.
(C) To keep abreast of current events requires that one read conscientiously at least two newspapers daily.
(D) There would have been bitter opposition to the plan had its provisions been publicized.

17

(A) His tone clearly inferred that he was bitterly disappointed.
(B) Having lain on the beach all afternoon, he suffered a severe sunburn.
(C) We cannot but suspect his motive.
(D) The family groups chosen to represent our town were the Browns, the Evanses, and the Granbards.

18

(A) The zinnia has the more vivid color, but the violet is the sweeter-smelling.
(B) No sooner had he begun to speak when the audience started to boo.
(C) About three-fourths of the review was a summary of the story; the rest criticism.
(D) I shall insist that he not be accepted as a member.

19

(A) In China today, there is insistence upon the doctor's giving greater attention to traditional medicine.
(B) No one in the audience dares refrain from hearty applause.
(C) We sure hope you will be able to come to the meeting.
(D) Lest the traveler concentrate too much on his stomach, the author has included notes on history.

20

(A) We ought to have prepared the group for the excitement which followed.
(B) Award the cup to whoever receives the majority of the judges' votes.
(C) She was promoted because she was more discrete than the other secretary.
(D) All he said was, "Please set it down over there."

21

(A) What you earn is nobody's business.
(B) Swimming is a healthful pastime.
(C) Mr. Brown was accidentally omitted when the invitations were issued.
(D) The boss insisted on no one else for the assignment but you.

22

(A) Do you think that the alumnae are helpful?
(B) I suggest that you send the document to the local library.
(C) Their comments being so indistinct, it's hard to say who's correct.
(D) They were happy to hear that the young piano student was liable to win the Tschaikovsky competition.

23

(A) He had a reputation for being an outstanding administrator, but he was not happy about being faced with too many dilemmas.
(B) Harry wants to be a good athlete like his older brother.
(C) We are quite enthused about his Ph.D.
(D) Maria is one of those pupils who frequently spend a good deal of their time in the detention room.

24

(A) Mary Lou incurred the enmity of the class when she revealed the secret.
(B) Being that she was a newcomer, Rose was shy.
(C) Though cleverer than her sisters, Louise is less trustworthy than they.
(D) Harassment of his employees is the mark of a tyrannical employer.

25

(A) The lecture finished, the audience began asking questions.
(B) Any man who could accomplish that task the world would regard as a hero.
(C) Our respect and admiration are mutual.
(D) George did like his mother told him, despite the importunities of his playmates.

26

(A) Oliver Wendell Holmes, Jr., decided to become a writer being that his father was a successful author.
(B) Adult Westerns on TV have neglected the great tradition of bronco-busting in the Old West.
(C) Nothing would satisfy him but that I bow to his wishes.
(D) The two companies were hopeful of eventually effecting a merger, if the government didn't object.

27

(A) Mrs. Mary Johnson Aldrich, only daughter of the late Senator Aldrich, disclosed today plans for her third marriage, to Dr. H. Walter Sloan.
(B) An excellent grade of synthetic rubber was discovered in 1954 by Goodrich-Gulf scientists.
(C) It's now clear that the largest number of votes may go to the incumbent.
(D) In the entire group, none was able to bear the heavy burden better than he.

28

(A) Few studied hard enough to achieve success in this challenging field.
(B) That there statue is one of the many that needs a good scrubbing.
(C) Larry practiced for a long time; consequently, he became quite proficient.
(D) His attempting to drive over the icy road surprised all of us.

29

(A) Look! Here comes Bruce and the rest of the team.
(B) Our students must write theses to qualify for the M.A. degree.
(C) You swim faster than he, but not so gracefully.
(D) Now kick your feet in the water like Gregory just did.

30

(A) After waiting for two hours, the audience left the hall, angry and disillusioned because of the author's failure to appear.
(B) In spite of the expense, it seems likely that more American men and women will be graduated from college this year than ever before.
(C) If you study for the test, you may get a good mark.
(D) If you do not know who owns the purse, leave the usher keep it until the owner appears.

31

(A) Michael has been taking accordion lessons for more than two years.
(B) Betty and Sue formed the nucleus of the group.
(C) Several players complimented each other as they came off the field.
(D) The tragedy of Leningrad dwarfs even that of the Warsaw ghetto or Hiroshima.

32

(A) The professor wanted to do advanced work in hydrodynamics, in which he had taken his Doctor of Philosophy degree.
(B) Eisenhower preferred to use the word "finalize" even though it was proscribed by precise grammarians.
(C) Would that I had been allowed to stay a minute longer!
(D) No sooner had the batter stepped into the box when a fastball came right at his head.

33

(A) It was probably an innocuous remark, but can you blame me for feeling resentful?
(B) It is generally conceded that Lincoln's address at Gettysburg is an American masterpiece.
(C) Enclosed herewith is one copy of the book you ordered.
(D) Despite elaborate preparations, the plan soon failed.

TEST XXI. CORRECT USAGE

CONSOLIDATE YOUR KEY ANSWERS HERE

	A	B	C	D	E			A	B	C	D	E			A	B	C	D	E			A	B	C	D	E
1	▯	▯	▯	▯	▯		2	▯	▯	▯	▯	▯		3	▯	▯	▯	▯	▯		4	▯	▯	▯	▯	▯
5	▯	▯	▯	▯	▯		6	▯	▯	▯	▯	▯		7	▯	▯	▯	▯	▯		8	▯	▯	▯	▯	▯
9	▯	▯	▯	▯	▯		10	▯	▯	▯	▯	▯		11	▯	▯	▯	▯	▯		12	▯	▯	▯	▯	▯
13	▯	▯	▯	▯	▯		14	▯	▯	▯	▯	▯		15	▯	▯	▯	▯	▯		16	▯	▯	▯	▯	▯
17	▯	▯	▯	▯	▯		18	▯	▯	▯	▯	▯		19	▯	▯	▯	▯	▯		20	▯	▯	▯	▯	▯
21	▯	▯	▯	▯	▯		22	▯	▯	▯	▯	▯		23	▯	▯	▯	▯	▯		24	▯	▯	▯	▯	▯
25	▯	▯	▯	▯	▯		26	▯	▯	▯	▯	▯		27	▯	▯	▯	▯	▯		28	▯	▯	▯	▯	▯
29	▯	▯	▯	▯	▯		30	▯	▯	▯	▯	▯		31	▯	▯	▯	▯	▯		32	▯	▯	▯	▯	▯
33	▯	▯	▯	▯	▯		34	▯	▯	▯	▯	▯		35	▯	▯	▯	▯	▯		36	▯	▯	▯	▯	▯
37	▯	▯	▯	▯	▯		38	▯	▯	▯	▯	▯		39	▯	▯	▯	▯	▯		40	▯	▯	▯	▯	▯

KEY ANSWERS FOR THE FOREGOING QUESTIONS

1.C	6.D	11.B	16.A	21.D	26.A	31.C
2.B	7.D	12.A	17.A	22.D	27.B	32.D
3.B	8.B	13.A	18.B	23.C	28.B	33.C
4.D	9.C	14.B	19.C	24.B	29.D	
5.A	10.D	15.C	20.C	25.D	30.D	

EXPLANATORY ANSWERS CLARIFYING CARDINAL POINTS

The core of the Question and Answer Method . . . getting help when and where you need it. Even if you were able to write correct key answers for the preceding questions, the following explanations illuminate fundamental facts, ideas, and principles which just might crop up in the form of questions on future tests.

Bold-face references in the following answers direct you to paragraphs in the Arco Grammar Text, where fuller explanations are provided.

ANSWER 1.

    C   His love for war is **contemptible**. REASON: **contemptuous** means feeling contempt. **(71)**

ANSWER 2.

    B   No sooner had he finished his studies **than** he dashed out to play. REASON: **No sooner . . . than** is the correct expression. **(71)**

ANSWER 3.

    B   Such talk **irritates** me. REASON: **to aggravate** means to make serious; **to irritate** means to annoy. **(71)**

ANSWER 4.

    D   Let's meet **about** six o'clock. REASON: **around** is incorrect for the idea of "approximately." **(71)**

ANSWER 5.

A   He lost a **considerable amount** in Wall Street. REASON: Don't use **considerable** as a noun.   **(71)**

ANSWER 6.

D   The scouts walked a mile **farther** than they had intended. REASON: **farther** is used for concrete distance — **further** for abstract distance (**I'll explain further**).   **(71)**

ANSWER 7.

D   That was a great **crowd** of people. REASON: We speak of people as a **crowd** — bananas, grapes, etc., as a bunch.   **(71)**

ANSWER 8.

B   **Take** all these books to the library. REASON: We **bring to the speaker** — we **take from the speaker**.   **(71)**

ANSWER 9.

C   Please see me **regardless** of the time of day. REASON: There is no such word as **irregardless**.   **(71)**

ANSWER 10.

D   Sandy is a very **attractive** girl. REASON: Avoid this over-used word (**cute**).   **(71)**

ANSWER 11.

B   If we can make an **arrangement**, I'll buy your paintings. REASON: **deal** means quantity.   **(71)**

ANSWER 12.

A   I think that Report A is as **good** as Report B. REASON: **equally** should be omitted since it is redundant — or replace **equally** with **just**.   **(71)**

ANSWER 13.

A   I prefer **this kind** of books to that kind, REASON: **kind**, being singular, requires the singular demonstrative adjective (**this**).   **(71)**

ANSWER 14.

B   Do you think she is **likely** to win the fellowship? REASON: **liable** means subject to some undesirable action.   **(71)**

ANSWER 15.

C   Although Richard **graduated from** high school with honors, he failed three subjects as a college freshman. REASON: We **graduate from** a school — also **are graduated from** a school. The verb **graduate**, when followed by a direct object, means to mark with divisions, as a thermometer.   **(71)**

ANSWER 16.

A   I can read almost anything, but these **childish** books disgust me. REASON: **childlike** means **innocent**.   **(71)**

ANSWER 17.

A   His tone clearly **implied** that he was bitterly disappointed. REASON: The speaker **implies** — the listener **infers**   **(71)**

ANSWER 18.

B   No sooner had he begun to speak **than** the audience started to boo. REASON: The correlative conjunction is **no sooner . . . than**.   **(71)**

ANSWER 19.

C   We **surely** hope you will be able to come to the meeting. REASON: **sure** may not be used as an adverb.   **(71)**

ANSWER 20.

C   She was promoted because she was more **discreet** than the other secretary. REASON: **discrete** means **separate**.   **(71)**

ANSWER 21.

D   The boss insisted on **no one** for the assignment but you. REASON: **else** is superfluous here.   **(71)**

ANSWER 22.

D   They were happy to hear that the young piano student was **likely** to win the Tschaikovsky competition. REASON: **liable** implies harm; **likely** refers to probable occurrence.   **(71)**

ANSWER 23.

C   We are quite **enthusiastic** about his Ph.D. REASON: **enthused** is poor usage.   **(71)**

ANSWER 24.

B   **Since** she was a newcomer, Rose was shy. REASON: **Being that** is incorrect because **Being**, a participle, does not modify a noun in the sentence.   **(71)**

ANSWER 25.

D   George did **as** his mother told him, despite the importunities of his playmates. REASON: The conjunction **as** (not the preposition **like**) must be used to connect the main clause and the subordinate clause. **(71)**

ANSWER 26.

A   Oliver Wendell Holmes, Jr., decided to become a writer **since** his father was a successful author. REASON: **being that** is incorrect as a substitute for **since**.   **(71)**

ANSWER 27.

B   An excellent grade of synthetic rubber was **invented** in 1954 by Goodrich-Gulf scientists. REASON: Man **discovers** what has already been there—he **invents** something that had no prior existence.   **(71)**

ANSWER 28.

B   **That statue** is one of the many that needs a good scrubbing. REASON: The expressions **that there** and **this here** are unacceptable.   **(71)**

ANSWER 29.

D   Now kick your feet in the water **as** Gregory just did. REASON: **as** is used as a conjunction which is required since the verb **did** (kick) follows. The preposition **like** is incorrect when a verb follows.   **(71)**

ANSWER 30.

D   If you do not know who owns the purse, **let** the usher keep it until the owner appears. REASON: An infinitive does not follow **leave**—an infinitive such as **(to) keep** does follow **let**.   **(71)**

ANSWER 31.

C   Several players complimented **one another** as they came off the field. REASON: **one another** refers to three or more— **each other** refers to two.   **(71)**

ANSWER 32.

D   No sooner had the batter stepped into the box **than** a fastball came right at his head. REASON: The correct expression is **no sooner ... than ...**   **(71)**

ANSWER 33.

C   Enclosed is one copy of the book you ordered. REASON: **herewith** is unnecessary in this case.   **(71)**